CommonWealth

CommonWealth

A Return to Citizen Politics

HARRY C. BOYTE

THE FREE PRESS
A Division of Macmillan, Inc.
NEW YORK

Collier Macmillan Publishers
LONDON

The Free Press
A Division of Macmillan, Inc.
866 Third Avenue, New York, N.Y. 10022

Collier Macmillan Canada, Inc.

Printed in the United States of America

printing number
1 2 3 4 5 6 7 8 9 10

Library of Congress Cataloging-in-Publication Data

Boyte, Harry Chatten
    CommonWealth : a return to citizen politics / Harry C. Boyte.
       p.   cm.
    Bibliography: p.
    Includes index.
    ISBN 0-02-904475-8
    1. Political participation—United States. 2. Citizenship—United
States. 3. Democracy. I. Title.
JK1764.B694 1990
323′.042′0973—dc20   89-12055
                                           CIP

For ELIZABETH KAMARCK MINNICH
and the pedagogical tradition that she
retrieves, illumines, and crafts
with brilliance and humor

A popular government, without popular information, or the means of acquiring it, is but a prologue to a farce or a tragedy; or, perhaps both. Knowledge will forever govern ignorance, and a people that mean to be their own governors must arm themselves with the power that knowledge brings.

—JAMES MADISON

Contents

Preface and Acknowledgments

CommonWealth is a book about the American political tradition of active citizen politics and its reemergence today. I argue that several developments make citizen politics increasingly relevant and important. There is growing alarm that the fundamental tasks of our whole society—from repair of bridges to care for the natural environment—are not getting done. At the same time, signs of recognition appear across the political spectrum that large institutions and technical expertise cannot by themselves solve our problems. Observers and activists of very different persuasions have begun once again to focus on the responsibilities and capabilities of the citizenry itself.[1]

The central idea of "the people in politics," associated in recent years with populism, has an older connection to the tradition of "commonwealth" in American history. In fact, populism, in its more democratic American forms, is a modern version of this older commonwealth heritage of politics. When popular movements and groups used the term "commonwealth" to describe their aims and vision of a good society, it involved the concept of the people as the independent agency of democracy. But today the term "commonwealth" is almost forgotten. Its ghostly, if alluring, quality says a good deal about our current political condition.

In American political history, "commonwealth" was, confusingly but powerfully, a descriptive and at the same time a prescriptive and evaluative word, much like "democracy." Thus, the very use of "com-

xi

monwealth" was an act of political drama and partisanship. Invoked by New England Puritans to express their commitment to create an exemplary communal model for the world; hurled defiantly at British loyalists by American revolutionaries; used by labor organizers, nineteenth-century utopians, women's rights crusaders, and populist farmers to describe a radical alternative to the cultural values and politics of large-scale capitalist enterprise, "commonwealth" was also used by tycoons like Andrew Carnegie to describe corporate philanthropy. In short, "commonwealth" meant radically different things to different people and groups, even within the same historical period and local environment. But in the past there was a fiery contest about the word. Whatever people meant when they used it, "commonwealth" referred to the fact that what was being contested *mattered*, in some deeply communal, supra-individual way. It conveyed passion, even political life or death.

Now "commonwealth" is an evocative but fuzzy murmur. And its fate mirrors the frayed and attenuated quality of public life and politics more generally in the United States. In an important sense, groups like the Baltimore citizen organization BUILD—whose campaign to revitalize the schools (called the Baltimore Commonwealth) I examine at some length in Chapter 7—are "creating the word over again," to borrow from Tom Paine. They draw on an old but largely neglected conception of politics as a public life of active citizens.

As the rise of technocratic models, based on the ideal of the detached scientist as the highest judge of truth and the most accomplished problem solver, came to dominate every field of social and economic policy, politics and public life became progressively thinner, not only in practice but in intellectual inquiry as well. Today, conventional understandings of politics do not incorporate concepts of an active civic life. Mainstream political science attempts an empiricist definition that views democracy as a political system in which different parties compete for electoral support and the most significant form of citizens' public activity is the act of voting. Neorepublican theoretical discussions of more active participation by citizens too often convey an idealized, nostalgic, and ahistorical view of politics, as if the nineteenth-century world of small communities were still with us. Both empiricist and neorepublican approaches reflect the uprootedness of modern theorizing from politics, understood as the actual, multidimensional civic decision making taking place in communities.

To retrieve a conception of citizen politics grounded in real life conditions requires a twofold project. First we need to recall the active traditions of public life in American history, now largely forgotten. Second we need to explore what citizen politics might actually mean today, in a world far different from that of our ancestors.[2]

Alasdair MacIntyre's imaginative beginning to *After Virtue* depicts a future in which scientists, their practices, and their tradition have been destroyed. Future generations seek to revive science and borrow from the language and the terms of the past. But the radical chasm created by the obliteration of a tradition means that the terms are disembodied, without clear referents. MacIntyre used the fable to position our contemporary plight, where the meanings of the terms that shaped strong conceptions of civic and moral community through most of the history of the Western world have been largely lost.[3]

The problem of revitalizing any strong concept of public life today is compounded by the detachment of theorizing from contemporary activity. It is as if future thinkers, in their effort to revive science, not only had little or no inherited tradition to draw on, but also avoided discussion with anyone engaged in practical experiments. With some important recent exceptions—such contemporary writers as Sheldon Wolin, Benjamin Barber, Hannah Pitkin, Michael Walzer, Jane Mansbridge, Christopher Lasch, Cornel West, and a few others stand out—mainstream political theory still avoids engagements with the turbulent world of actual politics in favor of analysis of language and terms, exegisis of past theories, and discussion of methodology. The rare exceptions to this pattern, like the short-lived but lively and important journal *democracy*, published in the early 1980s, have underscored the pattern by their very atypicality. Meanwhile, the left and other critical traditions, such as feminism, in their dissenting theoretical views of what *is* political, have made important analyses of the ways in which enormous groupings are rendered invisible in traditional constructions of politics or public life. But they have also tended to slight what the public realm, or politics, might mean today as an arena that has its own distinctive dynamics, imperatives, and rhythms.[4]

Important strands of social and political theory today, in evolving an approach that is neither radically historicist and relativist (refraining from *any* claims or arguments beyond specific time periods and social contexts) nor foundationalist (developing grand historical schema, on the basis of some presumed transhistorical method that allows a privileged viewpoint about the truth of the human condition), point strongly in the direction of practical engagement. As such they recall an older generation of democratic philosophers, progressives, and social democrats, like Thomas Hill Green, William James, Jane Addams, Walter Rauschenbusch, Max Weber, and John

Dewey, whose views took shape around the turn of the century, before the rise of the modern welfare state and the crystalization of its political culture.[5]

Thus, many theorists now emphasize the need for attentiveness to what is called "practical reason," or the development of thought about politics from a constant and rigorous reflection on actual experience. Communal life and traditions in real historical contexts necessarily form the dynamic referent for exploration of the meanings of "politics" and "public" and "justice" and "freedom" in the broader world. As Richard Bernstein pointed out at the conclusion of his work *Beyond Objectivism and Relativism,*

> At a time when the threat of total annihilation no longer seems to be an abstract possibility but the most imminent and real potentiality, it becomes all the more imperative to try again and again to foster and nurture those forms of communal life in which dialogue, conversation, phronesis [practical reason], practical discourse and judgment are concretely embodied in our everyday practices. This is the telos that is common [for instance] to the visions of Gadamer, Habermas, Rorty, and Arendt.[6]

CommonWealth is one response to such exhortations for engagement with the world. Its method is grounded in my observations of contemporary citizen initiatives over the last decade and a half. Through this period, I have become convinced that the historical and contemporary legacy of citizen efforts has crucial implications for democratic theory about change and action in modern societies that have as yet gone largely unexplored.[7]

CommonWealth goes considerably beyond my earlier works. Responding to the challenges of reviewers like Robert Fisher, who urged more detailed theoretical attention to "the successes and failures, the virtues and limits of grass-roots populism" today, *CommonWealth* locates contemporary civic action in an older tradition. It explores the reasons for that tradition's eclipse through most of the twentieth century. And it subjects current citizen organizing efforts to a sustained theoretical examination and critique.[8]

———

Indeed, the process of producing this work has itself been an odd mixture of practice and theory. In the course of its development, I have benefited greatly from many sorts of conversations, and activities.

I have an old intellectual debt I want to acknowledge here. Edward A. Tiryakian at Duke University, my teacher many years ago, left me with the enduring conviction that conventional languages and categories of politics are often at least as misleading as they are helpful. I also profited greatly from his insistence on the cultural context of meanings and traditions that undergirds explicit politics.

In the last decade or so, the most important influence on my thinking has undoubtedly been Sheldon Wolin, editor of *democracy* magazine. My many discussions with Sheldon, about the magazine in general and the two pieces on which I worked, gave me the powerful example of an engaged intellectual who combines democratic passion with a keen capacity for critical judgment and candor about projects for which one has sympathy.

Enrollment in the eclectic, freewheeling, fascinating educational process known as Union Graduate School created the specific scaffolding around which my arguments took shape as a dissertation. Commentary from members of my committee—Benjamin Barber, Joan Scott, Colin Greer, Ben Shaine, and Sylvia Hill—proved constantly challenging and helpful. Michael Patton made several insightful comments about method. My correspondence, in the nature of a lively debate, with Ivan Illich was a fascinating stimulus. Regular luncheons with Mary Dietz, a feminist political theorist whose work and insight I greatly admire, were a delight and a considerable aid. And voluminous exchanges with my friend and core faculty, Elizabeth Kamark Minnich, created a remarkable opportunity to engage questions of political theory and philosophy across the centuries, from Aristotle and Plato to contemporary feminists. It also opened a window into the tradition of pedagogy about public affairs which Elizabeth illuminates and also reshapes. More than any other contemporary figure of whom I am aware, Minnich sustains the spirit and promise of her own teacher, Hannah Arendt.

The themes of this work have been developed in the Commonwealth Project that I direct for the Hubert H. Humphrey Institute of Public Affairs at the University of Minnesota. In this process, I certainly owe the most to Peg Michels. Peg's stubborn optimism has contributed greatly to my conviction that a democratic renaissance is a substantial possibility in our time. She has also demonstrated again and again in practice that the activities of professionals in community contexts need not be narrowly technical. Far more than her formal title of Field Organizer and Curriculum Director for the Commonwealth Project can convey, Peg recreates a sense of the possibilities of the public arena.

Over the last three years, our collaboration with David Mathews, Pat Scully, and others at the Kettering Foundation has proven highly productive. In particular, the seminar we cosponsored on the American commonwealth tradition in the spring of 1987 raised many of the questions this book is intended to address. I want to note especially the helpful contributions of Mathews, John W. Gardner, Robert Bellah, Jane Mansbridge, E. J. Dionne, Eddie Williams, Helen Ayala, Daniel Kemmis, and others at that meeting. There and in many other conversations as well, I have benefited from Harlan Cleveland's insights. Other colleagues at the Humphrey Institute have also been of considerable help on these ideas. I want to mention in particular the feedback of G. Edward Schuh, Barbara Nelson, Paul Light, John Brandl, Tom Dewar, and Earl Craig.

We have experimented with various themes (the concept of the commonwealth, public life as an arena of difference, free spaces, relational power, learning from political experience, dynamic conceptions of self-interest, the concept of professional as "craftsperson" rather than technician) in many projects. Efforts like our work in the small rural community of Rice, Minnesota; my consultations with Minnesota Cooperative Extension Service, the Georgia Advocacy Project, the Community Renewal Society in Chicago, and the C. S. Mott Foundation; and our statewide projects such as the *Citizens' Guide to Elections, 1988,* undertaken in collaboration with the Secretary of State and the *St. Paul Pioneer Press Dispatch* in 1988, and our Youth and Democracy Conference in the spring of 1989, cosponsored with the Department of Education, Minnesota 4-H, the Community Education Association of Minnesota, the National Youth Leadership Council, and the YMCA, all feed into this book. Members of our working teams in these efforts, such as Jayne Marecek, Suzanne Paul, Laurisa Sellers, Keith Morton, and Sue Tacheny, have contributed a great deal to my evolving understanding of what "commonwealth" can mean in our time.

I want to make several personal acknowledgments. My close collaboration with Frances Moore Lappé has been a pleasure and a stimulation alike. I want to express appreciation for the many conversations I have had with members of the IAF network about political themes—especially for the insights and critical thinking of Gerald Taylor. Jim O'Brien did yeoman-like work in the creation of the index. Roz Siegel, editorial consultant for The Free Press, Miriam Hurewitz, my copy editor, and Edith Lewis, the editing supervisor, notably strengthened the work. Janet Ferguson's suggestions made their mark on the final product. Joyce Seltzer, my editor, pushed me with astonishing intensity and talent toward clarity and accessibility of argument as I turned the dissertation into a book. For whatever obscurity remains, I take full responsibility.

Finally, for her constant personal support and intellectual engagement, I thank Sara M. Evans. The arguments in *CommonWealth* are my own take on the world. But they bear the overwhelming imprint of the more than two decades of our partnership.

Minneapolis
April 18, 1989

Civic Life and the
American Dilemma

"**B**ush or Dukakis—Coke or Pepsi," read the graffiti on the bridge near the Minneapolis campus of the University of Minnesota. The comparison with the long-running advertising battle between the two soft-drink giants made a point with a crispness absent from the punditry which preoccupied the media in the wake of the 1988 presidential election.

American elections have turned into ritualized formalities, with an electorate that seems unable to wed its capacities for critical thinking to the ability to act effectively. Today we live in a schizophrenic political culture, fraught with a conflict between our ideals and hopes on the one hand and the gritty realities of politics on the other.

Despite the debacle of the 1988 election, by the threshold of the 1990s signs of renewed public spirit could be found across America. Polls showed stirrings of reawakened voluntary activism in communities. Youth service movements mushroomed on college campuses and in high schools. More and more observers of the American scene were voicing the need for a strengthened civic ethos.

Reflecting such positive signs, *Newsweek* magazine declared that "The Eighties Are Over," citing a variety of polls that suggested growing discontent with the mood of greed and selfishness embodied in the idea of a "Me Decade." The venerable National Civic League proposed a "civic index" to measure things like citizen participation, intergroup relations, and levels of voluntary activity, all of which, it argued, are as essential to community health as are physical and

1

economic attributes. The Kettering Foundation, one of the nation's largest operating philanthropies, redefined its mission to stress the reinvigoration of public debate and public will. And both political parties' nominees in 1988 campaigned with calls for a renewal of the spirit of community. "Where is it written that we must act as if we do not care, as if we are not moved?" said George Bush to the Republican convention. "Well, I am moved. I want a kinder, gentler nation."[1]

The same period that marked such rhetorical championing of civic concern brought forth dramatic examples of corruption in the nation's politics. The graffiti near the University of Minnesota expressed the widespread anger, worry, and disillusionment that grew from the sense that Americans had become "consumers" and spectators of politics, not participants. The large systems and institutions of the modern world seemed far beyond our control.

In the 1988 presidential election, 30-second sound bites replaced authentic debate, while media packaging and manipulation of symbols crowded out thoughtful consideration of public policies. Voting levels were the lowest since 1924, and there was evidence that many of the most attentive and informed voters deliberately stayed away. "Voters dislike the choice they have been offered and regard the Presidential campaign as negative, uninteresting and insubstantial," wrote E. J. Dionne of the *New York Times* shortly before the election. In blunt language, citizens communicated discontent. "I am embarrassed, ashamed and very angry," wrote Deborah Hunter to the *Cleveland Plain Dealer*. "These four [candidates] have shown us that they have no business in politics since they are still in the sandbox." Polls showed that wide majorities shared such sentiments. Sixty-four percent felt that the 1988 campaign was more negative than past races. Two thirds believed that candidates were manipulated by their handlers. After the election, a majority expressed dissatisfaction with the way candidates had explained themselves and their positions, while a striking 30 percent declared that they would have voted "neither" if such had been an option.[2]

The gap between our formal political values and the actual practice of our political system found its roots in what was, perhaps, a more profound disarray in the American body politic itself—a disengagement from politics and public life. Thus, not only did Americans participate less in the political system, many also lacked the basic information necessary to judge and analyze events, issues, and rhetoric. "Citizenship" was boring and "politics" had become, for many— perhaps most—teenagers and young adults, a disparaging epithet. Studies suggested a widespread lack of knowledge about history, geography, and political structures. Americans endorsed democratic norms in the abstract, but support for elemental liberties dropped precipitiously when people were asked to consider specific, emotion-laden cases or even the Bill of Rights. Signs of heightened racial and religious conflict and intolerance mounted. "Home Roulette," a parody of the board game Monopoly whose manual declared, "Yes, we hate most everybody," singling out especially blacks, homosexuals, the homeless, and women, was a best-seller in Washington, D.C., novelty stores.[3]

Across the political spectrum, analysts and critics pointed to the crisis of civic culture. The conservative think tank Free Congress Foundation issued a manifesto on the need for a renewed sense of public virtue and civic purpose to counter the selfishness of the Reagan years. "Both liberals and conservatives have been disturbed by America's cultural drift," declared their document. "The absence of a moral base breeds indifference, a 'me first' ethic of greed and ostentation, and a loss of the concept of the common good." Warnings about the state of our public life appeared on the left in works like *Habits of the Heart,* a best-selling examination of American culture which concluded that a "cancerous individualism" was destroying the country's older languages of civic commitment.[4]

Around a series of issues having to do with basic communal needs like education, housing stock, health, transportation, energy, communications, water supply and waste treatment, and drug control, a growing sense emerged that only new levels of citizen "stakeholding" could reinvigorate the sort of political commitments essential to get things done. The congressionally mandated National Council on Public Works Improvement expressed this view in its 1988 report, *Fragile Foundations:*

> The quality of a nation's infrastructure is a critical index of its economic vitality. Reliable transportation, clean water, and safe disposal of wastes are basic elements of a civilized society and a productive economy ... Now [our] inheritance is in danger ... the National Council on Public Works has found convincing evidence that the quality of America's infrastructure is barely adequate to fulfill current requirements, and insufficient to meet the demands of future economic growth and development.

The Council studied eight specific infrastructural areas—highways, mass transit, aviation, water resources, water supply, wastewater, solid waste, and hazardous waste. But its discussion of infrastructure acknowledged that the concept could appropriately "be interpreted to include communications, energy facilities, schools, hospitals, prisons and parks" and that "a considerable portion of its research findings and policy conclusions may apply to other areas." And the report emphasized repeatedly the need for broader civic participation: "Building and maintaining public works requires . . . a new public consensus . . . a shared vision, commitment of time and energy, and the skills of people throughout the public and private sectors."[5]

The dangers of widespread citizen disaffection and withdrawal were especially clear in cases like the intertwined issues of education and the future economy. In many urban centers, dropout rates among young people reached 50, 60, or even 80 percent of those entering ninth grade. Students who graduated from high school, taught by educators battling a deadly combination of student apathy, violence, numbing workloads, and bureaucratic red tape, proved ill prepared for skilled and demanding jobs.[6]

Yet longer-range analyses of the educational system and prospects for the economy argued for the imperative that schools train adaptable, thoughtful, and imaginative students, if America was to compete successfully in the world. The Carnegie Forum on Education and the Economy proposed that as manufacturing became progressively less the foundation of the economy, only a major transformation of American education would allow new businesses to survive and prosper in an environment where knowledge itself was increasingly the central resource. Employees' and managers' capacities for cooperative work approaches, dialogue, and consensus building would be essential. In the high-technology and service industries of the future, workers would need to be able to pose and analyze problems, evaluate different outcomes, and anticipate unfamiliar alternatives: "people who have the tools they need to think for themselves, people who can act independently and with others, who can render critical judgment and contribute constructively to many enterprises, whose knowledge is wide-ranging and whose understanding runs deep." Both educational reform and economic change in the direction of a more competitive, decentralized business system would require considerably increased citizen involvement. And such civic engagement was, finally, a matter of citizens *wanting* to be involved—a motivation that would grow only from the perception that ordinary citizens can make a difference.[7]

In much of American history, this strong and active understanding of citizen involvement was expressed through the language, vision, and concept of "the commonwealth." For our ancestors—and for many of our grandparents and parents—"commonwealth" had, most typically, two powerful meanings. The word suggested an ideal: a commonwealth was a self-governing community of equals concerned about the general welfare—a republican or democratic government, where citizens remained active throughout the year, not simply on Election Day. And commonwealth also brought to mind the touchstone, or common foundations, of public life—the basic resources and public goods of a community over which citizens assumed responsibility and authority.

Over the last generation, the language of the commonwealth has largely disappeared from our public vocabulary; indeed, its fate reflects the erosion of a strong and active sense of citizenship itself. But here and there one sees a revival: the Catholic Bishops invoked the commonwealth ideal in their Pastoral Letter on the Economy; several large citizen coalitions have formed recently using "commonwealth" in their names; the nation's most ambitious program for reform of an inner-city school system—the Baltimore Commonwealth—has resurrected the term, with the meaning, especially, of the common goods essential to community vitality. These revivals parallel the more general, growing attention to our civic culture and citizenship.[8]

It is the central thesis of *CommonWealth* that new possibilities for a wider, more active democracy are beginning to emerge in the modern "information age." Effective citizen action in our times is possible if—and only if—citizens develop the abilities to gain access to information of all kinds (from the roads and sewers to educational, environmental, and economic patterns) and the skills to put such information to effective use. Moreover, the possibilities for a reinvigorated popular sovereignty are dependent not only on information and knowledge but also on what might best be called "wisdom": the ability to *guide* and frame action with integrative concepts and a clear, if flexible and evolving, set of public values and purposes. Thus, "commonwealth" in our times points especially to the importance of knowledge itself as a resource that needs to be shared, shaped, and governed by the political community of citizens.

Such an argument builds on a lively contemporary revival of arguments about the importance of public life, community, and active citizenship. It also goes beyond them, highlighting the need to think carefully about what such things might actually mean in a modern, complex, technological society.

We have traditions of active citizenship close to the surface of our public memories that are sometimes invoked today. They illustrate the shortcomings as well as the appeal of what we remember about public life—its roots in a world of small towns and homogeneous communities that has largely disappeared.

———

Daniel Kemmis, former speaker of the Montana House of Representatives, grew up in a small town in the eastern part of the state. Kemmis likes to tell a story that he sees as conveying "the politics of cooperation," an understanding of a community-based public life forged out of the necessities of rural survival.

When he was a child in the early 1950s, the wind blew down the family barn. Neighbors came from around the area to help rebuild it, including the family of Albert Volbrecht, whose "hat was the biggest ... voice the loudest ... language the foulest ... intake of beer the most prodigious." Daniel's mother, Lilly, did not like the Volbrechts at all. He observes that she "would have done anything in her power to deny my brother and me that part of our education" that came from the young Volbrecht daughter, who regaled the other children with ribald stories while the adults worked. Yet in those years it was customary for a community to work together not only in crises like a fallen barn but in branding cattle and other joint activities—so that regular contact was unavoidable. "In another time and place, Albert and Lilly would have had nothing to do with one another," said Kemmis. "But on those Montana plains life was still harsh enough that you had no choice. Avoiding people you did not like was not an option. Everyone was needed by everyone else in one capacity or another. If Albert and Lilly could have snubbed one another, our barn might not have been built, and neither our calves nor Albert's branded." Personal likes and dislikes did not necessarily change from the interactions. Kemmis's mother remained angry every time the Volbrechts came by. But the community and his family gained other things: different "slants" on the world, as Kemmis put it; awareness that people could count on others in the community whatever their personal likes; an experience of community effectiveness in accomplishing difficult tasks.

Kemmis contrasts this story with another from Missoula in recent years. A group, considering ways to raise money for a music festival, cancelled their plan for an old-fashioned box lunch because of fear of a lawsuit if anyone got sick. To Kemmis, today's "litigious society" of confrontations and special interests results in "civic suffocation."[9]

There were limitations of the earlier world which are often easy to forget, in the roseate glow of our positive images: sharp cleavages and hierarchies along lines of ethnicity and race, for instance; circumscribed roles for women; an avoidance of discussion and debate about many controversial subjects. But the appeal of this kind of story also cuts across many contemporary divisions of politics, race, and gender. In the memories of many people alive today—not only in rural areas and small towns but in the stable ethnic communities of big cities as well—people learned an ongoing *connection* of their lives with their friends and neighbors. They developed a consciousness of mutual responsibility, and had ways to hold accountable

those who were too disruptive or violent. People of different ages—
the young, the middle-aged, the elderly—interacted every day, in a
fashion that allowed the transmission of values, perspective, and wisdom across generational lines. In sum, many people experienced an
ongoing education in a kind of "politics" of community life and action that was much more than elections alone. Daniel Kemmis's story
of his boyhood reminds us of a society when the ideal of "commonwealth" had real power, at least on local levels.

Kemmis's story and the concerns it conveys are paralleled by a
recent generation of what is sometimes called neorepublican scholarship. Historians like J. G. A. Pocock, Gordon Wood, Linda Kerber,
Bernard Bailyn, and a number of others have drawn attention to
the "republican" currents of our political culture, derived from the
classical tradition of Greek and Roman political thought, filtered
through the Renaissance experiences of Europe, and taking specific
shape in this country, especially at the nation's founding. American
republicanism furnished a set of political themes different from the
concerns for rights and individual liberties inherited from the Enlightenment. In republican thought, civic participation was understood to be the foundation of a free society. Thomas Jefferson used
the example of Indian groups like the Iroquois to make the point
that communal values and a sense of mutual obligation form the only
sure foundation for democracy. Europeans, argued Jefferson, "have
divided their nations into two classes, wolves and sheep," while for
the Iroquois, "controls are their manners and the moral sense of
right and wrong." More conservative men among the Founding Fathers like James Madison similarly emphasized the necessity of "virtue"—a strong sense of obligation and responsibility to the community. "No theoretical checks—no form of government can render us
secure," Madison declared in his speech before the Virginia ratifying
convention, June 20, 1788. "To suppose that any form of government
will secure liberty or happiness without any virtue in the people is a
chimerical idea."[10]

Contemporary neorepublican political theorists like Benjamin
Barber, Michel Sandel, William Sullivan, and Alasdair MacIntyre
have complemented such historical scholarship with the trenchant
criticism that modern liberalism has adopted an excessively individualist flavor. Liberalism today detaches the concept of "citizen" from
any communal ties or obligations. In the dominant liberal view, the
citizen is seen mainly as a bearer of rights, like the freedom to worship or not worship, to speak and assemble, or to vote. "Freedom"
itself, in these terms, is defined in a negative sense, as the protection
of individuals against interference and infringement. The political
arena resembles a marketplace, where the point is a competitive pur-

suit of goods and resources on the part of special and separated interests. Democracy is understood mainly as a representative system,
where elected officials are chosen by "political consumers" with different needs and wants. Such an individualist conception of politics
neglects the moral wellsprings of public life, the values like responsibility, fairness, and concern for others that were widespread at the
nation's founding.[11]

Neorepublican theorists today, like Kemmis's narrative, remind
us of vital civic resources that we are in danger of losing entirely. But
efforts to develop a positive theory of what renewed "public life"
might actually mean in the 1990s and beyond flounder because they
derive their terms still from the experiences of small towns and rural
societies, where most people knew each other and many shared similar cultural heritages.

William Sullivan, a prominent republican theorist, illustrated
this problem in his criticism of conventional liberal theory, *Reconstructing Public Philosophy*. Sullivan argued that the loss of a sense of
personal participation in political life spurs what he called a new
privatism—a focus on personal matters on the one hand, and a decline in voting and political involvements of all kinds on the other:
"Part of the meaning of the current American retreat to privatism is
a continuing search for what counts in life, a hunger for orientation
that neither the dynamics of capitalist growth nor the liberal vision
of politics provides." In contrast to liberal concepts, Sullivan urged a
richer view of citizenship tied to what he termed a "commonwealth"
understanding of political culture: "The notion of citizen is unintelli-
gible apart from that of commonwealth, and both terms derive their
sense from the idea that we are by nature political beings." For Sullivan, commonwealth means a "covenant morality," the agreement
that "as citizens we make a . . . promise to show care and concern to
each other." Such a "way of life," in his terms, "begins not with self-
interest but with the moral culture of justice, dignity and fellowship."
Indeed, "it stands in opposition to the life of self interest." It is "possible only when the members of a community trust and respect one
another." And its aim is "universal sympathy" that grows from a "mutual commitment to a common good."[12]

The problem is that trust, respect, and a mutual commitment to
the common good of communities are just what we have lost. And
they cannot be reintroduced into our political culture simply
through exhortation. In a contemporary environment of sharpening
economic and racial divisions, massive institutions, and profound
economic changes that render most citizens feeling largely like spectators, public-spirited rhetoric all too often takes on an ethereal quality, seemingly far removed from the fears, self-interests, angers, and

loyalties that usually motivate people. Calls for renewed civic engagement too often become merely nostalgic.

A practical theory of effective public action and strong citizenship for our society needs to take into account the changing nature of power, resources, and social life. At the same time, it requires a close examination of the broader lessons that can be learned from the citizen initiatives of recent decades.

Despite the general decline in civic involvements over the past decade, a number of strong, lasting, large-scale citizen organizations have developed in some of the poorest communities in the country. These furnish abundant material to explore how civic participation can be woven back into our highly fragmented and mobile society.[13]

The intersection between changing social structure and citizen activism highlights the importance of *knowledge* to successful citizen action, and points to the usefulness of the concept of an emerging "information society." The characterization of our country as an information society grows particularly from the work of theorists like Raymond Aron and Daniel Bell. Bell and others draw attention to the increasing role of knowledge as a resource and source of power in its own right. Energy generated by steam and electricity transformed preindustrial societies into industrial societies. Money capital replaced raw materials as the main strategic resource. Today, data-transmission systems—computers, telecommunications systems—and theoretical knowledge—the organization of information and data by complex frameworks—have progressively become the driving forces of innovation, strategic resources, and power, shaping a world economy, changing the pattern of human relationships. "The industrial era was characterized by the influence of humankind over things, including Nature as well as the artifacts of Man," wrote Harlan Cleveland, an astute analyst of knowledge-as-a-resource. "The information era features a sudden increase in humanity's power to think, and therefore to organize." Such a process, in turn, puts those who do the conceptual organizing in a particularly powerful position. Bell sees a "knowledge elite" of scientists, mathematicians, economists, engineers, and professionals of all sorts progressively replacing the traditional governing groups of managers, capitalists, and business executives.[14]

One does not have to subscribe to the most extravagant arguments that we are entering a qualitatively new world, or that the forms of social organization and class structure associated with capitalist society are rapidly dissolving, to note the profound changes in patterns of power and politics that the growing centrality of knowledge and its use are bringing about. In many ways the current knowledge revolution represents a continuation and acceleration of trends that have increasingly shaped our world throughout the twentieth century.

We are at the end of a long period of time—what might be called "the managerial era" of the twentieth century, or the liberal welfare state approach to politics—in which citizenship was defined in weak and attenuated ways *because* of the centralization of knowledge. In the twentieth century Americans handed over to experts, technicians, and professionals the power to make the key decisions about our "commonwealth"—the basic public goods, or what is sometimes called the social and economic infrastructure, that were widely seen as essential to the society. This transfer of power was accompanied by an approach to knowledge that understood the most reliable and useful information to be "scientific," drawing its imagery and terminology from a positivist model of rationality that precluded its access to nonprofessional, ordinary people.[15]

Today there has begun to emerge the widespread perception that we need a new citizenship, a deeper and richer view of politics that highlights the importance of public life in its own terms. But developments in our world differentiate a modern democratic politics from nineteenth-century variants. Knowledge itself has become more and more central to patterns of domination, as well as to those of democratic action. Power is gathered not only in distant corporate boardrooms; it is as close as the doctor's office or the social service agency waiting room or the child-rearing advice manual on the living room shelf and the expert TV commentators talking underneath. In our educated, service society, most middle-class and professional people hold roles both as "power elite" and as "powerless."[16]

In the twentieth century, control over information-generating processes and over information has resided in large-scale institutions like governments and corporations which have the resources and personnel necessary for accumulating, processing, and storing specialized knowledge. Such centralization has been justified on the grounds that large-scale problem solving is simply too difficult for ordinary citizens: the highly trained specialist—the expert—has been touted as the appropriate handler of information. Centralized information patterns and institutions characterize almost all aspects of the managerial society, from the economy and national security systems to medicine, law, education, and child rearing.

As knowledge becomes increasingly a source of power, the struggle regarding its accessibility and use becomes more and more central to democracy. The success of contemporary citizen activism in a variety of contexts depends upon the ability to ferret out key information, often against the efforts of powerful interests to restrict information access. From the parent who worries about local school dropout rates to the rancher fighting to preserve the open range from energy conglomerates, from community activists organizing around toxic waste to small businesspeople trying to increase the pool of resources available in their areas for entrepreneurial start-up projects, people need information to act. They also need "knowledge"—the organizational and communicative skills to organize. Studies of grass-roots leaders have found that the most successful have developed considerable talents at gaining access to information and to the organizing skills that facilitate action.[17]

But there is a broader problem with the structure and pattern of knowledge in our society that is harder for citizen activists to overcome. Large organizations and bureaucracies not only centralize information; they also fragment it, in ways that mirror the excessive specialization we learn in academic life and the professions. In the process, information is stripped of larger meaning. Data about housing, for instance, is rarely related to crime statistics, or health care patterns, or demographic information or environmental problems. "Issues" are separated from the larger context in which they appear. And we have lost the longitudinal knowledge needed to see questions in long-term perspectives.

Narrow specialization breeds a historical forgetfulness that has disastrous consequences for democracy. A character in the novel *The Book of Laughter and Forgetting* by Milan Kundera, the great Czech novelist, raged against the obliteration of history in communist nations: "The struggle of man against power is the struggle of memory against forgetting." Shoshana Zuboff, one of the most perceptive observers of the information revolution, echoed such sentiments in a different context. *Without* an active, informed, thoughtful citizenry, she told *Harvard Magazine,* new technologies create a "social amnesia" that obliterates any strong value perspective. "As the sense of how things were fades from awareness, we may be oblivious to what we're losing in the quality of our world." Zuboff maintained that education's role is more crucial than ever:

> to remind students of the classical themes in human experience,
> create a sense of kinship between present and past, and
> heighten understandings of the continuities in the human
> condition. What we're talking about is preserving our humanity
> and our human values in a world whose forces and pressures
> and seductions tell us to believe in technology and technological
> solutions.[18]

Knowledge needs to be guided by wisdom: broader frameworks, concepts, and values that integrate information and the knowledge of how to use it, that contextualize, prioritize, and guide action. But it goes against the grain of the times to think broadly and conceptually about civic practice. Much of citizen activism of recent years, on both local and national levels, has addressed itself to fairly narrow issues. Activists have not often asked what their work "means" in a larger sense, where they are going in the long run, or how their particular efforts might add up to more than the particular or localized campaigns they engage in. Citizen activism has frequently gained voice for marginal, poorer, minority, or relatively powerless communities historically left out of most decision making. It has done so, in large part, by generating effective ways of getting information citizens need, and teaching the skills to organize significant numbers of people. But like conventional politics, much of grass-roots activism has spoken a thin, sometimes cynical language of narrow interests and protest detached from any enlarged social and political vision. This kind of activism also neglects the ways in which citizen politics is an art, requiring such abilities as good judgment, skillful use of power, critical thinking, imagination, and rhetoric.

Interest-organizing often succeeds in particular issue fights or local struggles, but it does little to change the wider pattern of power relations in communities, nor does it affect to any significant degree the political culture. In fact, citizen organizing without larger purpose simply reflects the terms of politics-as-usual.

Technology, science, and the knowledge and political modes of thought they generate, in themselves, are detached from human ends and values. In a technological world, Kundera's dictum can be reordered: the struggle to remember, and to build the communal frameworks through which to remember, constitute central ingredients of the struggle for power. Lasting, large-scale citizen efforts that begin to revitalize a strong sense of public life renew communal traditions and value frameworks as crucial elements of what such efforts are all about. And they revive an understanding of the art of politics.

If an information society is fraught with dangers, it also offers opportunities. Knowledge is unlike capital or land as a resource. It is hard to centralize: one of the distinctive features of the "knowledge revolution" today is that information is harder and harder to hoard (community-organizing lore abounds with stories of the "inside sympathizer" who leaked information at critical moments of a community struggle against a bank or developer or chemical company). Information is not used up if it is given out. In many cases, it increases in value. Efforts to hoard information, in fact, lead to inertia and stagnation—a lesson learned most recently by Soviet bloc officials. Information lends itself to sharing transactions, rather than the exchange transactions of the marketplace. And if it is unusual to think about the values and concepts that frame and guide activity in our age of excessive specialization, skillful efforts to do so produce considerable power in their own right. Information without values is, in itself, a barren form of communication. Citizen initiatives which add such values, in turn, speak to the immense hunger that has developed in our society for a reintegration of large systems and technological modes of thought into a sense of human agency. And they generate a capacity to control the information flow of the modern world, by clarifying what people actually need to know and why they need to know it.[19]

Citizen groups and initiatives that engage in such work revive conceptions of politics as the activity of equal citizens, engaged in argument, debate, dialogue, conflict, and common work. And they provide a schooling in politics adapted to a heterogeneous and technological society, through which individual citizens and small communities come to understand the interconnections of their lives and aspirations with those of others unlike themselves. In short, they develop the consciousness, once incubated in small communities like Daniel Kemmis's, that a measure of mutual responsibility for "the commonwealth" is possible and even necessary, whatever one's personal likes and dislikes, specific communal history, and values.

Politics among equal citizens and assumption of responsibility for such public goods makes up the commonwealth tradition in American political culture, an old and rich, if largely forgotten, understanding of politics. To understand the possibilities for revitalization of this tradition, it is important to have a sense of its history and distinctiveness. Put simply, the commonwealth tradition forms an alternative to the politics of modern capitalism and socialism alike, one that has a renewed relevance for the years ahead. Commonwealth politics shifts the main focus of politics from the question of redistributive justice to the issue of who wields power over the fundamental structures of our common life.

recently—prompted, in part, by worldwide alarm about looming crises like the greenhouse effect—many arguments that a stronger consciousness of human responsibility for such common wealths is an urgent necessity.[1]

Against such a background, attention to the commonwealth tradition points to a considerable irony. What has been seen as perhaps the major weakness in America's political culture has obscured what may well turn out to be our greatest strength.

The question posed in 1906 by the German sociologist Werner Sombart, "Why is there no socialism in the United States?" (or more recently, why is there no strong socialist or labor political party?) has been, through the twentieth century, explicitly or implicitly, the central puzzle of most reformers, historians, and political scientists in America and Europe who have sought to explain twentieth-century American politics. A variety of answers have been suggested: the excessively utopian quality of American socialists' politics; the western frontier as a safety valve; the ethnically and racially divided nature of the American working class; the relative wealth of American workers; the absence of a feudal past; the relative lack of American workers' experiences in class-conscious political (as opposed to on-the-job) mobilization. A few observers—Richard Hofstadter and Michael Harrington stand out—have rephrased the problem by pointing to the absence of an explicitly socialist or social democratic *vocabulary* of politics to describe what was, increasingly, a social democratic set of policies championed by American liberalism since the New Deal. In Europe and America the modern welfare state had important similarities.[2]

But the intellectuals' and reformers' focus on what was "missing" eclipsed what was there instead. Today, the world we are entering is helping the American *alternative* to socialism, the commonwealth tradition, to resurface with heightened interest.[3]

This tradition did not revolve around calls for equalization of material circumstances (the "socialization of property")—the leitmotif of socialism and social democracy that has led to an emphasis on the state as the principal mechanism for redistributive justice. Rather, commonwealth politics was mainly concerned with different questions: Who wields power over the commons, or infrastructure of communal life? And, in populist terms, what are the instruments for power wielding by ordinary citizens? This question of power is the basic problem of democracy in the information age.

The commonwealth tradition took a distinctive American form in the eighteenth and nineteenth centuries. As we will see, it then became associated with Populism in the late nineteenth century and continued as a kind of "underground" tradition in the twentieth, when it retained a popular appeal despite relative programmatic marginality in the welfare state. Commonwealth themes shaped a mainstream political oratory which continued, periodically, to stress more activist notions of citizenship—for instance, John Kennedy's inaugural call to "ask not what your country can do for you. Ask what you can do for your country." Meanwhile, those who practically addressed and amplified the main commonwealth idea of active citizen power in the twentieth century have created a legacy that has much to teach democratic struggles and movements of all kinds in our age.[4]

The word "commonwealth," like "democracy," gains its meanings and its power from the specific ways it has been employed by different groups. The ensemble of such uses—understood only through a look at what the actors thought they were doing in their own terms—constitutes a dynamic tradition. It is worth looking at this tradition in some detail because the concept of citizen authority over "the commons" is resurfacing today as the alternative to technocratic, top-down politics, both in initiatives where the word "commonwealth" is present and where it is not.[5]

When the American rebellion against Great Britain broke out, the insurgent colonists used the language and tradition of the commonwealth to express their ideals. Drawing especially from English history, colonists meant "commonwealth" in two main senses. In the first instance, it suggested a republican government—the idea of a popular alternative to the monarchy, or as Edmund Pendleton put it, a "state belonging to the whole people rather than the Crown." John Adams urged that every state declare itself a commonwealth, and four eventually did so officially: Massachusetts, Kentucky, Pennsylvania, and Virginia. Commonwealth also was associated with a particular view of property—both private goods and public resources—which highlighted its social nature. Together, ideas of popular government and the social quality of property combined in the term "commonwealth" to suggest the concept of a democratic government that sees as its aim tending to the general welfare, especially in opposition to selfish economic interests.[6]

Commonwealth comes from the old English words "common" and "weal," and, used interchangeably with "commonweal" (and associated with Latin terms like *res publica*), originally meant the common well-being or good of the community. Early English uses include Harding's from 1470: "He dyd the commen wealthe sustene," in the first sense of common well-being.[7]

Commonwealth early became identified with the concept of the public, the whole body of the people or the state, and thus the classical tradition of politics, especially the idea of republican government in which "the whole people" had voice and interest. English writers of the Renaissance drew on classical notions of republic, like Cicero's definition of the commonwealth as "the people's affair," where "the people is not every group of men, associated in any manner, but is the coming together of a considerable number of men who are united by common agreement about law and rights and by the desire to participate in mutual advantage."[8]

By the seventeenth century, commonwealth customarily conveyed the idea of government of and by free citizens, instead of the Crown. Thus, the parliamentary act of May 19, 1649 ending the monarchy declared that "the People of England . . . shall henceforward be Governed as a Commonwealth and Free State." Republican currents in the Cromwellian era were expressed by writers like John Milton, Algernon Sidney, and James Harrington, whose thinly disguised treatise on the proper form of government for England, *The Commonwealth of Oceana,* envisioned a government of balancing parts, based upon numerous small freeholders: "If the whole people be landlords, or hold the lands so divided among them that no one man or number of men within the compass of the few or aristocracy overbalance them, the empire . . . is a commonwealth." In the seventeenth century, Harrington and other English republicans drew upon English history—what they saw as an ancient struggle of free men, small property owners, against tyranny, stemming from the conflict between Anglo-Saxons and Norman invaders.[9]

Thus, English radicals had challenged not only the monarchy but the large nobility with the language of commonwealth. In America, the commonwealth conception of government similarly involved the specific themes of citizen autonomy and independence, based on a widespread diffusion of property, as well as self-government. John Adams believed the people were free "in proportion to their property" and if "a division of the land into small quantities" allowed many to hold property, "the multitude will take care of the liberty, virtue and interest of the multitude, in all acts of government."[10]

In the American context, this ensemble of ideas and ideals gave a distinctive cast to the revolutionary cause. By the 1770s, to many English and colonial radicals alike, England seemed "one mass of corruption" and "tottering on the brink of destruction," while America was a land where the "ancient English tradition of liberty" might still survive through government's dedication to the public welfare. As the Trenton *New Jersey Gazette* put it,

> Here Governments their last perfection take.
> Erected only for the People's sake:

Founded no more on Conquest or in blood,
But on the basis of the Public Good.[11]

The radicals' mood combined exhilaration and anxiety in an uneasy mix. "By 1776, the Revolution came to represent a final attempt . . . even a desperate attempt . . . to realize the traditional Commonwealth ideal of a corporate society," one historian has observed.[12]

Yet the very constellation of themes that gave the American Revolution its elan and coherence was fraught with internal conflicts which unraveled the "republican spirit" of the young nation in the 1780s. In the first instance, the commonwealth ideal represented a white, property-owning, and decidedly masculine construction of politics which obscured social conflicts as much as it expressed common goals. Slaves and, in most states, even free blacks were not part of the citizenry. In the tradition of classic republicanism, intellectual leaders of the revolution employed a strikingly gendered language of politics which equated "male" virtues with public and "female" qualities with private life or (if they affected public activity) the corruption of politics. The ideal republic was filled "with all great, manly and warlike virtues," while "luxury," the great corrupter of public life, meant not only wealth but, in the words of Joseph Huntington, a tendency toward "soft effeminacy" with overtones of sexual vulnerability; it could leave "minds stupefied, and bodies enervated, by wallowing for ever in one continual puddle of voluptuousness." The first explosive line of fissure in the new republic proved its middle-class nature.[13]

During the revolutionary period, large merchant and landed interests split between loyalists to Britain and those, like the DeLancey party in New York, who participated in the independence movement but spent much of their effort fighting what they saw as dangerous signs of radicalism. The dominant tone was set by a middle-class constituency that included lawyers, some merchants, clergy outside the Anglican Church, small manufacturers, ship captains, and others. Such men, sympathetic to participation by an enlarged citizenry during the conflict with Britain, sought to balance economic self-interest with some conception of community responsibility and moral accountability. But they also resisted any *challenge* to the distribution of property, and viewed with contempt the civic potential of women, the poor, slaves, and the unskilled.

John Adams, spokesman for middle-class republican ideas and careful scholar of classic republican theory that he was, drew on older and more radical notions of republicanism in his first draft of the 1760s work *Dissertation of the Feudal and Canon Law,* when he wrote that "Property monopolized or in the Possession of a few is a Curse to Mankind. We should . . . preserve all from extreme Poverty, and all others from extravagant Riches." But his alliances with affluent Whig merchants might well have been troubled by the explicit advocacy of such ideas, and the passage was deleted from the published text. More generally, Adams urged that true citizens should not be seen as "the vile populace or rabble of the country . . . but the greater and more judicious part of the subjects of all ranks."[14]

In the 1780s, elites increasingly worried about the "chaos" and disorder engendered by decentralized government and the popular participation of groups of mechanics, artisans, small farmers, and the like. The Constitution and the Federalist argument both reflect this thinking, based as they were on the supposition that "public virtue"—a sense of what more affluent citizens viewed as the general interests and the commonweal—was in short supply. These arguments attracted the support of many dismayed by the turmoil they perceived in the decentralized confederation of states. By the time of the constitutional debates, John Adams vigorously disputed the natural inclination of citizens to put the commonweal over private interests: "Not only a majority, but almost all, confine their benevolence to their families, relations, personal friends, parish, village, city, county, province. . . . Very few, indeed, extend it impartially to the whole community." Alexander Hamilton put it more starkly, in terms that suggested a brutally Hobbesian view of human nature: "*Every man* ought to be supposed a *knave;* and to have no other end, in all his actions, but *private interest.* By this interest we must govern him; and, by means of it, *make him cooperate to public good,* not withstanding his insatiable avarice and ambition."[15]

But popular radicalism in urban and rural areas proved a force of its own, often overtaking the cautions of middle-class leadership, piquing the fears of the elite, and lending a radical democratic edge to the terminology of commonwealth politics. The evidence suggests that, at least in cities like Boston, New York, and Philadelphia, a growing disparity of wealth had taken place throughout the eighteenth century and had been accompanied by a striking increase in urban poverty, affecting about one fifth of the white population, by the time of the revolution. Against such a background, more popular conceptions of commonwealth emphasized the need for an active, mobilized citizenry. Especially in New England, the commonwealth ideal had long entailed voluntary traditions of mutual aid, town meeting government, and religious convenant. In the course of the constitutional debates and in their aftermath, these traditions came to be expressed in new ways. Thus, the Democratic-Republican societies that emerged in the 1790s in support of the French Revolution resisted a narrow and passive version of citizenship, where citizens simply delegated authority to elected leaders. "The power of government can only be kept within its constituted limits by the display of a power equal to itself, the collected sentiment of the people," declared Henry Kammerer in 1794. "The spirit of liberty, like every virtue of the mind, is to be kept alive only by constant action."[16]

Sharpening social divisions were expressed not only in differing theories of government, but also in differing conceptions of property. In popular terms, the language of the commonwealth conveyed both the *social* dimensions of individual property and also the tangible, ancient idea of the "commons." These views of property came to expression in struggles concerning grazing and fishing rights, land policy, pricing, and taxes.[17]

Commonwealth theories of property drew on religious values that stressed human custodianship of goods. In the "Jubilee" tradition, for instance, God instructed the Hebrew people that every forty-ninth year private lands should be returned to the common tribal pool, so that no large private accumulations could develop: "Your land must not be sold on a permanent basis, because you do not own it; it belongs to God and you are like foreigners who are allowed to make use of it" (Leviticus 25:23). Such a tradition—the "Year of the Lord"—continued as a major thread in Isaiah and in the New Testament, especially the Gospel of Luke. Thomas Aquinas, building on such traditions, stressed the social dimensions of property: individuals may own property, but they do not have the exclusive rights to use it as they wish. Property always entails the concept of social obligation. Aquinas's view formed the cornerstone of subsequent Catholic social doctrine.[18]

Secular, entrepreneurial leaders of the revolutionary cause held not dissimilar notions. Thus, Benjamin Franklin urged on the nation the example of the Iroquois Indian, whose "property . . . except the . . . temporary cabin, his bow, his matchcoat and other little acquisitions absolutely necessary for his subsistence, seems to me the Creature of Public Convention." Franklin argued that all substantial private property should be seen as "the creature of Society . . . subject to the calls of that Society."[19]

Complementing such theories of the social nature of private property was the concept of commons, or the collectively held goods of the community. Traditions and practices of commons were transplanted to the colonies with the first European settlers of the seventeenth century. Indeed, immigrants left England and other nations in some cases partly out of distaste for the spreading practices of "engrossing," which saw the gentry seize common lands by force or purchase. New England settlers typically created a pattern of one "house lot" from one to ten acres for each family, with shares in the common lands of pasture, wood, and meadow. A separate land was set aside for the church and meetinghouse, often adjoining the town green, or commons, "which provided a kind of physical axis of the community and served other community functions—militia muster, farmers market, even in some places, common pasture."[20]

In the first years of settlement, most crops were grown in common fields, but the soil and weather in New England proved to be less favorable to single crop planting, and soon individual planting of a variety of crops became the norm. Continuing immigration into towns also created sharp political tensions: Were newcomers to get a share in the commons, for instance? Did they receive land for a household lot, the very symbol of citizenship in English society?

But other patterns of commons—grazing of livestock, for instance, timber use, hunting and fishing rights, and village town halls and greens, often called "the common"—persisted in many areas, even to the present.[21]

During the revolutionary period, ideas of commons and the commonwealth concept of property as a social obligation served as rallying cries among lower-class groups. Thus, in the midst of the economic crisis in Philadelphia in 1779, artisans challenged Robert Morris, a wealthy merchant, for shipping grain outside the city. In view of the local scarcity of bread, they argued that Morris's property rights to use his ship were held in check by the social origins of property and the needs of the community. "We hold that [the shipyard workers] and the state in general have a right in the service of the vessel," they argued, "because it constitutes a considerable part of the advantage [the workers] hoped to derive from their labours." Property is subject to the commonwealth, they continued: "the *property* of the vessel is the immediate right of the owners," but "the service of it is the right of the community collectively with the owners."[22]

In Rhode Island, a series of fierce battles between farmers and mill owners took place over a farmer's common-law right "to enter the close of his neighbor, for the purpose of abating or removing the cause of injury" when owners built dams and thus damaged the fishing in the rivers, long regarded as a commons. In 1773, petition campaigns and agitation by backcountry farmers upriver from Pawtucket Falls caused the General Assembly to enact a law with the title, "An act making it lawful to break down and blow up Rocks at Pawtucket Falls to let fish pass up." In 1785, the Assembly limited the rights of sawmill owners in the Pawcatuck River Valley to dam the rivers during the spring runs. In other parts of the state, however, farmers were not as successful. Sixty-six farmers from Cranston and Warwick petitioned the Assembly on the ground that dams and commercial fishermen's nets were preventing alewives from spawning, adding that "before said obstructions said fish were taken in great plenty and were of infinite advantage to the Poor and middling sort of People." They claimed an "unalienable right" to fish in the rivers, but the Assembly ruled against them. Throughout this period, in successful struggles and defeats alike, farmers found in the commonwealth vocabulary of the revolution a way to frame their tangible concerns.[23]

The clashing understandings of government and property which began to widen in the 1770s and 1780s found expression in the Federalist and anti-Federal debates. Both sides stressed popular sovereignty—the concept that in America the people themselves created government. Moreover, both held to certain conceptions of commonweal, the mandate for government "to provide for the general welfare." But more affluent and powerful interests tended to stress the need for government to select out the few "men who possess most wisdom to discern, and most virtue to pursue, the common good of the society." In contrast, anti-Federalists resorted to a language of broadly participatory republicanism. "A republican, or free government can only exist where the body of the people are virtuous and where property is pretty equally divided," wrote Samuel Bryan in his "Letter of Centinel, No. 1" (1787). "In such a government the people are the sovereign and their sense of opinion is the criterion of every public measure; for when this ceases to be the case, the nature of the government is changed, and an aristocracy, monarchy or despotism will rise on its ruin."[24]

In short, differing views on who should have *power* over the commonwealth remained the central dividing line between elite and popular perspectives. These contending arguments set the basic framework for conflicts about the meaning of the American commonwealth legacy through the nineteenth century and formed the background for the emergence of "populism" as a distinctive politics as the century drew to a close.

In the revolutionary aftermath, artisans adapted republican themes to their own circumstances, interpreting their crafts as like property, and thus sources of virtue and independence. Such groups created a mass base for popular republicanism along the urban seaboard. In the eighteenth and early nineteenth centuries, artisan parades, great public events where each craft would march by banner, were symbolic celebrations of republican government and liberty as well as livelihood. But artisans in the new nation soon experienced threats from the emergence of national markets, which offered greater profits for contractors who parceled out portions of tasks to less skilled workers. By the 1830s, artisanal republicanism had begun to develop a challenge to emerging industrialists and commercial interests, arguing that the "commonwealth" of equal and cooperating citizens was threatened by concentrated economic power. In their view, speculative capitalists whose primary motives were greed and narrowly selfish interests represented a mortal danger to the American tradition.[25]

In popular republicanism, the independence—the "freedom"—guaranteed by widespread, modest landholdings joined with freedom from despotic and arbitrary political authority to create a commonwealth of productive citizens. Protection for small property owners or craftsmen and their rights, the importance of production for the community welfare as well as one's family, regular involvement in public affairs and community decisions—these were the cornerstones of a democratic tradition that largely shaped the early nineteenth-century language of politics.

The tradition was in a number of respects restrictive: republicanism defined citizenship in sharply gendered ways; it drew most directly from English experience, and part of its potency came from the contrast with "others" (slaves, the landless, the poor, many immigrants) defined as outside the orbit of "productive citizen"; its associations with an evangelical Protestantism carried images of America as the "New Jerusalem," a redeemed nation radically unlike the aged and corrupt nations of the Old World. But despite its restrictions, this set of themes also turned out to hold potent resources for challenges to concentrated wealth and power as the nineteenth century progressed.

Throughout that century, lower-class groups mounted struggles not only around their livelihood but around their home life, community institutions, and urban physical infrastructure as well. These conflicts, fought out in a civic vocabulary that poorer groups shared with middle-class and business interests, carried older themes of conflict over the commons into a modern, urban era. Schools and parks were striking examples. Thus, the Philadelphia Working Men's Committee in 1830, after conducting an investigation of schools, declared itself "constrained to believe that, until the means of equal instruction shall be equally secured to all, liberty is but an unmeaning word, and equality an empty shadow." In place of the existing system which schooled children of the wealthy, it declared itself in favor of "common schools" extended "throughout the Commonwealth," placed "immediately under the control and suffrage of the people" and open "to all classes . . . supported at the expense of all."[26]

After the Civil War, a range of radicals and reformers also used a vocabulary of commonwealth to challenge large-scale systems of concentrated power. Thus, former slaves proposed a distribution of land—"forty acres and a mule"—that would allow them full rights as citizens. "The great problem to be solved by the American people is this," wrote the African American poet Frances Harper in 1875, "whether or not there is strength enough in democracy, virtue enough in our civilization and power enough in our religion to have mercy and deal justly with four millions of people lately translated from the old oligarchy of slavery to the new commonwealth of freedom." Women's rights crusaders envisioned a "maternal commonwealth" as an alternative to the male-dominated public world, which they argued was increasingly brutal and corrupt. Similarly, labor organizers called for a "cooperative commonwealth" where small producers and cooperative enterprise would replace the new trusts and corporations.[27]

When the steelworkers at Andrew Carnegie's Homestead Steel Works went on strike in 1892 to protest a sharp wage cut for skilled workers whose jobs were threatened by new technologies, they declared that the centralization of emerging industrial and financial structures gave the rich "an enormous and despotic power over the lives and fortunes of their employees ... a power which eviscerates our national Constitution and our common law, and is coming to mean in effect nothing less than the right to manage the country to suit themselves." Their language of protest voiced fears about the destruction of the commonwealth and republican government which had been expressed countless times in a turbulent nineteenth-century history of working-class and agrarian struggles. Jacksonian artisans in working-class parties of the 1840s, former slaves, Knights of Labor assemblies—numbering at the peak perhaps ten thousand, in virtually every industrial community in the United States—farmers' cooperatives, women's temperance and moral reform organizations, railroad workers' unions, and an array of other popular organizations had all voiced similar themes, with a growing sense of urgency. After a tempestuous century of conflict about such ideas, the various strands of action merged in the Populist movement that challenged the emerging order of corporate capitalism.[28]

———

Populism has haunted the left as well as modern society for the last hundred years, simultaneously the bane of socialist and capitalist elites. Understood as "the people in politics," populism is a tradition with ancient roots, recalling themes that reach back to Greek and Roman popular revolts. More directly, it draws from eighteenth- and nineteenth-century traditions such as Jeffersonian democracy, European Romanticism, Scandinavian folk-school traditions, and the *sans-culottes* of the French Revolution. As a distinctive modern politics,

populism took specific shape in both Russia and the United States
in the late nineteenth-century agrarian movements that blended
modernist themes with peasant and rural traditions of commons and
communal solidarity, and had urban artisanal and working-class
counterparts as well. In the twentieth century, populist-type movements have appeared both in Third World countries and in advanced industrial societies. Historian Gianna Pomata, for instance,
has described how the populist tradition represented a powerful political alternative to Marxism in the Soviet Union into the 1920s, and
was ruthlessly suppressed by Stalin, who saw populism and populist
economists as perhaps his greatest practical threat and ideological
opposition.[29]

Populism, it is noted, has to do with a call for the "return of
power to ordinary people." Thus Richard Darman, deputy secretary
of the Treasury for Ronald Reagan, argued to conservatives that populism is "anti-elitist, opposed to excessive concentrations of power,
oriented toward fairness and toward a degree of levelling." On the
Democratic side, Iowa Senator Tom Harkin, founder of the Congres-
sional Populist Caucus, described populism as based on the conviction that "freedom and democratic institutions rest on the widest
possible dissemination of wealth and power—and we've come to the
point where too few people have too much and the rest of us have
too little."

But the breadth of the agreement on a rough definition of populism points to the problem in understanding its meaning. Democratic politicians from Jesse Jackson to Tom Harkin, Richard Geph-
ardt, Barbara Mikulski, and Jim Hightower have all been labeled
"populist" or have used the term in self-description. Republican politicians, from zealous right-wingers like Jack Kemp or Newt Gingrich
of Georgia to Ronald Reagan himself, have similarly claimed the
mantle. In 1988, the term was used to cover everything from Gep-
hardt's "get tough" with trade competitors policy to Pat Robertson's
calls for "moral renewal."

Populism as a journalistic label meant "little guys" against the
big shots. Political commentators agree that it forms a potent political language. Many have argued, in fact, that the outcome of the presidential election of 1988 suggests that populist themes—in contrast
to the managerial liberalism that Michael Dukakis reflected until the
very end of the campaign—provide perhaps the only hope for the
Democrats on a presidential level. But the complexities of whom
"the people" includes and what a return of "power" to the people
might entail in a technologically advanced and socially fragmented
society has led most observers to avoid any deeper exploration of
what "populism" means and has meant in practice.[30]

In fact, a good deal of social history is now available to use in reflecting on the dynamics that lead to radically different sorts of "populist outcomes." Especially, historians and theorists like Seymour Martin Lipset, Lawrence Goodwyn, Gianna Pomata, Alan Brinkley, and Steven Hahn have drawn attention to popular democratic *experiences,* or their absence, in public life and politics as the differentiator between more inclusive and democratic populism and authoritarian versions. Goodwyn, for example, observed that the organizing activities in the Farmers Alliances—the network of rural cooperatives of the 1880s—formed the foundation for the Populist party of the 1890s, and differentiated the "authentic movement" from its thinner, "shadow" versions that were simply electoral.[31]

Such experience in fact has been expressed, in the American case, by the language and concepts of commonwealth. When popular movements of "the people" aim at gaining power over the terms and instruments of the commonwealth, or the infrastructure of their life in common, such a struggle can occasion collective action among a highly diverse population. Such activity, in turn, opens political space far more tolerant of difference than social-change movements, on either left or right, which seek cultural and ideological conversion. When the struggle for power over the commonwealth is decisively defeated, or ceases to be part of a movement's real objectives— typically, along with the vocabulary of commonwealth itself—the charges that an "elite" has dishonored a people's folkways and "taken power" can become a politics of bitter grievance, not democratic hope. An exploration of the original Populists illustrates this dynamic.

"The stock law is the topic in this part of the country now," wrote a white dirt farmer named L. J. Jones in an 1885 letter to a local newspaper in Carroll County, Georgia. Jones argued that local planters' and merchants' effort to abolish the traditional "common law" rights of open pasturage for cattle and livestock threatened the spirit and virtue of the nation, and he envisioned a coalition in response to the danger that was, from the vantage of the white South, breathtakingly subversive in its intimations of multiracial action: "I want to say to the voters of Carroll county, that we as poor men and negroes do not need the law, but we need a democratic government and independence, that will do the common people good." Out of such sentiments, multiplied across the South and Midwest, American populism arose in the latter years of the nineteenth century as a movement to "restore government" to "the plain people."[32]

In urban areas and agricultural regions alike, the society which began to emerge in the last decades of the nineteenth century was a world removed from that of small towns and rural countryside in which American republican and religious themes had taken root and had some resonance. In 1830, the nation had twenty-three miles of railroad track. The telegraph was first used commercially in 1847. On the threshold of the Civil War, Cyrus McCormick's Harvester Works in Chicago was, he boasted, "the largest factory of its kind in the world," with 3,500 employees. The Pullman Company, a leading American industry, employed 200 workers in its plant that built sleeping cars. In 1870, more than two thirds of America's workers were found in agriculture, forestry, and fishing. Eighty percent of the population lived in cities or rural areas with less than 8,000 people. Government, similarly, was tiny by later standards. Only 14,000 non-postal employees worked for the federal government. Capital investment per worker was $700 in manufacturing.

By 1910, American society had changed dramatically. Only one third of the work force was still engaged in farming, logging, or fishing. New York City's population had increased fourfold between 1860 and 1910; Chicago had 2.2 million people. By 1920, half the population lived in cities. With a vast stream of immigrants entering the country each year, the population doubled between 1870 and 1900. More than a quarter of all male adults had been born overseas. Capital invested per worker had risen to more than $2,000, while the total investment in manufacturing had grown from $2.7 billion in 1879 to $20.8 billion in 1914. Hundreds of thousands of miles of railroads and telegraphs connected the country in transportation and communications systems that allowed a qualitatively different productive process.[33]

Popular movements understood the vast changes overtaking American society. Few imagined a return to a simple world of small towns and rural countryside. What American workers and farmers, small business interests, and middle-class reformers developed to replace the classical republican vision were new instruments for seeking popular control over the institutions that were reshaping the nation.[34]

Across the agricultural belt of the nation's South and Midwest in the 1880s, millions of farmers found themselves sinking ever deeper into debt as a result of a national monetary system and centralizing transportation systems that operated in the narrow self-interest of financiers and industrialists. Moreover, accompanying the emerging large-scale monetary, communication, and transportation systems was an attack on traditional "commons" like grazing lands and forest resources that lower-class groups used to sustain their independence and dignity.

Thus, in Georgia in the 1880s bitter conflicts arose about the meaning of "property." Affluent advocates of changes in the laws that would fence in livestock appealed to the "rule of law" about property, over against "custom." "When land belonged to the government it was right for all to pasture" their horses, pigs, or cows, argued the *Jefferson Forest News*. But once "government transferred those lands to different individuals," no one had a "right to trespass on another man's land." Or as the *Carroll County Times* put it, "What is mine I have a right to do as I please with and no man has a right to graze my land whether enclosed or not." In contrast, opponents of new laws like J. M. Green appealed to inherited commonwealth ideas about the social nature of property. The "idea of fencing a man's possessions against a neighbor's stock is a creation of local statute, and contrary to natural rights, nature and common sense," said Green. "The woods . . . were put here by our Creator for the benefit to his people," maintained W. D. Loworn. "I don't think it right to deprive a large majority to please a minority." As one farmer summed up the "fundamental principles" of rural opposition: "No man can deny that all the land of this country was once common property, belonged to all the people of Georgia in common as public domain. All once had a perfect right to graze it in common." He asked, rhetorically, "How or when did any of them loose [sic] that right?" In his view, "as citizens of this grand old commonwealth . . . they still . . . have that RIGHT."[35]

Desperate to retain their land, escape tenantry, and maintain their independence, the nation's farmers devised a new method of cooperatively marketing their crops and purchasing their supplies. They formed organizations called Farmers Alliances to buy and sell on a large scale, in an effort to avoid especially the local merchant interest rates which reached levels of 30 percent or even higher a year.

A gospel of "large-scale cooperation" swept the South and West in an enormous social movement, populism. Supported by their own system of more than a thousand insurgent newspapers, a vast lecture circuit with tens of thousands of itinerant speakers, and revival-like encampments, the farmers constructed a phalanx of cooperatives and made alliances with groups like the Knights of Labor. When the very existence of the cooperatives was threatened by the refusal of banks to extend credit, they created the People's party to challenge policies of government.

The People's, or Populist, party mounted the last truly serious challenge to the two-party system in American political history. It did this, especially, through a series of struggles around the concept of "cooperative commonwealth"—their vision of a future community in which citizens would once again exercise power over the basic foundations of communal life.[36]

The cooperative commonwealth was not hostile to private property. Rather, the thrust of the Populist platform proposed large-scale cooperative and social control over basic elements of the nation's economic foundations, those features like transportation, money supply, and land policy especially seen as essential to independence and small business survival. Populists viewed the loss of popular control at the hands of monopolies and concentrated financial interests as threatening the essentials of civic life and democratic government. Thus, challenges to elite control over money supply, transportation and communications systems, land policy, schools, marketing, and a series of similar areas formed the central thrust of the program. Frank Doster, a well-known populist in Kansas who later became chief justice of the Kansas Supreme Court, voiced the plight of the producers and their ideas for remedy at Topeka on Labor Day, 1894:

> Everything which goes to sustain his physical life, which enables him to conduct his daily toil, which makes existence possible . . . have become the monopoly of others. . . . Now the terrible elements of physical nature which the gods can scarce bridle or control—steam, electricity, compressed air . . . the common property of all, have been made the monopoly of the few, have been turned aside from the beneficent ends for which designed, to serve the selfish purposes of avarice and greed. . . .
>
> Against the tyrannical exercise of this power the People's Party in behalf of the laborers of the land protests. . . . The Populist Party . . . says that the subjects of those monopolies and trusts are public in their nature. . . . It would have the government, that is, the people, assert their rightful dominion over the same. . . .[37]

Academic and left-wing critics commonly have charged that populism's idea of *agency*—the "people" or ordinary citizens—in the nineteenth century and in more recent manifestations is a loose and ill-defined concept compared to the theoretical rigor of class. Moreover, populism is often described as a *reformist* strategy, focused on practical goals like popular control over resources, with only vague long-run objectives.[38]

But in fact, populism's purported weaknesses, seen from a vantage that is skeptical of elaborated blueprints for the future or sharply defined definitions of who appropriately leads the process of change, have proven to be considerable strengths. Thus, for instance, the very porousness of a concept like "the plain people" allows expansive and inclusive understandings when the movement is seeking allies in a struggle for actual power.

"The people" is not an indeterminate category, but a concept based on the idea of inheritance. Populist anger grows from a conviction that an elite has dishonored and abused a historically and culturally constituted group, its memories, origins, common territory, and ways of life. Thus there is a kind of class intuition in populism, a belief that common people are mistreated by the powerful. And there are boundaries: a "people" is defined symbolically rather than abstractly or quantitatively, as with class. But identity is conveyed nonetheless, through stories and legends, oral traditions, folk wisdom, foods, rituals, ways of speaking and remembering. A people normally has a point of origin and a moment of birth—the Hebrew Exodus, the mythic origins of Athens and Rome, our own Declaration of Independence. Such a founding moment allows for celebration and ritual connecting present to past and future.

Consciousness of being part of a national people coexists and sometimes conflicts with separate "peoplehoods," especially in a nation as immensely variegated as the United States. This is a tension especially striking in the case of African Americans, for instance. But for oppressed groups, claims on a common peoplehood can be a powerful resource. In Martin Luther King's terms, for instance, the civil rights movement represented the heart of the American tradition. Segregation was an evil "betrayal of the southern heritage" itself. The meaning of terms like "people," "patriotism," and "sacred values" can only be understood in context, from an analysis of who uses them and how.[39]

But the vagueness of the populist formulation, growing as it does from the sense of aggrieved peoplehood, leads to political ambiguity and volatility. How such a sense of grievance comes to final expression depends on a number of factors: the dynamics of the society that are responsible for politicizing the communities in the first place; the nature of the communities involved and their relation to others; the ideology, program, and effectiveness of those who seek to organize such discontent into a coherent social force; and the nature of the interior social and cultural processes at work in the specific subcommunities that make up "the people." In particular, when elite groups are able to manipulate parochial themes within the sense of "peoplehood" without effective contest from those who seek to create broader linkages among discrete oppressed communities, the outcome of the populist mood tends strongly toward authoritarianism.

The *experiential* dimensions of populist politics—the interior life of subcommunities as they are mobilized and transformed through the process of becoming a social movement—is an especially neglected subject, but one that bears directly on the outcome of group protests. A process of political activation normally begins as people

seek to defend established ways of life or perceived rights that they
have come to expect. In turn, how such inherited cultural resources
are sorted out proves the crucial variable. Whether popular democratic themes of civic idealism, cooperation, religiously motivated action on behalf of the oppressed, pluralism, and tolerance come to
be distinguished from themes of rapacious individualism, hedonism,
contempt, and fear of "others" depends on the evolution of groups
as they move from resistance to self-conscious opposition to centers
of power.[40]

In *democratic* populist movements, as people are moved to activism in *defense* of their rights, traditions, and institutions, they change.
They discover in themselves and their traditions new resources, po-
tentials, resonances. They repair capacities to work together for collective problem solving. They find out new political facts about the
world. They build networks and seek contacts with other groups of
the powerless to forge a more heterogeneous group identity. And
this whole process in turn helps to clarify basic power relations in
society. In sum, people deepen the meaning of what they are doing,
from understanding politics merely as a protest against threat to
coming to see the need for a struggle for new conceptions of rights
and participation and power. This kind of change is the identifying
mark, specifically, of a democratic movement that seeks a transformation of power relations, not simply a return to past conditions or
the replacement of one elite with another.[41]

Understanding the subtle, shifting nature of the experiences by
which people change, individually and collectively, enables us to begin to clarify and render comprehensible many dimensions of the
populist impulse and its possibilities. Depending upon how the institutional building blocks of populism develop over time and link up
with other groups—and depending on who organizes them and on
the organizers' program and vision—many different outcomes are
possible. The vision of the American destiny put forth by populism
can be inclusive, open, and cooperative—or it can be closed, static,
fearful, and bellicose.

The key to such a democratic resolution in the American context has been the concept of commonwealth. Late-nineteenth-
century populism was scarcely free of the prejudice and hatreds
woven through the dominant political culture; indeed, racial animos-
ities especially proved a fatal line of division in the face of a determined business assault. But for a decade, populism's practical reformulation of civic ideals as demands for public control over the
foundations and levers of community and economic life, embodied
in the language of "cooperative commonwealth," occasioned a public arena and language of change considerably more tolerant of dif-

ference than either the dominant culture or radical movements that aimed at conversion to a singular set of social and economic principles. Such a reformulation allowed the movement to garner wide support from diverse interests and social groups—African American farmers, white landowners, urban professionals and intellectuals, woman suffragists, ethnic communities, Hispanics in the Southwest, railroad workers, and a variety of others—who would have been far less likely to find common ground around a more detailed ideological program.[42]

Populist themes created the vocabulary for a variety of movements in the twentieth century and have reappeared in our time. But control over decision making by experts and managers also undermined populisms's foundations. And populism denuded of commonwealth concepts becomes the plaything of demagogues and authoritarians. At times, one can see the change in the rhetoric of individual leaders. Thus, Tom Watson, a Georgia crusader for black-white alliances and a nonimperialist foreign policy in the 1890s, ended his career as a virulent baiter of blacks, Jews, Catholics, and foreigners, when the commonwealth focus of the populist movement disappeared by the early twentieth century.[43]

Populist movements infused with strong commonwealth ideals have been rarities in our age. The main programs for reform in our time have come, instead, from socialism and social democracy— often with problematic consequences for democracy itself.

The Eclipse of the Citizen

*L*ate-nineteenth- and early-twentieth-century democrats held a contradiction in their theory of politics that ironically contributed to the long-range defeat of their participatory goals: by and large, commonwealth advocates combined a defense of community and participation with an uncritical celebration of science and technology as the highest form of knowledge and the key to human emancipation. Yet models of knowledge based on scientific epistemology—emphasizing a detached, rational, analytic observer as the judge of truth and the most effective problem solver—were inherently in conflict with the communal common sense, folk traditions, and appreciation for craft knowledge mediated through everyday life experience that were populism's wellspring.[1]

Moreover, concentrated capital, the major source of power in industrial society, seemed to demand an equally concentrated opponent—and to most reformers, the only serious instrument for taming the excesses of modern capitalism appeared to be government. But as the government, rather than the citizenry, became the active agency, the thrust of reform politics marginalized active citizenship rooted in local communities.

The results in America proved far-reaching. Elements of commonwealth and populist language, with ancient roots in America's political culture, continued powerful as a *rhetoric* of progressive reform. But as hopes for the exercise of genuine popular power over the commonwealth eroded, the thrust of the progressive program increasingly focused on redistributive justice through the state, not active democracy. Twentieth-century liberalism in the United States came to have similarities with the programs of socialist and social democratic governments in Europe. And across a range of political systems, experts, professionals, technocrats, and managers—purportedly far more qualified than the citizenry at large—acquired growing authority as the vanguard of scientific decision making.

———

The socialist movement emerged in Europe in the period from 1770 to 1840, when critics began to describe the ravages of industrial capitalism, the trend toward sharpening class divisions, and ideals of an alternative social system. John Stuart Mill and Karl Marx both used typologies of classes that included landlords, capitalists, and laborers. But for Marx this division was increasingly superseded by the categories of bourgeoisie and proletariat, or working class.[2]

In Marx's hands, the idea of class acquired a double meaning that was to shape subsequent socialist history. First, it formed a category of description. Class was a way of depicting the forces that shaped and impacted on people in modern society. This was what Marx meant by "class in itself." But class was used by Marx and most of his socialist descendants as also a strategic concept, representing the agency of liberation from capitalist depredation: class was seen as a group organized, self-conscious, and in conflict with others. This is what Marxists have meant by "class for itself."

In the double meaning can be found great irony. As a category of description, the left-wing view detailed the wrenching changes of modern life: the development of modern communications media; the bending and reshaping of the spaces in which people lived and worked; the uprooting and destruction of settled and traditional communities and connections; the sense of powerlessness that afflicted growing numbers of citizens at the hands of vast, distant, seemingly impersonal forces. At the same time, class has been used in politics to propose a homogenized instrument of emancipation that accepts such uprooting as painful but essential if a truly classless society is to emerge.

Such irony is clear in the work of Karl Marx and Friedrich Engels and in the conceptions of their theoretical and political progeny. Though less chiliastic, mainstream American progressives—whether they called themselves socialist or not—came eventually to have a not dissimilar view of change as the work of uprooted citizen-experts. And although few envisioned a classless society as a likely eventuality, the content of their reform efforts focused on redistribution of wealth and income in the direction of greater equality of circumstances, not on popular empowerment.

In the first instance, it was the remarkable project of Karl Marx to give historical concreteness to age-old conflicts of groups; indeed, the historical and analytical work of Marx and Engels sparkled with insight about the structural conditions which hindered or aided group formation. For example, in the *Communist Manifesto* they described the process of the working class's aggregation into factories, the growing disparities of wealth, the routinization of the work process—all forces which tended to increase collective solidarity. In a dramatic section of the *18th Brumaire,* by way of contrast, Marx recounted circumstances which hindered the French peasantry in forming common bonds, like bad communications. In their treatment of cities, Marx and Engels suggested that workers' new freedom of motion and contacts with a diversity of subcultures might create new conditions for a broader solidarity. Thus for Engels, "the driving of the workers from hearth and home" that accompanied urbanization and industrialization was "the very first condition of their intellectual emancipation." In his view, "modern large scale industry . . . has turned the worker, formerly chained to the land, into a completely propertyless proletarian, liberated from all traditional fetters, a free outlaw."[3]

Although the two thinkers saw such developments as laying the basis for broader association and group identity, they also described with feeling the suffering involved. According to Marx, in the modern factory "men are effaced by their labor." Workers' contributions and individuality become destroyed: "the individual characteristics of workers are obliterated." The mechanical world of machines and work schedules seemed to take on a life of its own, "quite independent of and divorced from the individuals." In contrast, "standing over against these productive forces we have the majority, robbed of all real life-content, abstract individuals."[4]

Insights like these gave Marxism a tremendous power and appeal. They named people's experiences of anomie, homelessness, and injustice. And they led to a tradition of left-wing support for forms of association which people created out of shared suffering and attempts to act together in the face of modern structures: benevolent associations, cooperatives, trade unions, and finally electoral parties.

Yet the socialist movement did more than analyze the rending tendencies of modern life and stand in solidarity with those who struggle against them. In its dominant theoretical tradition—and here one should certainly separate out a scattering of alternative voices, like William Morris and Martin Buber, who articulated more populist themes—the socialist left drew its theory of agency and its imagery for the future from the very terms of capitalist rationality and uprootedness. It remained caught by the language of the system with which it struggled.

Thus most socialist thought has assumed that a sundering of people's communal and historical identities—of "their roots"—is the indispensable prerequisite of freedom. It has proposed, in place of a community weakened or lost, a community based on "new" relationships. The international working class not only "will be" the human race, as the Internationale puts it, but *has to* become the human race for the escape from devastation to take place. In sum, Marxism, and the broader socialist left which shared its essential view of change, has assumed that people become that to which capitalism tends to reduce them. It is a theory that is profoundly flawed.

Marx often and clearly articulated such a political theory. In his view, workers' very detachment was the *basis* of their revolt. As he argued in the Introduction to his *Critique of Hegel's Philosophy of Right,* the workers' "complete loss of humanity" forces them to a "complete redemption of humanity." Or as he put it in *The Holy Family,* "since the abstraction of all humanity, even of the semblance of humanity, is practically complete in the full-blown proletariat, it follows that the proletariat can and must free itself." Both Marx and Engels described workers' relation to the past with ferocity. For Marx, there had to be a "radical rupture" with what had gone before. For Engels, "tradition is the great retarding force . . . but being merely passive is sure to be broken down."[5]

If such views reflected only the notions of nineteenth-century theorists, it would make little difference in the present. Indeed, in their political ideas, Marx and Engels were by and large merely expressing the abstract rationalism of the Enlightenment, applied to working-class instead of middle-class experience. Karl Marx was born into the world of the middle-class Enlightenment. His father, Henrich, counselor-at-law to the High Court of Appeal in Trier, was a model representative of "the new middle classes" and a founder of a literary society which discussed Enlightenment ideas at length, according to Eleanor Marx, Karl's youngest daughter: "steeped in the free French ideas of the eighteenth century on politics, religion, life and art," and sharing the faith in the power of reason and contempt for "backwaters of superstition." Moreover, working people in nineteenth-century Europe themselves often eagerly debated and adopted Enlightenment ideas, struggling as they did against the backdrop of feudal reaction and clerical authoritarianism.[6]

The point is that the basic theory of insurgent consciousness as requiring an agency infused with an abstracted and uprooted cosmopolitanism continued to hold sway over the left and has shaped the dominant discourse of social change and protest in the modern world ever since. Thus it appeared in Lenin's theory of revolutionary consciousness as the worldview of middle-class, radicalized intellectuals that must be "introjected" into the working class. It surfaced in Leon Trotsky's contention that the Bolshevik party must be a "moral medium" of its own, guarding against ideological contamination and implicitly forming a socializing agency for its members in order to detach them from all prior loyalties.

In our time, the left view of liberated consciousness as a process of radical separation lay behind Michael Harrington's gentler but still uprooted view of a "rational, humanist moral code" that should replace what he called "traditional moral values." It informed conventional criteria used to distinguish social movements. Thus, E. J. Hobsbawm contrasted "primitive" protests grounded in communal ties with "modern, secular" movements like trade unions and socialist parties that supposedly severed such connections. Ralph Miliband meant much the same thing when he argued that "the Marxist notion of 'a most radical rupture' with traditional ideas signified a break with all forms of tradition, and must expect to encounter the latter not as friend but as foe." This view of social change and agency was succinctly summarized by Stanley Aronowitz in his 1974 essay entitled, appropriately enough, "The Working Class: A Break with the Past." According to Aronowitz, all particular identities—of "race and nationality and skill and industry"—are obstacles to consciousness. As he argued, "they constitute antagonisms which still act as a brake on the development of revolutionary consciousness."[7]

Such perspectives were essentially strategic arguments for how changes come about—arguments which in fact flattened and rendered invisible the actual cultural and historical resources that are employed in the course of real social conflict. The left theoretical language has also been reinforced by—while it also partially constitutes—a range of experiential settings which undergird a subjective experience of "rootlessness." The basic experience of large portions of the modern middle class—from childhood in the suburbs through college to work in professions or large corporate and governmental bureaucracies—tends to shift identifications away from any historical, religious, or geographical ties.

However powerfully the dominant left-wing language of deracination tended to shape socialist movements, it fails on a number of counts even to explain its own agency. As a strategic theory of social change, the model of protest as emerging from radical uprootedness is simply at stark odds with the material of social struggle: contemporary social history has demonstrated in immense detail the ways in which people draw on a range of ethnic, kinship, religious, and other relations in fighting back and sustaining solidarity. Thus the biases of socialist theory slight just those sources of power—traditional values and popular memories—which often prove most resistant to the characteristic patterns of domination in our age, bureaucracy and technocratic rationality.[8]

Such views of political emancipation as involving uprootedness have also been associated with a vision of the good society, reflected in the range of socialist ideologies. "Socialism" is a word that first appeared in the writings of Robert Owen as a militantly secular alternative to any religiously based visions of the future. It came to mean, most formally, the "socialization of the means of production" accomplished by government action. The concept of "socialization" itself entails a basic theory of social transformation that retained its attraction for modern intellectuals who have long since developed doubts about the simple nationalization of industry. Although more rooted socialist perspectives periodically emerged, the view of "the new man" (and more recently "new woman") has customarily rested upon the conviction that a future community replacing the atomization of capitalism will be a new association of women and men. People's motivations will be kinder and more generous than the dog-eat-dog morality of capitalist institutions today. But their ties to the past and to continuous communal connections will be sundered, in ways that resemble workplace social environments. Thus, even the most democratic and humane expressions of socialist policy, like the social democratic programs of Europe, envision the state as taking on more and more functions previously performed by communal and voluntary institutions.[9]

The left-wing theory of agency and the future created great obstacles in politics. To see emancipation as an intellectual shedding of the past produces a strong tendency toward condescension and a subjective distancing from large parts of the social fabric: religious institutions, ethnic groups, small business, geographically based identities, and so forth. In Marx's own time, it led to depictions of "the idiocy of rural life" and the description of shopkeepers and artisans as "reactionaries who seek to roll back the wheel of history." In our own time, it leads to characteristic left-wing lack of interest in multiple forms of association with "traditional" overtones, from mainstream Catholic parishes to Southern white Protestants, from Conservative and Orthodox synagogues to Eastern European immigrant groups.

At points, left-wing organizers have overcome such condescension in practice. In fact, such *practical* supersession of the dominant theoretical tradition has proven the key to moments of left-wing success. Popular communist struggles like Maoism in China, the movements of Southeast Asian Marxists, African and Latin American guerrillas, and a host of others have gained their support through populist appeals. Yet there is inherent, ineluctable movement toward crisis and tragedy when left-wing parties which have in practice come to identify themselves with and claim the mantle of popular traditions win power. This can be seen as the cultural contradiction of socialist societies across the world. Behind populist language, socialism holds a vision of the future that subordinates interest in empowering the citizenry to the dynamics of modernization, economic growth, and material equality.[10]

American progressives never achieved the power—nor, customarily, did they seek it—to recreate the world in such totalizing terms. But in milder fashion, American liberalism in its main variants in the twentieth century came to focus on redistributive justice as its central concern. At moments of their greatest success, progressives drew directly on the commonwealth legacy. But they also most often acquiesced in the growing power of a technocratic elite.[11]

In America, even the most radical leaders spoke a language of commonwealth politics, not socialism. Eugene Debs, the leader of the American socialist movement during the years of its greatest popular success, up to World War I preferred to call his vision of the future a "cooperative commonwealth." Indeed, until experiences with violent repression of the labor movement led him to join socialist groups, Debs distinguished between the cooperative commonwealth, which he favored, and socialism. Thus, testifying before the U.S. Strike Commission in 1894, he said: "No sir, I do not call myself a socialist. . . . I believe in the cooperative commonwealth upon the principles laid down by Lawrence Gronlund." Throughout his leadership of the Socialist party, moreover, Debs continued to root his politics in an alternative, civic tradition. "Quote as he might Marx, Engels, Lassalle, or Kautsky," explained one noted biographer, "the roots of his own social thought remained deeply enmeshed in a different tradition. . . . For Debs, that demanded an appeal to the individual's right to share fully in the value of his or her work, to participate equally as a citizen with others, and to rear his or her family accordingly."[12]

More mainstream political figures of the twentieth century like Theodore and Franklin Roosevelt similarly spoke in commonwealth accents in rhetorically confronting "the mighty forces" of commerce and industry that dominated the American economy. Teddy Roosevelt in a famous speech in 1908, given at the dedication of a memorial to John Brown, challenged the "sinister influence or control of special interests," which he identified with ancient threats to democracy. "Exactly as the special interests of cotton and slavery threatened our political integrity before the Civil War," he said, so now the great special business interests too often control and corrupt the men and methods of government for their own profit. . . . The true friend of property . . . is he who insists that property shall be the servant and not the master of the commonwealth. . . . The citizens of the United States must effectively control the mighty commercial forces which they have themselves called into being. . . .[13]

Similarly, Franklin Roosevelt declared before the Commonwealth Club during the 1932 presidential election that "we are coming to a view that private economic power is a public trust [and] enjoyment of that power by any individual or group must depend upon the fulfillment of that trust." Both Roosevelts recalled concepts of property as a public obligation associated with commonwealth ideals.

But they also envisioned "control" over commercial interests in a sense far different than did the populists of the nineteenth century. For most progressives, citizens acted by proxy and through the state, with no broad popular involvement. Indeed, Theodore Roosevelt borrowed his understanding of politics and government largely from Herbert Croly, the *New Republic* editor who explicitly redefined "democracy" away from any local, civic activity to what he called the "great community" of the state. Democracy, for Croly, no longer meant that citizens "assemble after the manner of a New England town-meeting"; instead of the communal experience of small towns, the nation as a whole must be bound together by "a comprehensive social ideal," mediated by modern communications systems. Actual, direct civic encounter was not necessary since "the active citizenship of the country meets every morning and evening and discusses the affairs of the nation with the newspaper as an impersonal interlocutor," providing "abundant opportunities of communications and consultation without any meeting" at all. As Walter Lippmann, another architect of mainstream progressive thought, put it, the growth of citizens, large-scale industry, communications, transportation, and so forth "has upset the old life on the prairies, made new demands upon democracy, introduced specialization and science . . . destroyed village loyalties . . . and created the impersonal relationships of the modern world."[14]

In a world where citizens no longer meet, the concept of "public" becomes increasingly thin and specialized—the preserve of representatives, guided by the advice of experts and professionals. Citizens became, in mainstream reformist thinking, detached from particular identities of all kinds. By the 1950s, Louis Hartz could argue with few challenges that individual detachment from older, communal ties was the touchstone of American politics: "The master assumption of American political thought has been atomistic social freedom." Infusing both European and American politics was a view of the middle-class professional, manager, or technician, endowed with a specialized and "objective" body of knowledge, as the ultimate problem solver and decision maker in the modern world.[15]

A democratic strand of liberalism continued to exist. Such a political vision, identifying with and seeking to collaborate with independent citizen initiatives, led Paul Douglas to argue in the 1940s that without "the organization of those who are at present weak and who need to acquire that which the world respects, namely power ... we are likely to find the permanent benefits of Rooseveltian liberalism to be as illusory as were those of the Wilsonian era." Indeed, a host of federal, state, and local government programs, from Harry Hopkins's Work Projects Administration (WPA) in the New Deal to more recent government efforts that have supported and helped catalyze independent citizen and community initiatives, reflect such a strand of democratic politics. But the reins of power in the construction of twentieth-century reform have been held by self-described liberals who had little use for an active, independent-minded citizenry.[16]

Most reformers accepted corporate models of management. "The folklore of the business elite came by gradual transition to be the symbols of government reformers," concluded J. B. Shannon's study of municipal reform. Shannon described a pattern evident elsewhere during the progressive period, from labor relations to resource management: "Efficiency, system, orderliness, budget economy, saving, all were injected into the efforts of reformers who sought to remodel municipal government in terms of the great impersonality of the corporate enterprise."[17]

Yet the corporate model itself was partly shaped by a new generation of managers and technical specialists who drew their basic metaphors and language from science, and the authoritarianism of progressivism came to fullest expression in the outlook of that new, technocratic middle class whose rise has been chronicled by anticapitalist apologists for its role such as Thorstein Veblen. A "culture of professionalism" detached knowledge from communal contexts in field after field, emphasizing rationality, methodical processes, and objectivity that suggested, to an anxious middle class, ways of reimposing order on a fast-changing, turbulent environment.[18]

The technocratic strains of liberalism have been a consistent theme throughout the twentieth century, above all the preference for what are called "value-free" techniques that in fact veil quite specific views of power and decision making with a scientific pose. Simply, a singular focus on "scientific" techniques in the area of social and ecomomic policy has left decision making to experts and administrators. For instance, the movement for "domestic science" sought to make housework a profession by applying scientific management techniques from the factory setting to the home environment. "Old functions of child welfare and training have passed over into the hands of sociologists, psychiatrists, physicians, home economists and other scientists dealing with problems of human welfare," wrote two child guidance experts in 1934. "Through parent education the sum of their experiments and knowledge is given back to parents in response to the demands for help." Employing educational media that ranged from settlement-house classes to home economics departments in colleges, domestic science stressed themes like nutrition, scientifically planned kitchens, and sanitation that conveyed the image of a remade, rational, homogenized, and well-regulated society. As historian Sara Evans described, "White sauce found an analog in the concept of the American melting pot which dissolved the pungent spiciness of diverse immigrant cultures. Women in settlement houses and clubs actively participated in 'Americanizing' immigrants through classes in language, decorum, and cooking."[19]

A technocratic perspective which saw professionals, experts, and managers as the key decision makers spanned a wide range of liberal and reform opinion. In the 1950s, Gunnar Myrdal could argue that "increasing political harmony . . . [is emerging] between all citizens in the advanced welfare state. The internal political debate in those countries is becoming increasingly technical in character." The technical, managerial pattern of social relations and social change created institutional similarities across political systems like communism, social democracy, and capitalism. "From the standpoint of the employee," remarked Arnold Toynbee, "it is coming to make less and less practical difference to him what his country's official ideology is and whether he happens to be employed by a government or commercial corporation." State-owned businesses under social democratic nations produced those same patterns of hierarchy, efficiency-minded management, and labor fragmentation that could be found in the most capitalist of American firms. And social policy in countries like Sweden—long a model for progressively inclined Americans—was if anything further advanced toward a technical, radically instrumentalized view of politics. Myrdal, drawing on Swedish experience, depicted welfare-state populations as simple *objects*—"like domesticated animals . . . with no conception of the wild life." Ordinary citizens no longer bore resemblance to sovereign actors.[20]

In such an environment, older republican themes of active citizenship and public life became radically weakened. The citizen was now reinvented as the oxymoron "private citizen." Home ownership, seen by community activists like Mary Follett earlier in the twentieth century as analogous to Jeffersonian small freeholds, foundations for involvement in the public life of the community, had dramatically changed in meaning. The house was a refuge, a private retreat, a fortress from the world "out there." A "man's home" was "his castle," while for women the "feminine mystique" bore an eerie resemblance to the concept of the feudal, helpless lady. The ideal became isolated nuclear families tied together by the consumer culture of the suburbs. And the very language of commonwealth had all but disappeared. It appeared on the surface of politics that a technocratic elite held virtually unchallenged sway. "The fundamental problems of the industrial revolution have been solved," declared Seymour Martin Lipset. Even those who felt greater unease with the world around them saw little prospect for much change. "For the first time in history, the engine of social progress has run out of the fuel of discontent," remarked Adlai Stevenson at the decade's end.[21]

Apparent complacency masked rising currents of discontent which had been building for years and which suddenly erupted in the social protests of the late 1950s and 1960s. Commonwealth and populist themes, feeding into the language of such movements, had been nonetheless eclipsed throughout the twentieth century. The commonwealth tradition did not have the force to affect in a major way the methods of civil rights or the revolts of the young. By the late 1960s, the legacy of a decade of social turmoil seemed, in many respects, to be a strengthening of the similarities between an American trade union–led reform movement and European socialism. "In their support of the Democrats as a mass, pro-welfare state party," observed one historian, "American trade unions have forged a political coalition with important—though hardly complete—structural and behavioural similarities to the Socialist Party–trade union alliances of Western Europe."[22]

But the impression of confident progress for an American-style social democratic politics was misleading. American liberalism was about to experience a prolonged crisis of faith and direction—followed, later, by a crisis in European socialism itself. And commonwealth ideas had in fact retained a subterranean power in corners of America's political culture. In the 1930s, '40s, and '50s, in particular, the populist tradition had produced a highly creative if also only partially successful attempt to adapt citizen politics to the challenges of the modern world, taking the form of a new generation of community organizations begun by the late Saul Alinsky. Alinsky, often seen as the dean of modern community organizing, deserves a larger reputation. Over the course of a long career, he constantly asked and sought to answer what active democracy might actually look like in sustained *practice,* in a complex, industrial, managerial society. Chapter 4 treats his role as a major bridge figure in the history of citizen politics, connecting the earlier legacy of populism to citizen initiatives in our time.

The Politics
of Everyday Life

*P*opular commonwealth currents in America had a different axis
from the concept of socialized property that forms the central
motif of left-wing politics. The fundamental line of social division
for American lower-class struggles was the question of power, in particular the argument that vast dissymmetries of power and wealth
threatened the fundamentals of public life, civic virtue, and commonwealth government.

In the nineteenth century, American popular movements—including those of freed slaves, women's rights crusaders, and farmers,
as well as the urban working class—developed an alternative to large-
scale capitalist institutions and culture that did not posit extensive
state ownership. In the cooperative commonwealth of workers and
farmers—or the maternal commonwealth of suffragists or the commonwealth of freedom envisioned by former slaves, sustained by
"forty acres and a mule"—government had a role to play. But it was
not the "solution" envisioned by socialism and social democracy.
Rather, it was seen as the instrument of an active and virtuous citizenry. As historian Leon Fink described the understanding of civic
agency prevalent in the century's major labor movement, the Knights
of Labor, they "looked to self-organized society—not to the individual and not to the state—as the redeemer of the American dream."[1]

In the twentieth century, massive institutions and rule by experts
have seemed to be far more inevitable features of the social land-

scape. The basic problem in renewing citizen politics has been the question of how people can regain sufficient power and confidence to make strong citizenship a serious possibility. A number of democratic theorists in America—from Walter Rauschenbusch, Jane Addams, and John Dewey to Martin Luther King, Jr.—have addressed the problem; none has done so with more skill and thoroughness than the late Saul Alinsky.

In the sixteenth year of the Peloponnesian War, Thucydides recounted, Athens sent an armada of thirty-eight ships and several thousand warriors to the island of Melos, in the Aegean Sea. Unlike most of the islands, Melos had allied with Athens's chief enemy, Sparta, because, said Thucydides, ancient though distant ancestral ties existed between the two. Athenians had a simple demand: the Melians must switch sides.

As the Greek historian depicted the encounter which took place in the fifth century B.C., the Athenians were unswerving. From the beginning, they spoke a language of power. "We on our side will use no fine phrases," said their envoys:

> We recommend that you should try to get what it is possible for you to get, taking into consideration what we both really do think; since you know as well as we do that, when these matters are discussed by practical people, the standard of justice depends on the equality of power to compel and that in fact the strong do what they have the power to do and the weak accept what they have to accept.

Thucydides's vivid account sets up an encounter between abstract ideals and power politics that resonates across time and space. The Melians repeatedly argued on the basis of their hopes, appealing to the Athenians' own ideals: a "long-range" understanding of Athenian concerns for honor and stability in its empire; the possibility of last-minute help from Sparta or from the gods; the integrity of their seven-hundred-year history. The Athenians referred to the concrete realities of the situation: "do not be like those who, as so commonly happens, miss the chance of saving themselves in a human and practical way." Not eager to destroy or even humiliate the Melians, they suggested that their rule of power politics was to "stand up to one's equals, to behave with deference towards one's superiors, and to treat one's inferiors with moderation." They proposed that alliance with their cause need not mean abject surrender: "there is nothing disgraceful in giving way to the greatest city in Hellas when she is offering you such reasonable terms—alliance on a tribute-paying basis and liberty to enjoy your own property." But they were immovable in their demands. The Melians were "true to their ideals"—and blind to other realities. The Athenians laid seige. The Melians resisted for a time. Then, recounted Thucydides, "the Melians surrendered unconditionally to the Athenians, who put to death all the men of military age whom they took, and sold the women and children as slaves. Melos they took over for themselves, sending out later a colony of five hundred men."[2]

Saul Alinsky, dean of the American community organizing tradition, used this account by Thucydides as a basic training document. The Industrial Areas Foundation (IAF) Training Institute, which he and his associates formalized out of a loose network of groups in 1969, developed from the story a drama to begin every training session. It was intended to shock the new trainees. Shock them it did.

Alinsky's recruits came to the field of community organizing out of a range of settings—civil rights, religious activism, student involvement, and other causes—flushed with zeal to advocate the cause of the powerless and poor. The eager students would, of course, side with the Melians. They suggested "better arguments" the Melians might have advanced. They speculated that the islanders may have lost at the moment but "won" in some sense as lasting martyrs to the cause of liberty. And, inevitably when asked, they would argue with vehemence that the Melians had "done the right thing" in defending their autonomy and principles even at the cost of their lives. When IAF teachers called them romantics, operating out of a perspective of "victims," they would be greeted with offended outrage.

Student outrage was precisely the expectation of the IAF educators. Their use of Thucydides was a dramatic device to have students refocus from what Alinsky called "the world-as-we-would-like-it-to-be" to the "world-as-it-is." Alinsky-style organizers drew from Thucydides's story the lesson that the Melians' "all or nothing" approach failed to understand the process of conflict, power, self-change, self-interest, and negotiations that always is the medium for the expression of ideals in politics. At the end of the 1960s, the IAF was speaking about the interactive nature of power in a way that had been largely forgotten in a protest politics that counterposed "power elite" to "power to the people," with little understanding of the dynamic interaction.[3]

In those years Saul Alinsky had become famous but not popular: he was a discordant note among the voices raised on behalf of or against the tempestuous currents of social change sweeping across the country. Critics were legion, on left and right. "Saul Alinsky has possibly antagonized more people—regardless of race, color or creed—than any other living American," declared *Time* magazine, in what was perhaps only modest hyperbole. The man was charged with being variously a communist, fascist, dupe of the Catholic Church, racist, segregationist, and integrationist determined to "mongrelize Chicago." Ironically by the late 1960s, Alinsky was also sometimes lauded by the very establishment he loved to excoriate. *Crisis in Black and White,* the best-selling book on America's racial conflict by *Fortune* magazine editor Charles Silberman, pointed to The Woodlawn Organization that Alinsky and his staff had organized in Chicago as "the most important and the most impressive experiment affecting Negroes anywhere in the United States." *Time* argued in a 1970 essay that "it is not too much to argue that American democracy is being altered by Alinsky's ideas."[4]

What Alinsky's supporters most appreciated about the man was his approach to power, which differed significantly from the dominant culture's obliviousness toward the question and what he saw as the New Left's romanticism about "the people." As Silberman noted, Alinsky's driving passion was to help poor and minority communities develop the actual, existing resources and capacities they had available, in the face of social service bureaucracies and professionals who, in the name of "doing good," infantilized the lower classes. "Society stands in the same relation to [welfare recipients] as that of parent to child," said Raymond Hilliard, director of the Chicago Department of Social Services in 1961. " 'Social uplifting' . . . cannot expect to meet with success unless it is combined with a certain amount of 'social disciplining'—just as it is on the preadult levels." Alinsky not only saw views like Hilliard's as "crap"; he believed passionately that the poor could be mobilized in successful revolt against what he termed "welfare colonialism." Throughout his life, Alinsky sought to develop methods that would aid poor people in getting power. This focus marked him as a pivotal figure in the history of citizen politics, a bridge between nineteenth-century movements and our own time.[5]

———

Saul David Alinsky, born in 1909 to an Orthodox Jewish lower-middle-income family in Chicago, was from the beginning of his organizing career irreverent about settled conventions. "In little ways I've been fighting the system ever since I was seven or eight years old," he told *Playboy* magazine in 1972. "I was the kind of kid who'd never dream of walking on the grass until I'd see a KEEP OFF THE GRASS sign, and then I'd stomp all over it." Such iconoclasm emerged particularly in his fierce scorn for intellectual abstractions which seemed to him to impose arbitrary categories on everyday life-worlds. "Saul thought experts studied communities theoretically but that their approaches were mostly bullshit," recounted Ed Chambers, Alinsky's successor as the director of IAF. "Talk about 'social disorganization' and social pathologies with no face-to-face analysis he saw as irrelevant."[6]

For Alinsky, focusing on the "world as it is" demanded candor about power: "the power concept must be seen nakedly, without the sordid raiment which serves more as disguises for our own inability or unwillingness or timidity," he told a group of housing officials. Power became the animating principle for Alinsky. "Power is the very essence of life, the dynamic of life," he declared, in language intended to shock and unsettle middle-class audiences. Reminding his public that Lord Acton's famous remark that—"power *tends* to corrupt, and absolute power corrupts absolutely"—was customarily misquoted, Alinksy argued that "the word power has through time acquired overtones of sinister, corrupt evil, unhealthy immoral Machiavellianism, and a general phantasmagoria of the nether regions." Such derogation of the concept was simply paralyzing: "We prefer to keep it framed in the popular context of corruption and immorality as a defense, an excuse, to avoid entering the arena of conflict." Power was the active principle, the honest rationale for involvement in politics.[7]

Alinsky called himself, simply, an "urban populist" or a "democratic radical" and saw himself as functioning within a vivid, dynamic American tradition. His first book's identification of "the radical democratic tradition" remains a dramatic detailing of democratic advocates in American history. "What is the American radical?" Alinsky asks in a statement of faith.

> The radical is that unique person who actually believes what he says. He wants a world in which the worth of the individual is recognized. He wants the creation of a society where all of man's potentialities could be realized. . . . The American radicals were in the colonies grimly forcing the addition of the Bill of Rights to our Constitution. . . . They were in the first union strike in America and they fought for the distribution of the western lands. . . . They were everywhere, fighting and dying to free their fellow Americans regardless of their race or creed . . . in the shadows of the Underground Railroad . . . in the vanguard of the Populist Party . . . with Horace Mann fighting for the extension of educational opportunities.

For Alinsky, Americans' lack of attention to the methods and theories of practical democracy was a great frustration. "Communists are completely committed to change. They have a developed literature, organizational principles, a Communist philosophy," he complained to a class of priests in 1964. "But we have no literature on [our own theory of democratic] change whatsoever in this country."

It was his life work to rectify the absence in pragmatic terms that people could understand and put into practice. In particular, he sought to adapt earlier commonwealth, populist themes to the strikingly different world of the twentieth century. Alinsky recalled the temper of the earlier Knights of Labor, populists, and other radical movements at the turn of the century. But he was most directly a child of the 1930s popular movements, when populist themes of older movements had come alive again on a massive scale, in new ways.[8]

In the nineteenth century, citizen politics of the commonwealth drew its strength from connections to everyday life. The loyalties of religion, ethnicity, neighborhood, craft, or simple day-to-day interaction forged in the ethnic and working-class communities of large cities or the small towns and countryside of rural areas produced the commitments that moved people to action when ways of life seemed threatened. And experiences in voluntary effort—building a church together, raising a barn, helping the sick or elderly—generated a confidence that people *could* work together cooperatively and effectively. But these everyday-life "roots" of politics taught skills of cooperative action which were gravely weakened by the fragmented, mobile, technocratic world of the twentieth century. The starting point for citizen politics in the twentieth century has thus been a strengthening of such ties, as the foundation for empowerment. The successful movements of the 1930s accomplished precisely such a reconnection of politics and everyday life, and Alinsky learned from them that key lesson.

After the defeats of the Knights of Labor and the Populist party, artisanal and rural traditions of popular protest continued, but their main organized institutions, like the American Federation of Labor (AFL), turned to an increasingly narrow and craft-conscious style of organizing that severed the workplace from communal ties. The result was a fragmentation of the work force between native-born, relatively skilled workers of English, Irish, Scottish, and German descent and the growing numbers of unskilled immigrants, largely from Eastern and Southern Europe, who flooded the growing mass industries.

The structure of such industries has shaped labor struggles and much other protest in the twentieth century. Techniques of scientific management splintered assembly-line activity into small components over which few workers had significant control. Meanwhile, growing numbers of clerical and service workers sustained expanding corporate bureaucracies and service structures of government in white-collar "factories" that paralleled the mass mobilizations of the basic industry. Work became increasingly instrumental, something one did in order to "live," but "liberty" was something mainly to be experienced off the job, in home and community.[9]

Where union organizing proved effective it drew on and reinforced ethnic heritages which shaped workers' identities and reintegrated workplace organizing with the community. Abstract appeals to "class solidarity" apart from such roots simply did not work. In New York City, for instance, an early-twentieth-century generation of Jewish immigrant organizers imbued with European theories of socialism and committed to a purely secular radicalism failed to create any significant popular movement. Only when a new group arrived that was able to blend socialist language with labor organizing and Yiddish culture did Jewish workers become a leading force in the creation of industrial unionism. They led the massive strikes in the Garment District of New York: the "uprising of the 20,000" in 1909 and "the uprising of the 50,000" in 1910.[10]

The unions which grew from these uprisings—the International Ladies' Garment Workers Union (ILGWU) and the Amalgamated Clothing Workers—laid the groundwork for a new sort of unionism which was to combine conceptions of large-scale, industrywide action with older themes of community and civic action and involvement. In particular, the wave of industrial militancy which led to the formation of the Congress of Industrial Organizations (CIO) in the mid-thirties began as an outburst of protest against deteriorating working conditions and wage cuts. Workers reconnected with and reinvigorated older traditions of community action which had largely disappeared from view in the 1920s.

Thus the demand for civil rights at the workplace used the language of the revolution to brand its opponents "Tories" and to stress active citizenship. Mary Heaton Vorse wrote that "there has been a social awakening through the country, the coming of democracy in towns and industrial valleys where the Bill of Rights, such things as free speech, free assembly and even the right to vote as one pleased had been unknown."[11]

Through the 1930s and '40s, the specific language of "commonwealth" infused the largest popular movements in both Canada and the United States. Political campaigns like the Nonpartisan League, the Farmer-Labor Parties of the Midwest, the End Poverty in California campaign, the Washington Commonwealth Federation, Commonwealth College in the American South, and the Canadian Cooperative Commonwealth Federation all called for a "cooperative commonwealth" which would seek social control over basic physical and economic community infrastructure (capital sources, roads, bridges, transportation and energy and communications systems, and the like) while it supported voluntary action, small business, and cooperatives. As Floyd Olson, the fiery governor of Minnesota's Farmer-Labor movement, described its objectives: "We propose a cooperative commonwealth as an ideal society, under which the government would own and operate public utilities and key industries. . . . The Farmer Labor Party is no enemy of the so-called small business man. It is his champion."[12] Such language went against the grain of twentieth-century technocracy. But the combination of wide local organizing with a deep connection to American traditions lent active democratic themes a believability, even in a world of mass institutions.

At both national and local levels, key organizers of the CIO had been schooled in practices which led them to combine militant, confrontational, and imaginative tactics with distinctive cultural themes particular to the groups with which they worked. "We made every effort to make the councils part of their neighborhoods," explained Steve Nelson, a leading activist in the Communist party, describing the accumulated organizing lessons that radicals of all political stripes applied to their work in creating Unemployed Councils to work on neighborhood issues and issues affecting the unemployed. "For fund-raising we tried to stage events that fit into the cultural life of the community. Most councils relied on bingo, raffles, picnics, and block parties. [In Chicago] since the Catholic Church was always sponsoring such affairs, they were part of the natural way of life." Harlem council meetings organized by radicals began with a prayer, in deference to the black community's strong religious orientation. Council events in the heavily Catholic anthracite coal areas of Pennsylvania included "Hail Marys" and "Our Fathers."

Especially in the aftermath of the left's "popular front" strategy of 1935, which sought to unite a variety of progressive political efforts and organizing campaigns under the broad themes of defense of American democracy and defeat of fascism, various ethnic languages were melded together by a general republican vocabulary. Progressive political groups with names like Thomas Paine and Abraham Lincoln appeared across the country. Thomas Jefferson was described as the ancestor of all those "Americans who are fighting against the tyranny of Big Business with the revolutionary spirit and boldness with which he fought the Tories of that day." The African American singer Paul Robeson produced an anthem for the movement in his song "Ballad for Americans," which lauded the American democratic tradition and recast it in a way that included the full range of immigrant cultures and even atheists and agnostics as "true Americans." "We used to celebrate every holiday and use all our events as ways of educating people about their heritage as Ameri-

cans," recalled Terry Pettus, a radical leader in the political movement called the Washington Commonwealth Federation of the 1930s
and '40s. "Later I used to argue with the activists of the sixties. Why
give away symbols like the flag and the Fourth of July?"[13]

Thus, the key to successful popular action proved to be organizing methods that took into account the uniqueness of each community, connected politics to local ties, and revived the larger commonwealth traditions which sustained citizen politics. But left-wing
theorists and liberal professionals alike found huge obstacles in the
way of their raising such a practice to a central and explicit part of their
theory of social change. Beyond the rigid and hierarchically organized structure of groups like the Communist party (which took its
political approach, or "line," from the Soviet Union), left-wing theory
was formed around a model of political consciousness and change
that systematically eclipsed local cultures and particular identities:
the vision of the "new socialist man." Liberal technocracy shared
with the left a view of the detached observer as the best judge of
"truth" and the most sophisticated analyst of community politics.
Saul Alinsky, however, was to pioneer in the development of a different point of view.[14]

After attending the University of Chicago, where he became interested in welfare issues, Alinsky went on staff in 1931 at the Institute for Juvenile Research, a service agency directed at problems of
juvenile delinquency. He worked with its Chicago Area Project, begun by Clifford Shaw. Shaw's model of "problem solving" differed
notably from the conventional approach to professional service
work, which defined the professional as the most important actor
and his or her knowledge as derived largely from a "scientific" methodology detached from communal experience. In contrast, Shaw believed that communities held within themselves the resources and
capacities to solve problems like juvenile delinquency: the professional's appropriate role was more catalyst and facilitator than problem solver. Thus Shaw sought to create efforts based on local groups
and leadership rather than outside case workers. Such projects were
intended to address underlying problems as well as immediate behavior. In 1938 Alinsky wrote a paper reflecting Shaw's approach.

Meanwhile, Alinsky had also begun to do volunteer organizing
with the CIO, where he became deeply influenced by the labor leader
John L. Lewis, "one of the most outstanding figures of our time," as
he put it. At the CIO Alinsky saw firsthand the tactics of ridicule,
confrontation, and irreverence which organizers had practiced for
decades.

Late in 1938, Clifford Shaw assigned Alinsky to the community
called "Back of the Yards" in Chicago, an area of ninety thousand

impoverished, mostly Eastern European, Catholic immigrants in the shadow of the meatpacking companies that had become legendary through Upton Sinclair's depiction of it as *The Jungle.* The CIO was beginning another round of organizing in Back of the Yards, seeking to revive a tradition of unionism that had been crushed with the defeat of an Amalgamated Meat Cutters strike in 1922. It was a complicated task. Despite academic observers' view of the community as chaotic and unorganized, in fact it had a highly elaborated, though sharply divided, structure of interests and groups, based largely on nationalist identities.[15]

Working closely with Joe Meegan, a young Irish resident who had already sought to build an areawide community group, Alinsky helped organize a wide array of elements in the Back of the Yards Neighborhood Council (BYNC) around a campaign to support an organizing drive in the packinghouse industry. Back of the Yards brought together priests, small business interests, housewives, youth, communist organizers, the American Legion, and labor rank and file in an unlikely, freewheeling mix. The first "community congress" of the organization was held with fifty organizations represented on July 14, 1939, Bastille Day, about five months after Meegan and Alinsky started organizing—and two days before a scheduled strike by the packinghouse union for recognition. Its founding statement expressed its aspiration to become a new sort of community forum:

> This organization is founded for the purpose of uniting all of the organizations within that community known as "Back of the Yards" in order to promote the welfare of all residents of that community regardless of their race, color or creed, so that they may have the opportunity to find health, happiness and security through the democratic way of life.

Community support allowed the union to achieve a significant victory over the packinghouse industry. Meanwhile, the broad base of BYNC allowed it to fight effectively for a range of community issues throughout the 1940s, from hot lunch programs to recreational projects that involved teenagers directly in their planning and implementation. A byproduct was a sharp decline in juvenile delinquency rates.[16]

Alinsky's first book, *Reveille for Radicals,* sought to codify the experiences of Back of the Yards and several other communities where he had begun working under an umbrella institute, the Industrial Areas Foundation (IAF), which he began in 1940 to fund his organizing. The book remains today a fascinating compendium of organizing principles, full of psychological insight into the processes of conflict and "empowerment" of the dispossessed and the importance of drama, action, and participation in grass-roots activity. In particular, Alinsky develops two main themes: the need for popular organizations to be rooted in and reinforce the local community and its institutions; and a psychology of popular empowerment that depends on flamboyant tactics and the experience of concrete victories.

At the center of the book is Alinsky's insistence on the importance of careful *listening,* and investigation of the community where "the organizer" is engaged. "The foundation of a People's Organization is in the communal life of the local people," argued Alinsky.

> Therefore the first stage in the building of a People's Organization is the understanding of the life of a community, not only in terms of the individual's experiences, habits, values and objectives but also from the point of view of the collective habits, experiences, customs, controls and values of the whole group—the *community traditions.*

Alinsky urged that there was no specific model or blueprint of his paradigmatic "People's Organization": "the form, the character and the purpose of all the local agencies reflect the traditions of the community," and a People's Organization built on such agencies would reflect the idiosyncracies of the communities where they were.

Particularized methods were, in Alinsky's view, essential. The organizer "should have a familiarity with the most obvious parts of a people's traditions." Moreover, a careful balance was necessary for organizers with a democratic aim: often they would find themselves disagreeing with local traditions or groups. But efforts at democratic transformation and change must always be undertaken in the terms and histories given. "The starting of a People's Organization is not a matter of personal choice. You start with the people, their traditions, their prejudices, their habits, their attitudes, and all of those other circumstances that make up their lives." Organization must be "rooted in the experiences of the people themselves." Change should never be shortcut through ignorance or carelessness.

> To know a people is to know their religions. It is to know the values, objectives, customs, sanctions and the taboos of these groups. It is to know them not only in terms of their relationships and attitudes toward one another but also in terms of what relationship all of them have toward the outside.... To understand the traditions of a people is ... to ascertain those social forces which argue for constructive democratic action as well as those which obstruct democratic action.[17]

Against the background of the left wing's focus on the "new socialist man" and liberal technocrats' language of scientific decision

making detached from communities, Alinsky's strong, explicit advocacy of a rootedness in popular traditions, local cultures, and communal ties acquired a strikingly original character. He sought to revive citizen politics in the first instance by reviving its connections
to the everyday experiences that give people confidence in their own
power.[18]

In the second instance, Alinsky was a skillful psychologist of the
dynamics of popular empowerment. In his work with trade unions
and in Back of the Yards, he had observed that for poor and immigrant workers who felt powerless and frightened, dramatic encounters were often a precondition for action, a way of "bringing them
[foremen] down" to the level of ordinary human beings. "We didn't
hesitate to expose, to ridicule, and to be very, very critical, even in
the personal sense," said Herbert March, an organizer with whom
Alinsky worked.

These observations formed the background for Alinsky's stress
throughout *Reveille* on self-help, confidence-building collective success, and dramatic encounter. "It is impossible to overemphasize the
enormous importance of people's doing things themselves," he wrote
in his chapter on "Psychological Observations on Mass Organization." "The objective is never an end in itself," Alinsky continued:

> The efforts that are exerted in the actual earning of the
> objective are part and parcel of the achievement itself. This is so
> important that the actual definition of the objective itself is
> determined by the means whereby the objective was
> obtained. . . . What you get by your own effort is really yours. It
> is a part of you, bound and knit to you through the experiences
> that you have undergone in securing it.

Alinsky's book highlights the necessity for conflict (of the nonviolent kind), using a variety of dramatic and unexpected tactics to
"keep the opponent off guard," divide the opposition, use their rules
against them. It sketches the idea that "action is in the reaction"—
that is, the main consequences for a "people's organization" of any
course of action or tactic need to be thought through with careful
foresight, because what one's *opponent* does will affect not only the
issue but also the group. It details the importance of small victories
for people who have had consistent experiences of defeat and powerlessness.[19]

By the late 1950s, Alinsky had gathered a group of close associates attracted by his reputation and his theories of organizing. Beginning with Fred Ross, the group of skillful organizers included men
like Ed Chambers, Richard Harmon, Nicholas Von Hoffman, Tom
Gaudette, and Father John Egan. It was this group that created the

famed organizations for which Alinsky gained visibility, especially The Woodlawn Organization in Chicago, Community Service Organization in California, and FIGHT in Rochester. In fact, Alinsky served mainly as a consultant, constantly on the road giving lectures and speeches.[20]

Alinsky's organizing evolved over the decades into a distinctive approach which built on the methods that formed the basis for Back of the Yards. In simple terms, this community organizing divided cities into two units, the neighborhood and the "enemy" power structure outside. Poor, minority, and working-class communities, in this analysis, were victimized by the ability of affluent, powerful downtown connected interests to bestow social services and economic largess on the relatively privileged areas of the city. Within neighborhoods, the basic Alinsky model involved creating an organization of existing community institutions. In response to questions about unaffiliated individuals who belonged to neither religious nor union nor small business nor other civic groups, Alinsky pointed to pragmatic power wielding: poor communities had to start by unifying what "pockets of power" existed. Other approaches, he argued, simply did not generate as much power. And in fact, this "institutionally based organizing" has, over a period of several decades, proven far more effective in mobilizing poor communities than competing models. For instance, the Association of Community Organizations for Reform Now (ACORN), a network that has avoided such institutional foundations and sought out previously disconnected community residents as its core leadership, has been consistently plagued by rapid turnover in leadership and transience of local affiliates. After nearly two decades, ACORN's fifty thousand or so members in chapters scattered across the country are fewer in number than any one of the larger, local IAF projects.[21]

Thus, Alinsky-inspired community groups brought together community building blocks—religious groups, unions, ethnic and civic groups, small businesses, and political organizations—and through confrontation and other means this consolidated community group or "people's organization" would challenge specific, visible targets in the local power structure to produce concrete, tangible results. Alinsky and his associates relished the use of outrageous tactics. A community organization in the Woodlawn area of Chicago called The Woodlawn Organization, or TWO, once threatened to tie up the bathrooms at O'Hare Airport with hundreds of members holding "the country's first shit-in" to pressure Mayor Daley into an agreement. "Imagine for a second the catastrophic consequences of this tactic," Alinsky told *Playboy* magazine. "Constipated and bladder-bloated passengers would mill about the corridors in anguish and desperation, longing for a place to relieve themselves." TWO did not follow through on the threat. "We leaked the news to an informer for the city administration, and the reaction was instantaneous. The next day, the leaders of TWO were called down to City Hall and informed that the Mayor certainly had every intention in the world of carrying out his commitments" to Woodlawn.[22]

These kinds of organizations generated experiences of success and unity, rare in poor people's lives, which in turn built new feelings of confidence and dignity. They also led often to improvements in people's actual situations. If skillfully put together, they could deliver real "goods" in the form of jobs, housing, city services, and other benefits for communities which had been left behind, sometimes devastated, by urban growth.[23]

Major problems in Alinsky's approach remained, however, that stood in the way of its generating a larger force for democratic change. When pushed, Alinsky called himself a "radical democrat" or "urban populist" as his only self-description. That meant to him values like diversity, the importance of conflict, participation, and empowerment of the poor and powerless. But in practice he sharply discouraged what he called "ideological" discussion of what the broader implications of such values might be in the groups with which he worked.

Alinsky often professed a hatred of what he called "ideology," or "dogma"—sets of fixed principles or ideals, which he believed undermined the actions of those committed to social change. "Those who want change must be against sacred cows and not only innately irreverent but outwardly, purposefully irreverent in their actions. They must be iconoclastic bulldozers willing to be regarded as profane spoilers of the sacred myths." Conventional progressive approaches to social change, in his view, were full of "sterilized synonyms cleansed of the opprobrium of the word power," that deflected attention "off the main, conflict-ridden, hard, bitter, brimy and realistic power-paved highway of life."[24]

In his later years, Alinsky discounted even the older democratic language he had once used and any relevance of religious themes with caustic, often sardonic quips. In a 1965 interview with Marion Saunders of *Harper's* magazine, Alinsky said, in what was to become a legendary quote, that he never talked to religious leaders about their values, religious ideals, or convictions because of the fundamental precept that organizing must be grounded in people's everyday life-worlds: "It would be outside of their experience, because Christianity and Judeo-Christianity are outside of the experience of organized religion." When longtime associates like Father Egan suggested more discussion of religious values in organizing The Woodlawn Organization in Chicago, Alinsky remarked, "You take care of the religion, Jack. We'll do the organizing."[25]

His approach to organizing, drawing on the practicality and realism of the thirties, had always placed preeminent stress on beginning with an understanding of "the world as it is." But by the 1960s, Alinsky's depiction of that world almost entirely denuded political life of the relevance of ideals and values. "Once we have moved into the world as it is then we begin to shed fallacy after fallacy." There, as he saw it, "the right things are done only for the wrong reasons," "constructive actions have usually been in reaction to a threat," "judgment among alternatives is made on the basis not of the best but of the least bad," "irrationalities play a significant part," and "morality is to a significant degree a rationalization of the position which you are occupying in the power pattern at a particular time."[26]

In sum, Alinsky's organizing lacked a larger, framing visionary dimension. As a result, his groups produced local power but not much broader change. Leadership often was concentrated among a few key male leaders. Organizations typically lasted only four or five years. And the "Alinskyite method" became synonymous with an anti-ideological tone that spurned discussion of "power for what" or the values and traditions that informed activities. Sometimes the results were deeply discouraging to Alinsky himself. His most famous organization, Back of the Yards, by the 1950s had reversed its earlier commitments to fighting discrimination and had begun championing restrictive measures to keep out blacks. This violated Alinsky's most basic principles, to his great dismay. But his approach offered few ways to address the problem.[27]

On balance, Alinsky's style of community organization did much to keep alive and adapt older populist themes of organizing for power to the twentieth century. But it was not enough. While developing important methods for citizen empowerment, it nonetheless failed to address the wider democratic impoverishment of America's political culture. Meanwhile, new social movements among African Americans and young people were germinating in American society that were to raise precisely this larger problem of the lack of active and participatory democracy. They furnished a dramatic contrast to the narrowness of Alinskyite groups' vision. But they also lacked Alinsky's methods for sustaining effective, broad citizen effort over time.

5

The Rise and Fall of
Participatory Democracy

*A*fter World War II, Saul Alinsky hoped his book *Reveille for Radicals* would help spark a renewed democratic movement. "The job ahead is clear," he wrote. "Every conceivable effort must be made to rekindle the fire of democracy. . . . Can man envisage a more sublime program on earth than the people having faith in their fellow men and themselves? A program of co-operation instead of competition?" he asked with a lyrical flourish, using the gender-specific language of his time. However sublime, his program of cooperation did not materialize in the 1950s.[1]

Under the surface of apparent political tranquility, however, strong currents of democratic discontent were building. The social protest movements of the 1960s quickly confounded the complacency of those who believed that "the problems of industrial society have been solved." Civil rights, followed quickly by a spreading revolt among the middle-class generation of young people that came to be known as the "Baby Boom," charted new ground in protest at the disruptions and injustices of modern managerial society. They succeeded in large measure because, like the Alinsky type of community organization, they were able to reconnect politics to everyday-life concerns. Local communities formed the base of civil rights. The immediate experiences of the young were reflected in slogans like "the personal is political." But they also *expressed* their hopes in a democratic vision and a critique of modern society that community organizing lacked.

The problem was that these sixties movements had few ways to *sustain* a more participatory politics. They did resurrect the populist commonwealth's key themes: concepts of "the people" rather than "the working class"; a vision of direct and active democracy in which citizens, rather than the state, would be the central agents. But their strategy for broader change was underdeveloped compared to older populist ideas. More and more as the decade progressed, vision *became* the source of power. "People's organizations for power," the strength of democratic action in the community-organizing tradition, turned into "power to the people." The politics of student protest produced a consumer-culture version of "community," "the people," and "commonwealth" that derived from the uprooted, ahistorical experiences of the suburbs and the youth culture. Detached from any sense of history, accountability, or diversity, youthful calls for community and participatory democracy substituted strident, overblown oratory for practical organizing. By the end of the decade, the vision of commonwealth advocated by the New Left—originally an updated, if idealized, American *alternative* to socialism—had become conflated with fantasies of the utopia that radicals imagined existed in what were, in fact, totalitarian Third World societies.

As a result, in the 1970s a considerable irony took shape. Those activists out of the sixties who wanted to put their values into continuing, effective practice were desperate for an antidote to the hyperbolic rhetoric that had overtaken the New Left. They turned en masse to the techniques of Saul Alinsky, creating training centers across the country to teach his methods to activists in community groups, trade union organizing, environmental efforts, women's projects, and elsewhere. But by the early 1970s, Alinsky himself had almost completely lost whatever visionary dimensions his approach originally possessed. Thus a generation of new, progressive citizen organizations developed with an arsenal of effective techniques and methods for day-to-day grass-roots mobilization, yet with goals devoid of larger vision and purpose. In contrast, a right-wing version of populism—but without any conception of the commonwealth— proved far more effective in expressing older civic themes in the 1970s and '80s.

Citizen politics on a large scale had its rebirth in the civil rights movement of the late 1950s and early 1960s. The religious strands which sustained the hopes of African Americans intermingled with American democratic themes in an eloquent call for the nation to live up to its values and promises.

The civil rights revolt developed against the background of a rapidly changing social and economic environment. During World War II, the overwhelming majority of blacks in the South still lived in rural areas. But economic changes—mechanization of agriculture in the South, expanding opportunities in cities like Atlanta, Montgomery, Birmingham, Raleigh, and Richmond—prompted a mass migration from the countryside to urban environments. For a generation of blacks whose young men had fought for "American democracy" and were impatient for its fruits at home, cities also offered an alternative to the closed, paternalistic system of Southern agriculture. In cities, African Americans found new forms of economic independence and power, like their capacity to purchase consumer goods. Union traditions of self-organization, pioneered by leaders like A. Philip Randolph, had long nurtured an activist trade union leadership that complemented the black preacher. And in urban areas, extensive networks of voluntary associations, centered on the church, created further opportunities for leadership to emerge, information to spread, and ideas to germinate.[3]

The Montgomery bus boycott sparked by Rosa Parks's refusal to give up her seat for a white man on Friday, December 2, 1955, became the crucible in which the themes of the civil rights movement developed and first came to nationwide attention. "When Momma Parks Sat Down, the Whole World Stood Up," proclaimed the song commemorating the event. When the quickly formed Montgomery Improvement Association held its first mass meeting the next Monday night, the black community turned to the young, dynamic minister of Dexter Avenue Baptist Church, Martin Luther King, Jr., to give the major speech. His arguments set the stage for ten years of struggle.[4]

King had grown up in a professional family in Atlanta, Georgia, home of the largest and most prosperous black middle class in the South. At divinity and graduate schools, he had developed a distinctive philosophy that drew on popular African American religious traditions, the communitarian perspectives of the religious philosophy known as personalism, and Gandhi's belief in *Satyagraha,* or the idea that love and truth can be joined in a force for social change that disciplines and directs anger into constructive, nonviolent channels. King wedded these religious themes to the American democratic tradition. He rejected Marxism for its depersonalization of the individual and its doctrine of class conflict. And he dissented from the customary left-wing focus on government as the metaphor for the future, opposing any system which reduced the individual "to a depersonalized cog in the ever-turning wheel of the state." Rather, King held to a tradition of the "Christian commonwealth" that drew on older populist and biblical ideals.[5]

Martin Luther King used this distinctive philosophy to frame the struggle in Montgomery. "We're here," he declared, "because first and foremost we are American citizens, and we are determined to acquire our citizenship to the fullness of its meaning." King challenged blacks to discover in themselves a new "sense of somebodyness" that would transform the relations between whites and blacks. And he grounded his call in American traditions and religious faith. "If we are wrong," he said, "the Supreme Court of this nation is wrong. If we are wrong, God Almighty is wrong." Such themes continued to structure King's philosophy throughout his years as a civil rights leader. "One day the south will know that when these disinherited children of God sat down at lunch counters they were in reality standing up for the best in the American dream and the most sacred values in our Judeo-Christian heritage," King wrote in his central philosophical statement, "Letter from a Birmingham Jail." He portrayed the movement as "carrying our whole nation back to the great wells of democracy which were dug deep by the founding fathers." In turn, his language created a scaffolding for the grass-roots program crafted by leaders like Ella Baker.[6]

The Southern Christian Leadership Conference (SCLC), the organization which King headed, was formed in early 1957 out of discussions among King, Baker, Ralph Abernathy, Fred Shuttlesworth, Bayard Rustin, and others as an effort to spread "the Montgomery way" across the South. Its base was the black church. Baker especially, drawing on her own earlier experiences of labor union and co-op organizing, argued that a large-scale organizing program was needed to train laity and others. "Instead of 'the leader,'" she said, expressing skepticism of overreliance on black clergy, "you would develop individuals who were bound together by a concept that provided an opportunity for them to grow." Baker sought to develop SCLC's first program, called "the Crusade for Citizenship," into such an organizing effort, and her efforts took shape especially in an enormous program of "Citizenship Schools," organized in small communities across the South.

The Citizenship School program taught blacks, often illiterate, to read and write in order to pass arduous literacy tests that authorities used to disenfranchise poorer citizens of both races. But from its beginnings at Highlander Folk School, a Southern training center for organizers and activists, the strategy of Citizenship Schools had stressed the importance of connecting voting and literacy to a dynamic conception of citizenship itself. To that end, organizers of the schools avoided normal academic approaches and treated "students" as adults who could come and go as they pleased, bring sewing to classes, or chew tobacco. They used as their basic primers documents like the Constitution of the United States, the Declaration of Independence, and Scripture.

SCLC developed a training program for local "teachers" at Dorchester, Georgia, where the curriculum included much more than the mechanics of registering and voting. Students learned how to conduct voter registration campaigns, combat illiteracy, win government benefits for the poor, and talk about the meaning of American citizenship in ways that would inspire ordinary citizens. As Dorothy Cotton, a major leader of the movement, put it, they taught "a whole new way of life and functioning." Civil rights activists saw the movement as designed, in King's words, "to make real the promise of democracy." By democracy, moreover, they meant not simply formal rights but active citizenship. "The more important participation was to be not just at the moment when the ballot was cast but in all the moments that led up to that moment."[7]

In Citizenship Schools—and in analogous projects like the "Freedom Schools" sponsored by the Student Nonviolent Coordinating Committee (SNCC), the younger, more radical student-based wing of the movement—participants combined discussions about civil rights and voting with exchanges about the meaning of democracy, American history, and events in Africa. It was an often electrifying process that permanently changed the texture of countless small towns and urban areas. "We got our heads up now and we won't ever bow down again," explained one janitor. A study by a research team of psychologists discovered that levels of crime and social pathologies of all sorts had dramatically declined in communities involved in the movement.[8]

But the expansive democratic promise of civil rights was truncated. Few of those involved had any significant community or trade union organizing experience. Organizers were able to mobilize communities to end the rigid system of segregation, America's apartheid. But they simply did not know how to build organizations through which poor and disadvantaged blacks could continue to seek power, after the period of demonstrations and national publicity had ended. Movement activists were well aware of the dilemma; in fact, it formed a constant topic of debate and discussion across the organizing networks of groups like SCLC, SNCC, and the Congress of Racial Equality (CORE). In scattered sites, notably those organized by SNCC activists, efforts were made to build community groups of different kinds that would last, but with little success. In the face of tremendous repression and the overwhelming need for changes in federal law and support from other areas of the country, the strategic focus inevitably came to be placed on mediagenic events which would garner public sympathy for specific legislation. One incident summed up the dilemma of the movement. In 1966, SCLC sent several organizers to Saul Alinsky for training in organizing methods. But a movement "emergency" resulted in their recall, and they left after only a few days.[9]

Generally, the movement reflected its overt objectives. Despite the enlarged democratic vision of leaders like King, Baker, and many others, the movement was defined as the effort to end the bitter legacy of legal segregation. Like the woman suffrage movement a half-century before, it used a language of republicanism that stressed formal citizenship rights, not in an explicit sense the transformation of power relations. Civil rights succeeded in its own terms, abolishing the segregated statutes, registering millions of new black voters, and reviving a language of "democracy" that had far wider resonance. But it represented only one stage in democratic renewal. The efforts toward lasting poor people's organizing that King and others advocated by 1967 and 1968 were cut short by a rising tide of bitterness over the war in Vietnam, and King's death.

Democratic themes from civil rights found a responsive audience among those middle-class young people who seemed the apparent heirs of technocracy, yet felt themselves to be its victims. Stirrings of dissent from the bland political conformity and privatism of the fifties had also appeared among young middle-class Americans. In the main, alternative voices and currents found cultural forms. Millions of young people declared a kind of cultural independence from their elders with their embrace of the African American–influenced music of rock 'n' roll. In a more explicitly critical vein, the Beat poetry of Allen Ginsberg and others, the sardonic commentary of *Mad* magazine, the restless, angry views of writers like Jack Kerouac, all challenged middle-class, surburban, white-collar society—supposedly the very embodiment of the "American Dream"—labeling it hollow, fraudulent, and dehumanized. In 1955, Ginsberg read his poem "Howl" to an overflow audience and responded to a question about what he was rebelling against with an impassioned extemporaneous statement: "Moloch! Moloch! Nightmare of Moloch! Moloch the loveless! . . . Moloch! whose soul is electricity and banks! Moloch whose poverty is the spectre of genius! Moloch whose fate is a cloud of sexless hydrogen! Moloch whose name is the Mind!" Mingled with estrangement was identification with cultural rebels. "At lilac evening I walked with every muscle aching," wrote Kerouac in *On the Road,* "in the Denver colored section, wishing I were a Negro, feeling that the best the white world had offered was not enough ecstasy for me, not enough life, joy, kicks, darkness, music, not enough night. . . ."[10]

Overt political dissent had also survived, especially in campus environments like the YMCA and YWCA and religious centers and organizations. Even in the midst of the segregated South of the 1950s, for instance, Methodist, Baptist, Presbyterian, and Episcopal student centers on campuses were often seedbeds of discussion about the evils of segregation, specifically, and broader problems of "alienation," materialism, and apathy, more generally. In statewide and national networks like the Methodist Student Movement (MSM) and its magazine, *motive*, students with support and encouragement from sympathetic campus ministers created an insurgency within the broader world of Christendom. "The basic threat [facing the student today]," wrote Allan J. Burry, assistant Methodist chaplain at Duke University, "is the loss of meaning in an impersonal and destructive world." In 1958, the national committee of MSM on sociopolitical concerns attacked the church for irrelevant piety in the form of a confession: "We the Church have failed." It exhorted: "The Christian group on campus which does not promote involvement in political affairs denies [God's] authority in that area of life . . . to permit division within the church is to live in sin, and FURTHER, any form of segregation, discrimination or privilege within the church is an abomination. . . ."[11]

By the early 1960s, a web of connections developed between campuses and civil rights. Support committees sprang up at virtually every major university. They raised money, sponsored speaker tours, educated their fellow students. Students volunteered for service projects—tutoring, working on issues of hunger and poverty—in nearby communities. And thousands of students traveled to the South for support of demonstrations or for large-scale projects like Freedom Summer, a Mississippi voter registration effort in 1965 which recruited Northern volunteers.[12]

As the civil rights movement swelled across the South in the early sixties, African American and white students from every region of the country found in its themes, language, and vision ways to articulate their feelings of often inchoate discontent. In particular, the Southern movement's call to "make democracy real" in America resonated with young people, who adapted its meaning to their own situation as well.

The strengths and weaknesses of student hopes for a more active, direct democracy were articulated in 1963 in the document known as *The Port Huron Statement*, a manifesto of the newly formed Students for a Democratic Society (SDS). Largely written by Tom Hayden, a former student leader at the University of Michigan with strong ties to civil rights, the statement went through multiple printings and was perhaps the central expression of New Left political philosophy.

The Port Huron Statement bears interesting similarities to Saul Alinsky's *Reveille for Radicals*. Like Alinsky, SDS grounded its arguments in the search for a democratic alternative. "Today, for us, not even the liberal and socialist preachments of the past seem adequate to the forms of the present." The document addressed the specters of nuclear war, meaningless work, loneliness, and materialism. All were symbolized by a valueless technocracy that rendered most people without voice. "Our generation is plagued by program without vision," it declared, pointing not only to the political system but to higher education, suburbs, unions, corporate bureaucracies. "All around us there is astute grasp of method, technique—the committee, the ad hoc group, the lobbyist, the hard and soft sell, the make, the projected image—but, if pressed critically, such expertise is incompetent to explain its implicit ideals." The *Statement* sketched its alternative:

> We would replace power rooted in possession, privilege, or circumstance by power and uniqueness rooted in love, reflectiveness, reason and creativity. As a *social system* we seek the establishment of a democracy of individual participation, governed by two central aims: that the individual share in those decisions determining the quality and direction of his life; that society be organized to encourage independence in men and provide the media for their common participation.

Like *Reveille, Port Huron* stressed the foundation of democratic action in community. "The very isolation of the individual—from power and community and ability to aspire—means the rise of a democracy without publics," it read. "The vital democratic connections between community and leadership, between the mass and the several elites, has been so wrenched and perverted that disastrous policies go unchallenged time and again."[13]

In such passages, the student organization, echoing the evocative language of the civil rights movement, described dimensions of the contemporary condition and a vision of alternative possibility with an eloquence and critical sweep which Saul Alinsky had largely lacked. But their politics also missed what Alinsky had possessed in considerable measure: a way to *ground* democratic action in history, tie a critical perspective to actual, mainstream American community life, and develop a strategy for popular empowerment.

Like Martin Luther King, Saul Alinsky spoke in what can best be called a "prophetic mode." The prophet is not an outsider: he or she stands ardently in a tradition, claiming its insights, charging that present-day activities, leaders, or the society as a whole are tarnishing or destroying its own best ideals. Prophets challenge certain traditions and values at the same time that they invoke others. And the act of recalling the past for present-day action also transforms the traditions invoked, adding nuance and new dimensions. Alinsky had located his efforts in a dynamic democratic tradition that he argued represented the best values and spirit of the country. He had also sketched new strategies for effective poor people's organizing for power in a world where experts made the poor into dependent clients.[14]

The New Left's early theorists saw themselves within one strand of the commonwealth tradition, but it was the one most idealized and abstracted from actual democratic currents in American society. In particular, radical students were attracted to historian William Appleman Williams's interpretation of American frontier history as a conflict between utopian and more reformist readings of "the Christian commonwealth," and his zealous advocacy of a "viable Utopia" which would lead to the radical socialization of property. Such a version of "commonwealth" had antecedents in America's utopian communes and other communal experiments. But it was far from the pragmatic democratic politics expressed in movements like the Knights of Labor, the Women's Christian Temperance Union (WCTU), the Farmers' Alliances, or the civil rights movement.[15]

The Port Huron generation had grown up in suburban America in the aftermath of World War II—historically forgetful, privileged, assured of its own judgments, confident in its ability to "get heard" by its elders. Reflecting such a background, student radicals took the stance of detached *social critics*, outside American culture. In *The Port Huron Statement* there is virtually no reference to American *antecedents* of its quest for "participatory democracy," no recitation of prior movements, or mention of the aspirations of those who had gone before. Instead, the document expresses disillusionment mingled with arrogance. "We are people of this generation, bred in at least modest comfort, housed now in universities, looking uncomfortably at the world we inherit," it began. It continued with a series of unrelenting indictments: "worldwide amusement, cynicism and hatred toward the United States as a democracy is not simply a communist propaganda trick, but an objectively justifiable phenomenon"; "we are a minority—the vast majority of our people regard the temporary equilibriums of our society and world as eternally functioning parts"; "we ourselves are imbued with urgency, yet ... Americans [generally exhibit what] might be called a glaze." Even their most telling indictments were fraught with an absolutism that would make their words hard for most Americans to hear, on the one hand, and which, on the other, created a purist standard of rhetorical attack that would have dire consequences. "The white [American] lives almost completely within his own, closed-up world where things are tolerable," they said. "The awe inspired by the pervasiveness of racism in American life is matched only by the marvel of its historical span in American traditions."[16]

Complementing the student radicals' stance as cultural outsiders (and forgetting many of their immediate antecedents in groups like Y's and campus religious centers), their invocation of "community" conveyed the idea of something totally new and invented. Whereas Alinsky had based his strategy for power on a multiplicity of cultural groupings, arguing that

> a People's Organization is built upon all the diverse loyalties—
> to the church, to the labor union, to the social groups, to the
> nationality groups, to the myriad other groups and
> institutions. . . . These loyalties combine to effect an abiding
> faith in, and a profound loyalty to, the democratic way of life,[17]

Port Huron pointed to no *real* communities. Except for African Americans and the Third World, existing communities were portrayed as irredeemably corrupted. Community, the student radicals *imagined*, was to be achieved through an act of will. "Loneliness, estrangement, isolation describe the vast distance between man and man today," *Port Huron* read. "[H]uman brotherhood . . . must be willed . . . as the most appropriate form of social relations." Such a community was to be without constraint or obligation. In fact, in the reading of the early New Left (reflecting, perhaps, the predominantly male perspective on politics that was also evident in its gendered language), the pupose of community was seen as *independence:* "Men have unrealized potential for self-cultivation, self-direction, self-understanding. . . . The goal of man and society should be human independence: a concern not with image [or] popularity but with finding a meaning in life that is personally fulfilling."

This spirit infused the youthful counterculture in the later years of the decade, creating the simultaneous yearning for communal ties and the constant flight from them. As Todd Gitlin has observed, the counterculture was fraught with a pervasive "transcendentalist fantasy of the wholly, abstractly free individual, finally released from the pains and distortions of society's traps." Bob Dylan invoked this sense of radical individualism in "Mr. Tambourine Man," a song widely viewed as an ode to the counterculture:

> Yes to dance beneath the diamond sky with one hand waving
>   free
> Silhouetted by the sea
> Circled by the circus sands
> With all memory and fate

Driven deep beneath the waves
That may forget about today until tomorrow[18]

Critics who have pointed to the ineffectiveness of the New Left's constant, interminable preoccupation with group process—consensus meetings, endless discussion, hostility toward formal leadership structures, and the like—have missed the point. In the absence of genuine community, process itself necessarily became communal substance. "Community Now," expressed in events like "love-ins" (and echoing "Peace Now," or "Power to the People") was the spirit of the youth movement, substituting for long-term organizing campaigns. Exhortation to ideals and feelings was the only form of power that existed.

But democracy and community without history or constraints are only fantasies. Student politics bred an endless series of splits, divisions, and subgroups, each claiming its own rightness. If feeling itself was the touchstone of politics, who was to judge (besides "me") who was right? What were the criteria for action? And on what basis was the "other" not simply part of the all-encompassing system to be condemned? By the late 1960s, "the movement" had shattered into a myriad of factions. New Left rhetoric and posturing had escalated to wild dreams of guerilla-like operations in America (the "Weather Underground") and identification with revolutionaries abroad—the Vietnamese, the Cubans—whose rhetoric matched the student rage but whose authoritarianism made a mockery of "participatory democracy."

Yet the ideals and the discontent that had fed the student protest were not exhausted or spent by its rootless and abstracted politics. Indeed, for many who were inspired by the democratic values of the sixties, the challenge was to find ways to put these ideals into practice in more realistic and less self-righteous fashion. By the tens of thousands, sixties activists sought to rediscover an American reality to which their slogans—"Don't trust anyone over thirty"—had blinded them. Translation often involved personal change.

———

Susan Cobin, thin, intense, thoughtful, now teaches Jewish children their heritage at Talmud Torah School in St. Paul, Minnesota. But for many years, she had scorned such roots.

Susan had grown up in Springfield, Illinois, in a conservative Republican area where she felt constantly different. Her family were Democrats—she remembered being almost the only child she knew who was for Adlai Stevenson for president in the 1950s. She had felt pressure to assimilate to the Christian culture—many of her Jewish friends had been critical when she refused to say the Lord's Prayer in grade school,

In high school and college, like many of her contemporaries, Susan had become involved in civil rights and protests against the Vietnam War. When she and her husband, David, moved to Berkeley on Bastille Day, July 14, 1969, it seemed appropriate. By that time both were far removed from active connection to the Jewish community. Berkeley was a substitute.

Cobin became a teacher in a Free School, but she soon developed doubts about the school's freewheeling, antiauthoritarian culture. "They used to tell me that I was laying my trip on the kids. All I could answer was that if you don't want me to lay my trip on these kids, I shouldn't be teaching. For strictly social interaction, I'd rather be with my peers." She thought the normal school system also inadequate, belittling children of poor and blue-collar backgrounds. As an alternative, she helped start a prevocational school which taught skills that gave students basic self-confidence.

Having a baby transformed Susan and David's perceptions of the world. "Before Seth, we never noticed our neighborhood. But suddenly, it became important to think about playgrounds, schools, the kind of rental property in the area." Parenting also changed their attitudes about the future. "We started to think about leaving Berkeley. In Berkeley, there was a deep confusion about what it means to be a free person, a confusion between freedom and license."

When they moved back to the Twin Cities area of Minnesota, they also rethought their relationship to their heritage. "We began to think about how our children will learn about values, and what we wanted them to learn." With a friend, she put ads in the paper that invited a group to create a community "to think about how to be Jews in the 1980s." They met for celebration, discussion, support for social action. Through this process, she came to feel they were part of a "chain." "I was really touched," concluded Cobin, "at seeing my nephews have their Bar Mitzvahs before the Ark, just as their father had and my father had." She wanted the same for both their children, a boy and a girl. The chain had formed over eons. "I didn't want to be the one to break it."[19]

Like the Cobins, thousands of other activists who wanted to make "organizing for democracy" their life in some fashion were rethinking their approach. "Toward the end of the war while I was so angry, I realized I'm really a very patriotic person," explained Martha Ballou, who began to work with a group of senior citizens in an effort to help older people regain dignity and power. One of the leaders of SDS at Harvard, Miles Rapoport, left the campus to organize working-class white ethnics in Lynn, Massachusetts. He discovered that different kinds of skills and a different approach were essential. "The antiwar movement operated a lot on ideological and moral forms of persuasion," explained Rapoport. "We were outraged by the war, but we communicated that outrage best to people who shared similar perspectives about what a democracy should be. To people who were struggling to get by themselves, the argument didn't have the same force." A parallel development occurred in the Black Power movement that had succeeded civil rights. "In about 1972, we decided that we should take our resources and experiences and put them at the feet of the community," said Bill Thompson, a poet and black organizer who came to work for a large multiracial citizen organization, Massachusetts Fair Share. "No line, no Ho Chi Minh, Kim Il Sung, Che. We tried to get back to real, everyday things, to a calm style. We switched issues from Vietnam and Cambodia and just moved in with the community."[20]

The diverse networks of grass-roots citizen and community organizing and the dozen or so organizing training schools which emerged as a lasting legacy of 1960s activism looked to Saul Alinsky as the first great pioneer. His emphasis on building organizations of the poor and marginal, voiceless groups that would gather the power to win concrete, practical changes seemed a godsend to many sixties activists fed up with rhetorical posturing and abstract moralizing that never seemed to go anywhere. In particular, Alinsky provided a method and a language for those determined to reach new groups of the population and "dig in" for change over the long haul. "Saul Alinsky is to organizing as Freud is to psychoanalysis," said Heather Booth, a dynamic sixties student leader who founded the largest training center in the 1970s, the Midwest Academy. But Alinsky's method, by the time it gained a widespread audience, had developed further problems.[21]

Alinsky's public persona, his language, and the themes he emphasized had significantly changed from his earlier approach, developing a caustic tone missing in *Reveille for Radicals,* his first book. It was this sixties and early seventies "version" of Alinsky organizing which came to shape most directly the bulk of community and citizen activism in the following years.

"A generation has passed since I wrote *Reveille for Radicals,*" Saul Alinsky began the Introduction to a new edition of the book in 1969. "The angry, defiant, go-for-broke, irreverent youngster coming through in these pages seemed almost but not quite another person." Alinsky's reminiscences chronicled a number of changes he felt in his approach to organizing (he saw his later self as more dispassionate, cooler, more strategic). But he missed the most striking change: the dramatically different language he used to describe and justify the *point* of organizing.

In the 1940s, Alinsky's "anger, defiance, and irreverancy" had grown from perceptions that America was violating a set of tarnished but still present democratic and religious ideals. By the end of his life, his tone had grown markedly more sour and embittered. "In this world laws are written for the lofty aim of 'the common good' and then acted out in life on the basis of the common greed . . . where 'good' is a value dependent on whether we want it," he wrote in his second and last book, in 1971. "In the world as it is, the stream of events surges endlessly onward with death as the only terminus . . . the world as it stands is . . . no evil dream of the night; we wake up in it again forever and ever."[22]

A number of factors may have shaped Alinsky's change in tone. His audience had shifted. His first work was a call to revive a massive, popular, and largely working-class movement after World War II. By the late 1960s, he was reacting against what he saw as the middle-class naiveté, romanticism, and class condescension of youthful campus audiences before which he spent much of his time speaking. Moreover, his bitter and disillusioned tone may well have been accentuated by a series of wrenching personal experiences, like the early death of his first wife, to whom he was deeply committed, and the chill in public dissent he had witnessed during the McCarthy period of the 1950s.[23]

Whatever mix of forces shaped Alinsky's vocabulary of organizing in his last years, the approach associated with his name took on a series of clearly limned characteristics by the time of his death. Two main themes structured "Alinsky-style" organizing. "Organizing for power" was the point, but power without discussion of larger ends. Moreover, the motivational basis for popular organization shifted noticeably in Alinsky's speeches and writings. From a careful attentiveness to the "communal life of the local people" with its "habits, experiences, customs, controls and values"—a focus which in the 1930s and '40s had combined a reading of individual self-interest with a discernment of community traditions—Alinsky began to refer to "self-interest" understood in narrow ways as the wellspring of action. When he argued that in the world as it is "man moves primarily because of self-interest," he had in mind a utilitarian view akin to that of contemporary economists: people's dominant motives can be understood as self-centered calculation of gain or loss. Such a view led to a narrow focus on *issues* around which people could be mobilized, largely detached from reflection on the point of the issues, or the values involved.[24]

These themes shaped an entire generation of organizing efforts that emerged in the 1970s as sixties activists, searching for a more pragmatic, result-oriented approach, joined with growing numbers of Americans who were increasingly restless and discontent. For many like George Wiley, head of the National Welfare Rights Organization, an activist network of poor people's organizations, the changing political environment of the 1970s simply demanded different strategies. Wiley, paralleling and borrowing from Alinsky, formed the national alliance of grass-roots groups known as ACORN (Association of Community Organizations for Reform Now). "It was very simple," said Bert DeLeeuw, a co-worker of Wiley's. "Welfare recipients were getting clobbered because they were isolated. So we went out to organize this whole new constituency as allies."[25]

The problem was that organizers of such groups, motivated themselves by passionate ideals, buried their values in the process of organizing. They felt *themselves* to be motivated by powerful democratic aspirations. But in a process accentuated by class and racial differences (in the 1970s and '80s, most "organizers" continued to be upper middle class, college educated, and usually white), they saw the "people" they worked with in a far more narrow and even cynical fashion. The result was a characteristic culture of organizing that created great distances between organizer and community, and turned poor people into groups to be "mobilized," not listened to or learned from.

ACORN's language of power as its own rationale and its view of specific issues as the vehicle for power mobilization illustrate the common vocabulary of citizen organizing. As its organizing manual explains,

> When ACORN attacks a public utility for raising rates, the attack is not based on an analysis which holds that ACORN members, and other low to moderate income Arkansans (or Texans or South Dakotans) are, as consumers, getting nailed by high electric rates. Undoubtedly they *are* getting nailed that way, but even more important is the fact that they are getting boxed in because in reality rather than rhetoric a bunch of corporate directors and New York bankers have the power to unilaterally make decisions that affect the lives of ACORN members.

In ACORN's view, the pursuit of power was self-justifying. "The very nature of organizational growth and experiences in the process of producing power models its own ideology," said ACORN's chief organizer, Wade Rathke. Power itself, in other words, was the point. Issues like utility rates were the means.[26]

The organization that Alinsky started on a citywide basis to test

out his ideas, Citizens Action Program in Chicago, became the basic
model for scores of city and state organizing campaigns. Environmental, consumer, and working women's organizing efforts through
the decade drew heavily from his approach. And numerous training
centers and programs developed to teach these principles. Alinsky
did not single-handedly craft the language and themes of modern
mass organizing. Traditions like labor activism fed modern efforts,
and labor unions themselves by the 1970s had become largely detached from active membership control and participation, or from
the community environments which had nourished the organizing
of the 1930s. Moreover, by the 1970s, Alinsky's cynical, wry focus on
power and self-interest, detached from any broader vocabulary of
values and purposes, matched the tone of the political culture in the
aftermath of sixties assassinations, the war in Vietnam, Watergate.
Still his legacy had an immense impact.

Such organizing initiatives have produced a notable series of
legislative accomplishments. Even in the Reagan years, the networks
of grass-roots citizen action that Alinsky helped to shape were able
to win major national victories around issues ranging from energy
to toxic waste and water quality. But conventional "Alinskyite language" and its understandings of human motivation were a thin echo
of his earlier insights.[27]

Born largely of the passionate, if immature, revolt against a dehumanized and abstracted technology in the 1960s, by the late Reagan years progressive action had become largely technique. Michael
Dukakis's claim that the definitive issue in the 1988 election was com-
petence found a counterpart in the methods and vocabulary of those
on the left who thought themselves far more devoted to ideology:
The substance of *most* progressive citizen action and politics had become direct-mail operations, television advertising, packaged semi-
nars, and door-to-door and telephone canvass around narrowly defined issues.

Partly as a result of the impoverished progressive language of
politics and change, by the early 1980s—in ways Alinsky would not
have anticipated by the end of his life but may have understood at
an earlier age—the right wing in American politics found success not
only through the identification of "scapegoats." It wedded to such a
formula a vocabulary ironically and eerily reminiscent of populist
themes from the 1930s and earlier. "The quality of American neighborhoods is the ultimate test of the success or failure of government
policies," declared the Republican national platform of 1980. "We
are committed to nurturing the spirit of self-help and cooperation
through which so many neighborhoods have revitalized themselves."
Throughout his years in office, President Reagan justified proposals

ranging from budget cutting to the New Federalism by invoking the need for increased local control and a rebirth of voluntary community initiatives.

For most Americans, trapped in a world of demanding jobs, family responsibilities, and budget balancing, the calls for "participatory democracy" by New Left student protestors in the 1960s simply had not spoken to the practical problems of their everyday lives. Indeed, it seemed that the frequently anti–working class sentiments of middle-class radicals represented the same attitude that Middle Americans had come to expect from condescending professionals of many varieties. Yet popular resentment against the welfare state's bureaucratic authoritarianism and impenetrability had been building for decades and waited to be tapped. A poll of Americans in 1967 found that almost half believed that the gravest threat to the country's future was big government.

The political right responded first to the discontent against technocratic liberalism. By fusing popular frustrations and anxieties about the protests of those "below" in the social order—blacks, the poor—with anger toward the "pointy-headed bureaucrats" who "look down their noses at the average man," conservatives found a ready audience. They spoke in pseudopopulist accents—protesting powerlessness, with no program to help citizens regain control over political life. "Decisions have been taken out of the hands of the people," declared George Wallace's campaign platform of 1968. Or as Ronald Reagan put it a decade later, "Thousands of towns and neighborhoods have seen their peace disturbed by bureaucrats and social planners through busing, questionable education programs, and attacks on family unity." It was a time for "an end to giantism," according to Reagan, a "return of power to the people."[28]

The conservatives of the 1970s identified problems experienced by many Americans. But "power" was defined in negative and privatized terms: an end to "government interference" in traditional communal patterns, on the one hand, and the enlistment of government aid in the enforcement of "traditional" moral prescriptions in private lives, on the other. Reagan's focus on the marketplace as the key public space for citizen activity—as consumers, not citizens—obliterated ground for common action, and with it, the possibility of public life itself. Thus, the Reagan years reinforced people's sense of themselves as spectators of the political process. The rhetorical form of older civic and republican themes became drained of commonwealth content.[29]

In short, what the republican, civic themes of the dominant right-wing rhetoric obscured was the real dynamic of power: conservatives *named* people's experiences of being powerless, but sought to demobilize and deactivate even conservative popular organizations. "When you demythologize the rhetoric and look at the specific things the administration has cut, you find that they've specifically targeted all those programs that [are] essential components of self-help," explained Kathy Desmond, who conducted a study for the American Catholic Bishops on patterns of administration defunding. "The Reagan people didn't want the government to fund groups that were going to stir things up," she concluded. "Anything that was organizing or advocacy."[30]

Thus, a little understood but profound distortion of America's political culture had taken shape by the late 1980s: the older ensemble of populist, commonwealth, civic ideas that combined popular movements for power with a vocabulary of values, American traditions, and cultural themes had become split in two. On the one side progressive movements sought "empowerment" of ordinary citizens with little discussion about broader ends. On the other, a conservative Republican and religious vocabulary detached rhetoric from popular power entirely, resulting in a sentimentalized political language where public-relations image was taken for substance.[31]

Meanwhile, interestingly, it remained for the IAF organizing network that Alinsky himself helped establish to chart another route. After Alinsky's death, the network went back to older democratic traditions and began to build "people's organizations" that wedded the struggle for power to vision. The result has been a wealth of lessons for American democracy.

Reconnecting Power
and Vision

The Industrial Areas Foundation, or IAF, is a network of large-scale, successful citizen organizations made up of poor, minority, lower- and middle-class groups associated with a training center established by Saul Alinsky. It has reinvigorated an understanding of citizen action by taking advantage of the multiple resources and dimensions of power in the modern world. In particular, IAF groups have addressed a context where information itself is increasingly a central strategic resource and form of power.

IAF organizing went through two stages of development. Through the seventies, especially after Alinsky's death in 1972, organizers and local leaders explored new ways to ground the organizing process in a deeper connection with community institutions, preeminently local churches of mainstream Catholic and Protestant orientation. Such a development gave rise to a new approach, called "value-based organizing." Value-based organizing wedded the struggle for power to communal fabric and cultural traditions. Organizers enlisted groups of community sustainers—those they called "the moderates"—who rarely form the foundation of visible public action, in minority communities or elsewhere. As these groups experienced growing successes and began to think about their longer-range rationale, they added a second dimension to their self-understanding, coming to see themselves as "schools of public life."[1]

Schools of public life, in the IAF view, are self-funded citizen organizations where people learn the arts and skills of a politics far more multidimensional than voting. IAF experience is intensively debated and discussed throughout the affiliated organizations. Its approach to learning develops ways to overcome people's lack of access to civic knowledge as well as the ability to think about the meaning and values that must be added to information.[2]

The IAF network forges a thoughtful, constantly evaluated political practice out of the tension between "the world as it is" and "the world as it should be." It not only teaches people specific political details about legislation, issues, and the skills to cooperate and act together effectively, it also adds a dynamic intellectual life involving a practical *theory* of action, employing and constantly developing concepts like power, mediating institutions, public life, the meaning and management of time, judgment, imagination, and self-interest. Such concepts, in turn, are tied to discussion of the democratic and religious values and traditions which inform and frame their efforts—justice, concern for the poor, the dignity of the person, diversity, participation, heritage.

Of particular importance as these groups have evolved and developed is their concept of governance for sustainable citizen activity. IAF groups believe that it is not sufficient to simply protest; to "move into power" on a continuing basis in the modern world, citizens must also assume an important measure of responsibility for the basic public goods of their community. IAF leaders and organizers sometimes refer to such goods as the commons, or commonwealth. Sometimes they give them other names. In either case, it can have a major impact.

———

East Brooklyn Churches (EBC) is a citizen organizing project affiliated with the IAF training network that Alinsky and his associates established in late 1968. For a number of years, they had had local successes in the impoverished neighborhoods of the East Brooklyn area of New York City. In the early 1980s, they had taken on a housing building project on a scale that dwarfed not only their own prior activities but any other low-income housing development initiative in the country. Early in 1982, they had waited for weeks for word from Mayor Edward Koch about whether he would support their plans. It still seemed uncertain.

EBC envisioned an enormous undertaking: construction of 5,000 single-family, owner-occupied housing units designed for lower-middle-income buyers, built in the midst of the decimated and mostly black neighborhoods of East Brooklyn. Drug dealers ruled the streets, even in daylight. Block after block had been bulldozed into rubble, like some vast war zone. Most middle-income families had long fled. But EBC had lined up a remarkable group of financial backers, including Bishop Francis Mugavero, leader of Brooklyn's 1.5 million Catholics, and theologically conservative church groups like the Missouri Synod of the National Lutheran Church. And EBC had a long track record of smaller victories.

Their work had begun far more modestly in 1978 with a small group of Catholic and Protestant clergy and laity convened to discuss a formidable array of community issues. They followed the Alinsky dictum to start with small, "winnable," immediate issues around which poor and powerless people can experience confidence-building success. EBC members had forced cleanups in local food stores, pressured the city to install hundreds of street signs, forced renovation of local parks, and worked together to clean up vacant lots. And slowly through the process they had forged a sense of solidarity and potency. "We are not a grassroots organization," thundered the Reverend Johnny Ray Youngblood, a key leader in the organization, at one rally. "Grass roots are shallow roots. Grass roots are fragile roots. *Our* roots are deep roots. Our roots have fought for existence in the shattered glass of East New York."

EBC's turn to housing arose out of the conviction that only widespread home ownership could create the kind of "roots" essential for renewed community pride and freedom from fear. Teaming up with a well-known *Daily News* columnist and former developer, I. D. Robbins, they adopted his controversial argument that for half the cost of high-density, high-rise apartments, it would be possible to build large numbers of single-family homes that could create stable neighborhoods.

EBC had come to name their undertaking the "Nehemiah Plan," recalling the Old Testament prophet sent back the Jerusalem by the king of Persia in the fifth century B.C. to lead in the rebuilding of the city after the Babylonian captivity. "The story connected our work to something real, not something bogus," said Mike Gecan, lead organizer for EBC. "It got it out of the 'housing' field and the idea that you have to have a bureaucracy with thirty-five consultants to do anything. It made it a 'nonprogram,' something more than housing." Or as one EBC leader, Celina Jamieson, emphasized, "We are more than a Nehemiah Plan. We are about the central development of dignity and self-respect."

To the amazement of almost everyone in the housing field, EBC had secured funding nearly sufficient to begin. What remained was approval by the mayor of a plan for loans from the city for each house, payable upon resale, that would bring the prices low enough for middle-class families. Leaders held a press conference. "The first

question was about the mayor's support," Gecan remembered. They
could not speak about Koch's intentions, but they declared their intention to go forward.

One of the local TV network affiliates traveled to the site after
the press conference. Cameras rolled over block after block, building
after building. That night, as scenes of desolation appeared on the
screen, an announcer read from the Book of Nehemiah [2:17] to illustrate EBC's intent:

> You see the trouble we are in,
> How Jerusalem lies in ruins with its gates burned.
> Come, let us build the walls of Jerusalem,
> That we may no longer suffer disgrace.

Audience response was immense. The next day the mayor approved
the project. Koch, with the flair for publicity that had long been his
trademark, soon was comparing himself to the prophet Nehemiah
in speeches across the city.[3]

The Nehemiah story provides a window into the organizing approach of the IAF network. It testifies to major changes in its organizing over the years, from the scale of the effort—involving tens of
thousands of families—to the sorts of projects worked on—assuming
responsibility for a large-scale infrastructure effort like the creation of
a small township of houses. The language of the Nehemiah undertaking, resonant with the prophetic Old Testament imagery of the black
church tradition, is far removed from the nonideological vocabulary
of raw power and self-interest most often associated with community
organizations. Indeed, much of EBC's power comes from its capacity
to frame its action in a language with a widespread appeal: it adds
values to issues, in a way that reembeds problems like housing once
again in a sense of human agency. These changes suggest ways in
which IAF groups have evolved since Saul Alinsky's death in 1972.

In the context of a growing economy and the Great Society of
the 1960s, even through the mid-70s the classic Alinsky approach to
community organization often proved effective in the immediate
term, at least for those served by dominant organizations in poorer
communities. Sufficient resources, controlled by city administrations
or local economic power brokers, existed to provide a wealth of local
targets for campaigns for tangible benefits in municipal services,
housing, education, economic development, and a range of other
areas. There continued to be a broader public that poor and powerless communities might appeal to on the basis of their right to a fair
share. And at least until the early seventies, dense networks of local
neighborhood institutions continued to thrive in most inner-city ur-

ban areas which could be pulled together and mobilized through effective organization.

Yet the context for community organization changed dramatically through the seventies and into the eighties in ways that prompted changes in IAF methods. Innovations in telecommunications, urban growth and development patterns, the appearance of massive suburban shopping malls and industrial and office parks far from downtown areas, indicated a further erosion in the numbers of jobs available in inner-city areas and a transformation of the nature of jobs. Cities became less regional retailing and manufacturing centers than centers for administration, finance, conventions, and recreation. Those who moved to the suburbs—including, in the aftermath of sixties civil rights laws, much of the black middle class—were mainly those who could afford to move. Inner-city areas were left with large populations of the poor, new immigrants, working-class ethnics, and others whose traditional blue-collar jobs were fast disappearing. An increasingly large number of women-headed, single-parent households were trapped in welfare or low-paid, dead-end, or part-time jobs, which accounted for the growing percentage of woman and children among the poor.[4]

With the flight of jobs and the disappearance of many middle-class residents came a weakening in the elements that had furnished the foundations of traditional community organization: unions, political groups, ethnic associations, small business organizations. All lost ground, save only religious congregations, which remained centers of local neighborhood life. In view of such changes, the 1983 report of *U.S. News and World Report* on the next fifty years represented a plausible bleak scenario. The magazine envisioned "large, aging cities [where] vast neighborhoods housing the least mobile of Americans—the poor, the elderly, and new immigrants from other lands—will continue to crumble. The residential parts of central cities 'will be more a repository for those who have fallen off the train.'"[5]

At the same time, the growing conglomeration of the economy greatly limited the maneuvering ability of local power brokers. Between 1980 and 1985 alone, $380 billion was spent for corporate mergers and hostile takeovers, many involving the purchase of locally owned business by multinational corporations. Patterns of concentration reflected such merger activity. By the early 1980s, the assets of the largest two hundred companies matched the percentage of the economy held by the largest one thousand in 1941.[6]

The gobbling up of locally owned industries and businesses and the trends toward centralization of financial and economic power and wealth all meant transfer of effective authority to national or even global managers. Meanwhile, Reagan-era cutbacks in aid to cities have severely circumscribed the resources of the public sector.

These shifting terms of political and economic power greatly affected the IAF practice by the middle seventies, as organizers tried to cope with the changing community landscape. "We began across the board, working with middle-class whites as well as blacks and chicanos," explained Ed Chambers. "We began looking not so much at geography as at communities of interest." They discussed how to deepen the process of organizing, which led to an even stronger emphasis on community institutions, especially congregations. And they began to stress that citizens' organizations needed a clear independence from government funding, foundations, and corporate donors if local communities were to have a strong sense of "ownership" and power. "We became very strong on the need for the organization to be based on the people's own money or it won't last," said Chambers. IAF leaders and organizers began to stress the need for citizen groups to be largely self-financed through dues from affiliated groups and through membership fund-raising campaigns.[7]

The new focus on religious groups as the foundation for organizing came partly out of IAF organizers' readings of the changing urban environment. It was also made possible by the generational change in IAF leadership.

Ed Chambers, the organizer who took over as executive director of IAF in 1972, conveys something of Alinsky's legendary style. Brusque, often contentious, Chambers mingles the *persona* of "organizer" with Alinsky-like intellectuality: he seems something of a cross between political philosopher and stevedore. Recruited by the IAF in 1958 to work with The Woodlawn Organization, Chambers combines reflections on books he has been reading lately with profane observations about the state of American politics and society. He constantly uses stories from his three decades of organizing to make his points. At times, he interrupts the conversation to challenge you: "What do you mean by that?" "Why do you think so?" His early encounters with the sponsoring committee of EBC had this quality, participants remembered. "He stood up there and kept telling us that we were living in a garbage heap," explained Lutheran minister Dave Benke. At times, it made Benke furious, but Chambers also forced attention to things the community leaders had closed their minds to, "just to survive." "The man kept us in touch with reality and with our anger. He insisted that our people, pastors included, should be training in organizing skills. He demanded that we *research* every project or issue to be addressed. And he made us practice ahead of time for every important meeting or action."[8]

In ways that resemble Alinsky, Chambers radiates a "tough guy" organizer stance that is abrasive to many. But he has made sharp breaks in the IAF traditional approach to women organizers and leaders. Alinsky was renowned for his comment in the early 1970s to Marge Tabankin, a community organizer who later headed the ACTION program for the Carter administration, that "women couldn't be organizers." In contrast, Chambers has sought out women as paid organizers since his days with FIGHT in the sixties, and he has encouraged women like Christine Stephens and Maribeth Larkin to become leading, highly paid organizers in the IAF network. Chambers is also well known for encouraging women in IAF-affiliated groups to take on top leadership positions. And over the past ten years, IAF training sessions have come to depict the contemporary women's movement in a strongly favorable light—a notable difference from earlier times.[9]

Chambers brings a different set of passions to organizing than Alinsky did. A former seminarian, Chambers has strong interests in theology and religious thought, which have infused his perspective on what organizing is about. As a young man he traveled through Europe and was inspired by the example of worker-priest movements in the fifties. He is also driven by the concern for developing *organizing* as a respected, reasonably well-paying career with security. Today, IAF "lead organizers"—those who direct large organizations—make comfortably middle-income salaries, and "cabinet" members, the most senior IAF organizers, make more. (Such salaries, unprecedented elsewhere in the world of community organizing, are possible because of the strong emphasis on membership-based fundraising—mostly dues from member church, synagogue, union, and community affiliates of local groups—and because their new organizing approaches devolve most authority and tasks, eventually, on voluntary leadership themselves.) Perhaps most notably, Chambers is more "relational," as one young IAF trainee put it. He constantly encourages, prods, and supports the network of organizers for whom he feels responsible, and at the same time asks for criticisms, feedback, and reciprocity from others. Chambers is visibly a man who enjoys public life.[10]

Chambers pointed the IAF organizing network in new directions. The changes were given depth through an organizing effort called Communities Organized for Public Service (COPS), which proved dramatically successful in the sprawling, impoverished Mexican barrios of San Antonio.

Ernesto Cortes, COPS's first organizer, grew up in San Antonio in the 1940s and '50s. He had always felt, as a Mexican-American, something of a stranger in the town where the majority population

had been excluded from political and economic power for more
than one hundred years. "The struggle was to become American,"
Cortes remembered. "If someone called you a Mexican you were supposed to beat them up." For years he had been frustrated by the
ineffectiveness of traditional approaches to poverty, from the poverty programs to voter registration and economic development strategies. The underlying problem seemed to him the lack of power, reflected in the fact that there was no Mexican representation on the
City Council. He decided to get organizing experience.

Cortes had read *Reveille for Radicals* in the early 1960s and liked
the book, but he had thought Alinsky in person too cynical when he
heard him speak in college. IAF groups like Rochester FIGHT and
TWO were known as the best community organizing around, however. So Cortes went to Chicago in the summer of 1971.[11]

The need to listen to community traditions and individual self-
interests was becoming codified in IAF organizing in a constant practice of individualized, face-to-face meetings. Organizers and leaders
learned how to regularly interview people within churches or neighborhood groups and in the larger community alike, to find out "who
people are," what motivated them, what were their interests and concerns. IAF organizers see this structured listening process as the singular "genius" of their work, the key to their successes. They argue
that most organizing involves one-way communications between an
activist or group and a passive constituency; direct-mail fund-raising
appeals for causes or electoral politics or door-to-door canvassing
are familiar examples. By way of contrast, in IAF groups a constant
process of interviewing grounds organizing in an ongoing conversation. Sister Margaret Snipe, a copastor at a Hispanic parish in Brooklyn connected to EBC, illustrated the point. She said that the training
of a group of lay members of her church in the skills of listening
through individualized, face-to-face meetings worked a dramatic rebirth in the community. It created a group of church organizers who
were sensitive to others' points of view, more aware of their own
needs and interests, and skilled at interpersonal communication.[12]

In IAF projects in Chicago and Milwaukee, Cortes learned similar skills. "I learned the value of listening," he explained. "I had always had a tendency to jump down people's throats, to intimidate."[13]

When Father Edmundo Rodriguez, a priest in San Antonio,
asked for help from the IAF in putting together a local community
group, Cortes returned in 1973. He brought with him the IAF emphasis on detailed attention to community concerns—before doing
anything else, Cortes conducted hundreds of interviews in his first
months to get a mapping of local issues. It turned out that the chief
concerns were concrete problems close to home like substandard

housing and the drainage system that overflowed each time it rained—not the more visible issues like racial discrimination and police brutality which Chicano militants had sought to organize around. Father Rodriguez suddenly began to feel that this effort at organizing was different from earlier, unsuccessful campaigns. It was not that people were apathetic or unconcerned; they had rarely been asked what concerned them. "It was like one of those light bulbs that suddenly appear in cartoons," according to Rodriguez.

Ernie Cortes brought the conviction that it made no sense to organize in the Mexican-American community without an attentiveness to what people actually believed, as well as what issues were on their minds. "I thought a lot about a conversation I'd had once with Cesar Chavez," he explained. "Every organization needs an ideology if it is to continue." For the Mexican community in San Antonio, as for Chavez's United Farm Workers union, Christianity in the form of Catholicism was by far the strongest, most vital belief system, and it was hard to imagine successful civic activity that would not draw on the rituals and traditions of the church, as well its institutional strength.[14]

Combining careful listening to basic community issues with an organizing approach based on the core convictions of the community led COPS in San Antonio, and the IAF network more broadly, to several critical innovations. In the first instance, "self-interest" as a concept became considerably richer and broader. IAF training began to combine the two earlier Alinsky themes of listening to community culture and individual self-interests to gain a different view of what motivates individuals. It began to distinguish between "self-interest" and "selfishness," arguing that people's basic concerns are not only for themselves in an immediate, short-term sense. When people think about what they care about in the longer term they evidence a strong interest in the intangibles of their lives—their families' well-being, their own sense of contribution and dignity, their core beliefs, their friends and closest associates, and their sense of efficacy in the world.[15]

A more elaborated approach to listening to community needs also resulted in a change in the base of those organized. The IAF organizing method reached deeper into the community's institutional and social fabric than it ever had before. In the process it drew in conservatives for the first time and established the organization on the basis of community moderates, through attention not only to community issues but also to concrete needs of institutions such as religious congregations. COPS helped local parishes with tangible concerns such as membership rolls, fund drives, liturgy, and music.

Thus the organizational leadership also shifted, from the more visible "public" actors—most typically male—who had championed causes like an end to racial discrimination and police brutality, to a more invisible tier of leaders, frequently women, who had worked behind the scenes to keep school PTAs going, run day-to-day activities of churches, and the like. COPS organizers termed such community sustainers "moderates," in contrast to activists or liberals. COPS built on the basis of PTA leaders, parish council members, stalwarts of the church guilds: "Not the politicos, the people who have *been in* and defined public life, the people who have wheeled and dealed," said Christine Stephens, lead organizer of the organization in the early 1980s who is a student of American social protest and political theory.

> This approach builds around the people who have sustained the community instead. The women, for example, whose lives by and large have been wrapped up in their parishes and their children. What COPS has been able to do is to give them a public life and a public visibility, to educate, to provide the tools whereby they can participate in the political process.

In the process, "politics," "public life," and "leadership" became redefined.[16]

Janie Gonzalez, the sort of community stalwart to whom people turn instinctively in times of need, remembered Cortes's first approaches. "When Ernie was interviewing people in 1973, he always kept coming back to me. I said, 'Why?' " Cortes's reasoning was clear. For many years, Gonzalez had been active in her church parish and her school PTA. She still speaks softly—until she is in a public setting. In those years, Cortes would challenge her a little: "Ernie used to say you have to speak loud, from your stomach. I'd say, 'I'm sorry, I'm not that way.' " For COPS leaders like Gonzalez, the fusion of particular issues with values and faith created a potent alchemy. "We'd talk about what values come from our families and our faiths," she remembered. "Love, caring. Then we'd talk about the pressures on families nowadays: unemployment, drugs, the media, peer pressure, alcoholism. And we'd talk about how the church should be responding." COPS provided a new vehicle for *acting* on strongly held convictions that had had no outlet.[17]

Such new dimensions of the IAF approach had the visible consequence in San Antonio of delivering a series of stunning political and programmatic victories. The organization forced the city to act on drainage problems, dirt roads, and schools, and soundly beat a "Proposition 13" tax limitation initiative with a massive door-to-door campaign in 1987. Its network of affiliated Texas organizations also passed landmark statewide legislation around issues of school district financing, health care, and farm safety in the mid-eighties.[18]

In the early 1970s, San Antonio still had a "colonial" air whereby a small group of businessmen, most of whom belonged to the segregated Texas Cavalier Country Club, held sway. City Council members were elected at large, which meant that Mexican and African American candidates could almost never raise funds to compete. COPS "shattered San Antonio's established conservative order." The City Council now is elected from single-member districts; by 1977, five Hispanics and one black formed a new majority in city government. Henry Cisneros, rising to political leadership in the city in large part through his championing of COPS issues, gained national visibility as the first Hispanic mayor of a major American city.[19]

It became clear that in groups like COPS, the organizer played more of a catalytic role, encouraging others to take on increasing responsibility for getting people to meetings, planning strategy, doing research, and training itself. "No organizer comes in from the outside and organizes," said Cortes.

> All you can do in any situation is to identify those leaders who want to organize. I didn't organize COPS. The leadership did. I taught them; I trained them; I identified them; I challenged them; and I worked with them on a one-to-one basis. But they did the actual organizing. They had already the relationships for years and years, mostly built around the churches. The question for leaders is to what extent they feel serious enough about the problems to work the networks they already have and to build new networks. The basic process was developing the skills to act.[20]

Organizing, then, began to involve a much more extensive process of skill development in the IAF groups. "We began to see every action as an opportunity for education and training," described Maribeth Larkin, an organizer first in United Neighborhoods Organization (UNO), an IAF affiliate in Los Angeles, who later became lead organizer of COPS. "If you look at it in the right way, there are all kinds of opportunities for training—every presentation before city council, every meeting, every discussion with the media." Chambers saw this more elaborate focus on what the local organizational leaders were learning as a fundamental difference with the older Alinsky style: "The mistake of the first forty years of Alinsky organizing was the absence of political education. We were very good at the action, very clever and imaginative, but we didn't make a commitment to the growth process of the people. We never forced people to reflect. We never took retreats, or did extensive evaluation."

The IAF "iron rule of organizing" now is "Never do anything for people that they can do for themselves." Indeed, IAF's "iron rule," with its insistence on self-reliance and independence as a condition for self-respect, shows intriguing parallels with the step-by-step assumption of personal responsibility one finds in self-help groups like Alcoholics Anonymous or Al Anon, or the more political stress on "self-determination" found in movements like Black Power or Women's Liberation. But what is unique about IAF's approach is its *location* of this stress on autonomy in a specifically public environment, where public is understood as an arena of difference, not homogeneity. The combination of an emphasis on autonomy with one on the different, unique needs and motivations that bring each individual into politics furnishes a constant prod in the IAF organizations for people to acknowledge their mistakes and account for their actions—behavior that in most "public settings" renders the individual too vulnerable to sustain, or changes "public" back into a more personalized communal style. In IAF, public life is seen more as a particular kind of craft, an artful way of acting in a specific setting. With such an understanding, personal vulnerability is diminished by learning the political art. And people's experience of "transformation" comes most directly from public roles, connected to feelings of power which result from lessening dependence on experts, professionals, and even organizers themselves.[21]

Six years after Alinsky's death, the changing approach of the network was articulated in *Organizing for Family and Congregation.* "We are in a conversation about families, churches and institutional power," began the document, reflecting "the collective experience of lay leaders, clergy, women religious and professional organizers in twenty cities." The document situated IAF-style organizing in a far-ranging analysis of American culture and society, with something of the stark, even apocalyptic tone of Alinsky in his 1972 *Playboy* interview. "If we follow where our dollars go, we will find the institutions that shape our daily lives," it argued.

> Our dollars end up in banks and savings and loans, in insurance companies, in oil companies, in utilities, and in the hands of major manufacturers, real estate developers, retailers and organized criminals. . . . They buy the second level, the politicians, lawyers, the advertisers, the media . . . and other professionals [who] provide the rationales and jargon to perpetuate the top power institutions and screen them from the public.[22]

This sort of skeletal power analysis was vintage Alinskyism. It departed from the original method, however, in its depiction of the *nature* of the conflict and its prescriptions for achieving solutions. The document listed a number of consequences: economic pressures that result from families struggling to meet bills; community pressures like drugs, pornography, crime, violence against children; and more subtle cultural pressures as well. "Television tells people how to eat, how to look, how to love, and how to feel." People increasingly were subjected to "overscheduling" that eroded free time and family ties. All of these pressures, moreover, added up to a value crisis: "Our country is in the kind of crisis that both Madison and de Tocqueville warned us about. The intermediate voluntary institutions—including churches—are ineffectual in a power relationship with the powerful. As a result, the middle is collapsing, confused . . . sucked dry by a vacuum."[23]

The result, argued *Organizing for Family and Congregation,* was a "value war," fought over the

> fundamental question: who will parent our children? Who will teach them, train them, nurture them? How will they be taught and trained and nurtured? Will this parenting take place in a strictly secular setting where the system is said to be the solution, or time is money, or profit is the sole standard of judgment? Or will the true teachers and prophets—parents and grandparents, pastors and rabbis and lay leaders—win this war and continue to convey the best values of the Judeo-Christian tradition?[24]

Such a framing of the "crisis" in America pointed to the distinctive changes in IAF methods of organizing. Sixties-style movements' weaknesses, in IAF terms, included a reliance on charismatic leaders, an absence of ways to teach accountability, activism without careful thought and purpose, and an alienated cultural style which turned off most Americans. As an alternative, *Organizing* urged the growth of new forms of citizen organizations that had roots in a variety of institutions—from religious congregations to Lions Clubs. Such groups had to build on and respect the traditions and culture of the community, but also be open to diversity. The issues such new forms of organizations might address were not specified (although the nature of the institutional foundations put limits on what issues they were likely to raise: gay rights was not a likely cause for Catholic parishes, for instance). Rather, the document expressed the conviction that broad and inclusive citizen groups, deciding their own agendas but drawing and reflecting on religious and democratic traditions, would allow "a collection of families, a church or synagogue or an alliance of churches [to] break out of the materialist pattern" and "arm themselves for a value war."[25]

Such an approach spoke powerfully to minority, poor, and working-class communities, and it also had a wider appeal to Americans in the period of "me first" morality and consumer culture. By the end of the decade, the IAF was able to help local leaders build larger, more potent "people's organizations" than had previously appeared out of the community organizing tradition. Indeed, in many ways such groups were no longer "community groups," but broader, more diverse citizen organizations that drew especially from congregations.

The experiences and relative successes of such groups, in turn, brought new challenges and questions: How could they be sustained over time? How might new leadership emerge and develop? And, finally—since IAF had spurned the model of sixties-style social movements, which they saw as transitory and superficial—what was such organizing *about* in longer-range terms, in a world whose dominant institutions and culture palpably differed from their values and interests? The expression "value war" had specific content for participants in these groups. They saw justice, participation, the dignity of people, and other key values undermined by "me-first" selfishness. But it was unclear what they were proposing as the alternative. In the 1980s, out of a concern for the meaning and content of their broader vision, these groups rediscovered the language of public life.[26]

In the 1980s, the IAF network continued to be widely viewed as models for populist-style citizen organizing. No other local groups in the country could boast the thousands of delegates that IAF affiliates like COPS in San Antonio, BUILD in Baltimore, EBC in New York, or UNO in Los Angeles could turn out to conventions every year or two, or the scale of victories for poor, working-class, and minority communities that IAF groups sometimes achieved. San Antonio's COPS, for instance, had secured one billion dollars for roads, schools, sewers, parks, economic development, and other infrastructural elements in the once devastated barrios. Moreover, it was seen to be catalyzing broader political changes in Texas and in the Southwest generally. In Texas, the original COPS organization had led to a network which included groups like Valley Interfaith in the Rio Grande, EPISO in El Paso, Austin Interfaith, the Metropolitan Organization in Houston, and others.[27]

On the face of it—and even to many experienced grass-roots organizers—IAF continued to resemble Alinsky's "classic" approach. "Saul believed power was such a good thing that people should have it and lots of people should have it," said IAF Executive Director Ed Chambers to a reporter in 1988, explaining the animus of the mass-based organizations IAF helps put together. It was the sort of language Alinsky himself would have employed. But in fact, the IAF organizations developed basic themes in ways Alinsky could not have anticipated.[28]

In particular, the IAF approach transformed Alinsky's understanding of "self-interest" and "power" into far more dynamic concepts. Their evolving understanding of such terms now highlights the multidimensional motivations that initially *bring* people into organizations and the fashion in which any exercise of power is always relational, changing the actor as the actor changes the environment. Moreover, in elaborating Saul Alinsky's rhetorical dedication to "democratic values" like diversity, conflict, participation, and difference, the IAF has rediscovered older populist ideas of public life as a distinctive, vital arena in its own right, where citizens exchange ideas and power, achieve visiblity, engage in conflict and collaboration. Their organizations have also significantly reworked the practical theory of public life and its relationship to private life-worlds. The IAF theory of public life highlights in a novel fashion the dependence of the public realm on the private as well as the public realm's distinctiveness. And although groups like COPS have not solved the problem of organizational inertia and routinization, they have addressed it through an intense stress on the need for self-reflection and education if citizen organizations are to remain vital.

Some of these concerns were visible as early as the *Organizing for Families and Congregations* book. Leaders in citizen organizations were defined not simply as individuals but as those in relationship with others, who "recognize that leadership is not by nature a form of individual aggrandizement but rather a means to continually expand the number of their fellow leaders in the interest of collective power." A premium was placed on "leadership training," including skills that ranged from "how to listen to and affirm other people" to raising money and negotiating with decision makers. The question of how to hold leaders accountable—both within organizations and in the broader public environment, where they dealt with office holders and others—emerged as a central problem. All of these issues had to do with forms of public activity.

The tone of IAF's book, however, remained parochial. Little attention was given to building ongoing relationships with groups or individuals outside the citizen organizations. By the late 1970s, in fact, IAF had developed a reputation for unwillingness to work with other groups. Moreover, organizing was described in terms of its effects on families and congregations, not on the larger institutional patterning of communities or the dominant culture. But several things moved IAF to frame its work more broadly.

In part, the IAF was led to ponder the nature and distinctiveness of specifically public relationships out of the dynamics of organizing itself, as organizations lasted and matured. Despite attentiveness to "getting people to do things for themselves" and avoid staff domination or excessive responsibility, patterns of reliance on organizers like Cortes nonetheless developed. What would happen in COPS if he left? Could leaders "do it on their own"? And what happened to the possibilities for new leaders emerging if the same person kept the presidency of the group year after year? A remarkable feature of the IAF network is the extent to which such questions are constantly posed, in the name of a self-reflective, educational process intended to expand the number of leaders and keep organizations alive and dynamic. But it was still not an easy process.[29]

Furthermore, relationships over time with politicians had been a prod to thinking more carefully about the nature of "public." Attentiveness to power and self-interest led COPS to challenge politicians' personalized styles out of the suspicion that first-name relationships and expressions of endearment were in part a mystifying ploy to win voters' suppport. Moreover, COPS saw itself as creating a different sort of relationship, based on collaboration. As Stephens put it, "What we create in actions with public officials is a world in which leaders control the agenda for the space of that meeting. It is the people talking and the politicians listening, and not having the central place."[30]

Ed Chambers saw himself as having worked on the distinction between "private" and "public" out of his difficult experiences over the years with the organizing tradition. "Saul never paid attention to organizers' private lives. They were a mess." Indeed, Chambers spoke with visible pain of Alinsky's cavalier, dismissive attitude toward his associates' family life and retirement and security needs: "He called me up long-distance to order me to Rochester."[31]

All of this led to a major innovation in methods by the late 1970s: a basic workshop given in every national training session and reproduced countless times in local groups that IAF calls "public and private." In the typical pedagogical approach, making a distinction to be discussed, the trainer divides the board and makes a series of paired contrasts, corresponding to "appropriate behavior" in different realms:

Private	Public
family/friends/self	church/school/politics/work
sameness/commonality	diversity
fidelity/loyalty	accountability
givenness	choice
intimacy/closed	open/fluid
vulnerability	dramatic role
the need to be liked	need to be respected
self-giving	quid pro quo/self-interest

The distinction between public and private is always framed by IAF's basic rules of knowledge. "Universals," principles that seem to apply across widely varying cultural and communal contexts, need always to be contextualized to have any real meaning. Thus, IAF teachers argue that with public-private, as with other distinctions, nothing is ever completely "either-or." ("We're the same people, after all, whether we are in public or private setting," explained Gerald Taylor, the lead organizer of BUILD in Baltimore.) All categories should be seen as provisional and fluid, based on lessons from experiences; Taylor pointed out that "public" would have a qualitatively different meaning in most traditional African societies, for instance. And different settings partake of different "public" and "personal" or private qualities—a church, explained IAF cabinet member Arnie Graf, is far more personal than a convention or a political rally.[32]

But with all the nuance, the very outlining of this sort of distinction often has a large impact on participants, in a culture where such distinctions are regularly muddled or mystified. "The first time I gave the workshop in a training session with UNO in Los Angeles, I knew this was something very powerful," Chambers remembered. "The discussion could have gone on all day. And people lined up afterwards to talk about their lives." IAF has used this basic, working distinction for a decade now, and it always stimulates intense, sometimes agonizing reflection, as participants think through the ways such boundaries are obscured or confused in their lives. "It was the most meaningful experience I ever had, more important than seminary or college," said the Reverend Doug Miles, a dynamic minister who heads one of Baltimore's largest black churches, Brown Memorial Baptist. Miles described his emotions during an IAF 10 Day Training session in July 1982. After the workshop on public and private and a follow-up discussion of the way participants defined their own individual self-interests, he suddenly was overwhelmed.

> Preachers historically have problems in their personal lives at home because they're so busy in "public," taking care of everybody else. When I figured out what priorities I had been living by, I sat there and cried. My wife was fourteenth, after the NAACP. For the first time it dawned on me just how neglectful I was being.
>
> It also altered my view of the ministry. The church had been functioning so that if the pastor was not involved, the program did not go. I began to see the fallacy of that. The ministry was not something *I* was responsible for; it was something the church was responsible for. I began to see the need to share responsibility, not to be afraid of training people to become leaders.

After the training session, Miles instituted a program of leadership development in his church, tying 10 Day principles to scriptural and theological reflection. By 1987, the church had grown severalfold.[33]

This distinction proved significant in teaching leaders the dynamics of effective political action, from the parish level to the life of communities. "We would never have been able to challenge the priest to stop acting like our 'father' without this sort of training," said Beatrice Cortez, a president of San Antonio COPS in the early 1980s. "You learn what's appropriate and inappropriate for politicians. They shouldn't try to get us to love them, for instance." Cortez frequently tells a story about her daughter to illustrate how children can quickly pick up the point. During her tenure as president of the organization, Cortez had a COPS phone in her house. One day the mayor, Henry Cisneros—whom she had known for years—called up on the line. "My daughter answered and at first didn't know who it was. 'Who should I say is calling?' she asked." Cisneros said, "Tell her it's a special friend." "Then she recognized his voice," Cortez continued. "She said, 'On this line, you're not a friend. I know who you are. You're the mayor!' I told her, 'You've got that right, honey!'" Cortez subsequently found that in training Mexican communities in other parts of Texas in effective "public life," the distinction proved invaluable. "In these towns, politics has come to be equated with family ties. People get mixed up through marriage, godparents, and don't want to challenge close ties." Evocation of a public realm where dynamics of personal loyalty were not dominant did not undermine extended family patterns, or consign family concerns to the private realm. But it positioned them in a way that allowed common work with people *beyond* traditional family ties. Cortez conducts role plays built around Scripture to bring home the point.[34]

The self-conscious *recognition* of the public realm in which IAF organizations functioned as significant actors thus began to make explicit and clear what had often been known intuitively but never quite identified: public life had its own distinctive dynamics, its own principles like accountability, respect, diversity, self-interest, pluralism, "quid pro quo," visibility, and collaborative action. But public life, for the IAF groups, also stands in a different relationship to private life than has been classically conceived. Indeed, the groups partially reverse the traditional attributes of public and private and their corresponding valuations. The private, in IAF terms, is the more self-sacrificial and idealistic realm, while the public is the world of quid pro quo and self-interest. Moreover, public life in the IAF view, although it has an integrity and value in its own right, also is meant to serve the personal interests of families and individual persons.

The republican tradition across the centuries has accorded privilege to public life, sustaining in various forms Aristotle's metaphor that public life is like a body, while private life resembles limbs, which can be cut away if necessary.[35] In contrast, a more apt metaphor for IAF's construction of public and private is the BUILD organization's symbol of a tree. In these terms, roots serve as the private foundations of public life, while trunk and branches, symbols of the visible public world, are expressions of maturity, although they continue to draw sustenance and support from their roots. Such a set of conceptual reversals has its counterpart in the sorts of communal and family issues that are taken up by groups like COPS. And they have led to a radical recasting of the nature of leadership and politics which, for instance, encourages women to take new roles. After COPS's first, every president of the organization was female.

Finally, IAF groups shifted from simply *protest* organizations to the assumption of some *responsibility* for policy initiation and what they call "governance." Affiliates began to take on issues of infrastructure that affected the entire life of communities, in addition to those that concerned their own constituencies. The results included fascinating examples of how public life can combine difference with discovered commonalities, conflict with cooperation, around a renewal of citizen responsibility for the commonwealth.

7

Repairing the Commons

"We are of the humble opinion that we have the right to enjoy the privileges of free men, but that we do not will appear in many instances and we beg leave to mention one out of many," declared *A Petition to the State Legislature of the Commonwealth of Massachusetts,* delivered by a group of African American leaders in 1787, the year of the nation's Constitutional Convention. The right in question was "the education of our children which receive no benefit from the free schools in the town of Boston." A "great grievance," they argued, that made them "fear for our rising offspring." If not remedied, their children would be consigned to "ignorance in a land of gospel light . . . for no other reason [than] they are black."[1]

The petition served well as testimony to the painful ironies of American democracy. Since the nation's beginning, the ideal of public education has been inextricably linked with America's very definition of a republican, or commonwealth, government. And the distance between that ideal and the actual practices has proven the key to deciphering the unfulfilled promises of democracy. In few other cases has the contrast between myth and reality proven as stark as in the educational story of African Americans.

But the narrative is not one of unrelieved victimization. Blacks have often refashioned schools—or created their own—as instruments of community strength, cohesion, and the struggle for full citizenship, even in the face of considerable hardship. And today, Baltimoreans United in Leadership Development, or BUILD—the largest mainly black local organization in the country—has crafted what may well be the most ambitious plan for revitalizing public schools, called the Baltimore Commonwealth. It combines a remarkable incentive plan for high school graduates with a strategy for wide-ranging devolution of power and responsibility to teachers and the community. Moreover, it represents a potent redefinition of the very function of schools, reviving the old tradition which saw education as the instrument of democracy itself, teaching young people to be full, active participants in the life and decision-making processes of their communities.

The Baltimore Commonwealth of schools, furthermore, renews the old concept of *commons* as meeting ground. In Baltimore, collaborative work on schools by BUILD, the business community, city officials, unions, and others created a mechanism for an ongoing conversation about the city and its future, after a period of extreme division and polarization.

BUILD's Commonwealth initiative has old antecedents. It stands as an example of the prophetic role African Americans have regularly played in calling the country back to unrealized democratic promises. And the clout that BUILD assembled to press its plan constitutes a reminder of the regenerative possibilities still to be realized in American politics.

———

For the more democratic activists in the American Revolution, widespread public schooling was seen as the indispensable bulwark against tyranny. "Where learning is confined to a few people, we always find monarchy, aristocracy and slavery," wrote Benjamin Rush, a founding figure in American education, in 1786. Thomas Jefferson rested much of his hope for avoiding the corruption and decay of the American republican spirit in the spread of schooling. "Enlighten the people generally, and tyranny and oppressions of body and mind will vanish like evil spirits at the dawn of day."[2]

Such a faith in the democratic power of education had antecedents on the continent. As early as 1664, reflecting in part the Puritans' interest in teaching practical applications of the Bible, Massachusetts passed a compulsory education law, requiring all male European children in the colony to receive formal schooling. Five years later, enabling legislation required each township to provide schools and schoolmasters. A hundred years later, similar legislation had been passed in the body of the New England and Middle Atlantic colonies. The original religious purposes of education had taken on secular, practical ends of the sort advocated by Benjamin Franklin, who argued that any man might have to do anything in a frontier society; the point of his model school, the Philadelphia Academy, was to train male children to deal with unanticipated situations. It was to be a school out of which boys "will come . . . fitted for learning any Business, Calling, or Profession."[3]

In fact, relatively few children—even among the white male population—received more than a few years of public school education in the early republic. But in the first half of the nineteenth century, the public school ideal fueled an extensive movement, called the Common School Movement, which picked up the language of commonwealth and civic commitment. In this view, public school education was both an instrument of democracy—the means for enlightening the general "citizenry"—and, increasingly, a new form of social property: the very possession of an "education" in schools was seen as a foundation for independence and civic virtue, allowing active participation in the public affairs of the community. But as educational and social historian Colin Greer has pointed out in his book *The Great School Legend,* "public schools never really embraced the mass of the community."[4]

Whatever the rhetoric and intentions of reformers, common schools in the nineteenth century were not only meant to inform and increase access to citizenship. They were also seen by the powerful as instruments for sorting out virtuous citizens from others—females, blacks, the poor, immigrant workers—who were not to be included, and for training in the skills and attitudes seen as desirable. Thus schools became objects of sharp struggle over control, and urban elites most often emerged victorious from the fray. The result was that schools, in the main, sought to inculcate middle-class values of discipline, control, and deference to authority that would be useful in producing a tractable work force and citizenry.[5]

African Americans confronted educational obstacles even more daunting than white working-class families. Reading and writing had been illegal for blacks under the slavery system of the Old South. But the illicit tools were taken up in secret nonetheless. In Richmond, Virginia, after the Civil War, a petition of "20,000 colored people" seeking repeal of a hated pass system circumscribing the movement of former slaves highlighted subterranean practice. "Three thousand of us can read," it maintained, "and at least 2,000 can read and write."

The black population immediately undertook a zealous crusade whose twin goals of education and land challenged America's racially restrictive commonwealth and demanded full inclusion. Land was tied to education. "It was a whole race trying to go to school," recalled Booker T. Washington about those years in his autobiography, *Up from Slavery.* "Few were too young, and none too old, to make the attempt to learn. As fast as any kind of teachers could be secured,

not only were day-schools filled, but night-schools as well. The great
ambition of the older people was to try to learn to read the Bible
before they died." The Freedmen's Bureau in 1865 opened more
than four thousand schools across the South and, in the next five
years, almost a quarter of a million people attended them. Throughout the South, those with education became leaders during the early
years of Reconstruction. Thomas Allen, a former slave in Georgia
who had no property, explained that his literacy made him a leader.
"In my county the colored people came to me for instructions, and
I gave them the best instructions I could. I took the New York Tribune and other papers, and in that way I found out a great deal, and
I told them whatever I thought was right."

The drive for land, schooling, and full citizenship rights more
broadly animated a vast political movement for several years. One
Mississippi planter in 1873 observed, "Negroes all crazy on politics
again." "It is the hardest thing in the world to keep a negro away
from the polls," said another white in Alabama. "That is the one
thing he will do, to vote." African American women shared in the
new public world. Even though they could not vote for public office-
holders or take office themselves, in the black political movement
they voted on resolutions, organized mass meetings, and took part
in rallies and parades, sometimes to the dismay of males.[6]

But the expansive sense of political possibilities engendered in
the early years of Reconstruction soon eroded. The promise of land,
a central program of the Freemen's Bureau, was quickly rescinded.
And the reality of African American education proved far more incomplete than Washington's generation had hoped for. By 1870, the
bureau itself was shut down and its schools mostly ended. Although
Reconstruction legislatures in the South had been moved to establish
public schooling for blacks, the subsequent decades locked the population into a rigidly segregated system where their schools received
only a pittance. By the 1930s, the amount spent yearly for each pupil
in black schools by ten Southern states amounted to $17.04, little
over one third the amount, $49.30, spent for white children. In Mis-
sissippi and Georgia, school systems spent about $9 for each black
child in school and five times more for whites.[7]

As industrialization reshaped the nation, schools came increasingly to be understood as the handmaiden of the emerging corporations. U.S. Commissioner of Education William Harris put it briskly
at the turn of the century in his argument that graded schools represented the instrument for "training in the social habits . . . regularity,
punctuality, orderly concerted action and self-restraint." Schools also
were most often designed to teach more subtle forms of accommoda-
tion to dominant values: the effort to "Americanize" millions of im-

migrant children into a homogeneous white, Protestant, and largely English culture, where differences of national background would be marginalized. Ruth Elson's and Colin Greer's separate investigations of textbooks found that every minority cultural group except English, Scots, Germans and Scandinavians was depicted with similar stereotypes: Catholics, Jews, Italians, Chinese, Irish, Eastern Europeans, as well as blacks, were "mean, criminal, drunken, sly, lazy, and stupid in varying degrees."[8]

Finally, there was pressure for schools themselves increasingly to *resemble* factories in the emerging industrial, urban order. Teachers functioned as "line workers," whose work process was tightly regimented and divided into relatively narrow tasks. Students became the "product," stamped with the mark of homogenized and routinized learning of a given body of "facts," in ways that formed a stark contrast to the practical occupational flexibility envisioned by Benjamin Franklin and the education for citizenship foreseen by reformers like Jefferson and Horace Mann. Through the twentieth century, the trend has been toward larger and larger high schools. Curriculums have become increasingly fragmented, with students moving from room to room each hour. Teachers have less and less contact with individual students. And school administrations are progressively more concerned with questions of order, conflict management, and quantifiable measures of "output" like standardized testing. In such a setting, *most* students experience considerable failure.

The evidence suggests that for most immigrant groups through the twentieth century, economic mobility came largely as a result of access to entry-level industrial jobs where individuals could advance through seniority systems over time, not through formal schooling. Indeed, functional illiteracy rates are highest in the nation's "Rust Belt" urban areas, where generations of immigrants left school long before graduation to enter the work force, convinced of the school system's scant usefulness to their own lives. As New York school board member and education theorist Norman Fruchter has put it, "For the most part we produced a complex, interlocked system which produces failure for most kids. The debate is about who to blame." On top of the long-developing problems of urban schools, moreover, the migration of both black and white middle-class residents to the suburbs in the 1970s left central-city school districts in often desperate straits. Middle-class taxpayers were increasingly unwilling to fund school improvements. Schools were wracked by problems of drugs, teenage pregnancy, even gang violence and physical assault against teachers. Dropout rates—after declining for two decades after World War II—began climbing once again. The specter grew of school systems that were more like prisons, where poor and black populations were consigned to dramatically inferior education, locked into a culture of despair.[9]

By the early 1980s, such accumulating problems resulted in a widespread sense of crisis, captured in the 1983 report by the National Commission on Excellence in Education, *A Nation At Risk*. The report argued that America's very future was being undermined by the nation's deteriorating school systems. But its solutions themselves became objects of controversy. *A Nation At Risk* reflected the views of the Department of Education under Ronald Reagan. It proposed an upgrading of salary scales for teachers. But its main emphasis was toward a further centralization of power in school systems: new focus on discipline and strengthening of the hand of school administrators, sharply increasing attention to central core curriculum and standardized testing. Its approach came to be known as the "Accountability Movement." Accountable schools, heralded by Ronald Reagan's appointee William Bennett, quickly became a kind of orthodoxy across the country.[10]

But this strategy was challenged by critics like the Carnegie Commission and leading educators such as Vito Perone, Deborah Meier, and Theodore Sizer. They argued that the main thrust of these reforms could well end up making schools *more like* factories, where students were treated as unthinking, uncreative receptacles for a given body of information, and teachers' possibilities for innovative pedagogy and mentoring of kids would all but disappear. On the surface, Accountable Schools might appear to parents and children to introduce new elements of democracy into education by requiring, for instance, that students pass standardized tests in order to graduate. But in fact, the result would be a work force and citizenry ill equipped to respond creatively to complex problem solving in the ways essential in future decades. For instance, to put the sort of intense emphasis on standardized testing called for in Accountable Schools meant, in practice, the gearing of curriculums specifically to prepare students to pass narrowly focused tests—with little attention to the broader array of skills and critical capacities essential in a real-world environment. But it is Ben Franklin's old ideal of a flexible, creative, adaptable work force that in fact has a renewed relevance for the years ahead.

In contrast to the Accountable School approach, an alternative began to emerge with a number of dimensions variously called "Essential Schools," "Local Site Control," and the "Professionalization of Teaching." Together, this ensemble of themes stressed increased autonomy for teachers and development of a view of teaching as a *craft,* involving high standards and multiple skills, and rewarding teachers at the highest levels with professional salaries. They stressed decentralization of power and authority to the local school itself. To prove successful, the democratic school approach would require the breaking up of enormous schools into smaller units that would allow far more teacher-student interaction. Visitation with parents would also be considered part of teachers' regular responsibilities. Students would be required to meet rigorous standards, but the means of testing would be far more multidimensional than standardized testing allows. Sizer, for instance, proposed that students pass rigorous "exhibitions" in each core subject before graduation, combining written work, verbal presentations, and questioning by peers and teachers. In a number of school systems, indeed, there were moves toward at least experimenting with some of these elements.[11]

Thus a conflict began to emerge around the shape of America's education whose central issues involved questions of power and control. It was a complex and many-sided controversy, with arguments and obstacles on both sides of the debate. Accountability advocates pointed to research by Ronald Edmundson and others which showed that creative leadership by school principals was the key factor in effective educational reform. Democratic school organizers agreed that the principal's role was important, but they argued that schooling for America's future must involve a radically different, more collaborative sort of leadership than had traditionally been the case. But for democratic school approaches to work necessitated not only changes in the formal structure of education but also effective, skillful training and some clear public commitment to an alternative understanding of educational purposes themselves. Parents and community members were usually disadvantaged in school governance experiments. "I've had principals tell me they can always spot independent or troublesome parents in PTA meetings at the first of the year," recounted Norman Fruchter about his experiences on the school board. "They quickly move to isolate them."

In addition to traditional, hierarchical attitudes among school administrators and the lack of detailed knowledge about school functioning, minority and poor parents are discouraged from serious participation in school decision-making processes by various other obstacles. Great differences in class and cultural background may separate parents from school professionals. Community residents, overworked, trying to survive economically, encounter dificulties in even attending meetings, often held far away. Finally, minority or poor parents frequently have painful memories of school to overcome. "There is an enormously powerful tendency for parents to simply say, 'They're the experts,'" Fruchter summarized. "They just tend to stay away from any involvement." In sum, any serious effort aiming at substantive democratization of the school systems—especially programs that involve a greater degree of accountability and responsiveness to communities—faces considerable difficulties.[12]

But there are also traditions of resistance to draw upon. In Baltimore, Maryland—a city midway between North and South, shaped by a history that included both the sharply etched divisions of segregation and the largest nineteenth-century free black population of any city in the country—urban schools, like their counterparts across the country, had similarly suffered neglect and underfunding. But schools in the black community had also long stood as a symbol of black community pride, with a resilience forged by decades of battle against discrimination. In the 1980s, after a period of decline, the schools once again became the centerpiece for a renewal of black community power in a fashion that held lessons for the nation as a whole. The program for change, the Baltimore Commonwealth, reflected a threefold combination: incentive plans for high school graduates of the sort sponsored by business groups around the country; the ideas of the Essential School Movement and other democratic school advocates; and the methods for a vast public "schooling in democracy" developed by the IAF.

———

Moses said to the Lord, "Why hast thou dealt ill with thy servant? . . . Where am I to get meat to give to all this people? . . . I am not able to carry all this people alone, the burden is too heavy for me. . . ."

And the Lord said to Moses, "Gather for me seventy men of the elders of Israel . . . and I will take some of the spirit which is upon you and put it upon them; and they shall bear the burden of the people with you, that you may not bear it yourself alone." (Numbers 11:10–18)

In 1981, the Black Caucus of the network of organizations produced a new document, *The Tent of the Presence,* based on the passage from Numbers where Moses gathered a carefully selected group of elders at the "tent of meeting," the center of the Jewish community. There, Moses shared with them power and responsibiliity for leadership during the travels to the Promised Land.[13]

Tent of the Presence, rich with biblical symbolism and exegesis, also included the newly accented IAF themes of democratic public life. The document argued that the black community in America—and the black church in particular—stood at a crossroads, facing a dangerous movement to the right in American politics. In such an environment sixties-style "movement leaders," dependent on charismatic appeals and moral exhortation, were simply ineffective. For the black community to avoid an increasingly dangerous isolation and marginality, a new style of leadership would be needed, along with new organizational forms. Like Moses, the black clergy had to choose individuals with promising talents and abilities and "share some of the spirit" with them. A new form of collaborative leadership should emerge, spreading leadership, power, and responsibility more widely. And new "broad-based" organizations were needed, owned by the members, funded with their own money, aimed at gathering durable power over time. Baltimore was an ideal test case for the new approach.

Baltimore's African American community had a rich history to draw upon. The city had always had something of a mixed regional character, "caught midstream between the freedom of the North and the tradition of the South," as a Baltimore Urban Coalition report in 1934 put it. "The Negro rides the street cars in Baltimore as he does in New York, sitting where he finds a vacant sit. Yet . . . Negroes and whites attend separate schools and separate motion picture houses." Gerald Taylor, raised in Harlem and organizing in the New York City area for years before he came to the city in 1984, immediately felt the contrast. "There's still respect for property—you don't see a lot of graffiti in Baltimore," he observed. "Because it was a segregated city, there were a limited number of places that blacks could go. But you also see a lot of overlaps, friendship networks, a density of community ties to build on."[14]

Through the nineteenth century, the city was noted as a center of cultural and political strength: Bethel AME church was a founder of the African Methodist Episcopal denomination. The city had been home of famous abolitionists like Frederick Douglass and William Lloyd Garrison. As early as 1890, African Americans gained representation on the City Council. The black school tradition dated to well-known institutions like Sharp Street, established in the eighteenth century; African School, founded in 1812 by Daniel Coker; and black girls' schools like St. Francis' Academy, begun in 1828. In the decades of segregation, institutions like Frederick Douglass High School and Morgan State were seen as beacons of black education, turning out national leaders like Lillian Jackson of the NAACP, Clarence Mitchell, the lawyer, and Congressman Parren Mitchell.[15]

A long tradition of popular protest had emerged from the dense network of community institutions in black Baltimore as well. Abolitionists like Elisha Tyson had been prominent figures in Baltimore as early as the Revolutionary War. In the 1880s the State Supreme Court, prodded by the African American legal organization called Brotherhood of Liberty, admitted blacks before the Bar. During the Great Depression of the 1930s, activist organizations like the Young People's Forum, the People's Unemployed League, the Fellowship of

Reconciliation, and the Women's International League for Peace and Freedom combined protests against economic hardship with challenge to segregated educational and employment patterns. Every Friday night in the early 1930s, the Young People's Forum drew hundreds of people to its forum on controversial public issues, held at Bethel AME church. It led a widespread boycott to demand the hiring of black clerks in downtown stores, and petitioned the city and state for an upgrading of black schools in the city. During the civil rights movement of the 1960s, leading ministers like Vernon Dobson often consulted with Martin Luther King, Jr., and his staff, and helped spark a wide-ranging series of successful protests for desegregation of public facilities in Baltimore.[16]

By the later years of the 1970s, however, the civil rights movement had largely run out of steam. "I was becoming an old disillusioned preacher," remembered Dobson. "The last demonstration we called, we had had a press conference where we announced we'd have three hundred people. Ten came." For the Reverend Doug Miles, the memory of those years was more painful yet. Miles had led a group of ministers to meet with Alan Hoblitzel, president of Maryland National Bank, to protest the institution's plans for an increase in interest charges on credit cards. "Out of the ten who said they would come, four showed up. Hoblitzel escorted us to a classroom. Then he told us what he was *not* going to do—what we didn't have the power to make him do. I sat there and my blood boiled but I realized that was the truth. We didn't have enough clout." The credit card fees were instituted.[17]

Such defeats fed a gathering political discouragement in black Baltimore. "Reagan's message was becoming the message of America," Miles recalled. "Even the black community had adopted the philosophy of 'me, myself, and I,' the idea that I've got mine and if you don't have yours that's tough." In religious terms, the trend was strongly toward privatism. "The black middle class was eating up the message that you could go in and get saved, feel good about yourself." Politically it was a time of retreat. "For the first time I heard black people talking about 'those people in the ghetto.' It was a mental dissociation from the pain that none of us are more than a step away from." Miles himself prepared to pull his congregation back from social commitments and cut back his involvement with groups like the Black Ministerial Alliance.[18]

But leaders like Dobson and Miles, discouraged as they were, understood the perils of public apathy. Indeed, the same period marked a growing perception throughout the city of "two Baltimores"—a prosperous middle class increasingly distanced from a growing largely black underclass. The division took many forms. William Donald Schaefer, elected mayor in 1971, had led Baltimore to national prominence with a vigorous promotion of a downtown "renaissance" that took Norman Vincent Peale's philosophy of positive thinking on to hitherto unexplored terrain. Touting large-scale developments along the harbor—Harborplace, and a complex of office buildings, commercial spaces, and recreational facilities called Charles Center—Schaefer sponsored flamboyant public events. On "Sunny Sundays" at the harbor he led crowds in clapping for the sunshine; in "Pink Positive Days" he organized rallies to applaud the harbor improvements. Schaefer's exuberance undeniably aided corporate development. But he also fashioned a political machine built directly around his personality, brooking no opposition. "Schaefer didn't want anybody to challenge him at all, especially in a public way," said Michael Fletcher, who covered city politics for the *Baltimore Sun* after his arrival in 1981. When the mayor encountered resistance, reaction was swift. "Schaefer could act like a vindictive bully," added Michael Ollove, another newspaper writer. According to critics, the mayor combined a quick temper with a marked tendency toward a politics of denial. "Anything that raised negatives about Baltimore, he just did not want to hear," said Miles. "He didn't even acknowledge that there were homeless in the city."[19]

The consequences were mounting problems below the surface celebration. Housing for low-income city residents became scarce. Seventy percent of the officially unemployed 20,000 Baltimoreans were African Americans—and the actual numbers of unemployed ran much higher. Eighty percent of the school system was black, and increasingly the system divided into a few special programs for gifted students in magnet schools, contrasted with neighborhood schools, called "zone" or comprehensive schools, which were overcrowded and scandalously in short supply of basic materials like textbooks. "For the first ten years I worked here, the system was excellent," remembered Irene Dandridge, president of the Baltimore Teachers Union, or BTU. "The next ten years, the community lost its commitment to schools. It was very discouraging. Teachers began a mass exodus to the county and we couldn't recruit new teachers." Schaefer's own appointee as superintendent of schools, Alice Pinderhughes, echoed the diagnosis. "We had developed a few citywide schools with high-achieving students," she described. "But the majority are not. White exodus started. Then middle-class blacks began sending their children to private schools. The comprehensives lost their image of being community schools. There was a major morale problem there; they felt like second-class citizens."[20]

The erosion of city schools and, for many young people, decent job possibilities as well fed more subtle social decay. When Carl

Stokes grew up in the 1950s and '60s in a public housing project in the poorer black area of Baltimore, the East Side, it was a safe, intact community. "We had no drugs—we didn't know drugs. The project was safe. The project was a stepping-stone for a lot of families who would move out when they could; it was public housing as it was supposed to be." But just as he was leaving, the neighborhood went through marked changes. Drugs appeared on the scene. Shoot-outs between dealers and police would occur in the middle of the day. Desperate, unwed mothers and children populated the deteriorating apartments.

Perceptions about a growing crisis under the surface were shared by other parts of the community as well. Robert Keller, city and then metropolitan editor for the *Evening Sun* for thirteen years, took a position as the executive director of the main business group, the Greater Baltimore Committee, in the early 1980s out of the sense that the city had reached a crucial turning point. "The physical development of the community was under control, the harbor and further out" he recounted. "But there were major fundamental problems in jobs, education, the cultural infrastructure. I felt this was a community that was either going to be on the edge, on a new forefront of civic cooperation, or we were going to disappear into the bay." It was against this background that BUILD began shakily in the late 1970s, found its footing in the early 1980s, took on the problems of the public schools in 1984, and then crafted a wide-ranging alliance and strategy for school transformation and democratization, known as the Baltimore Commonwealth.[21]

The tenth anniversary convention of Baltimoreans United in Leadership Development—BUILD—convened at 2:30 P.M. on a Sunday afternoon, November 8, 1987, in the Baltimore Palladium with more than two thousand people present. By 1987 BUILD's membership, still mainly black, was also increasingly diverse: it was made up of forty-two churches (and was in the process of negotiating Jewish membership as well), including several white congregations; three labor unions (the BTU, the Community College Teachers Union, and 1199E of the Hospital Workers); the association of school principals; and the Murphy Homes Improvement Association, a public housing tenants' group.

The Palladium is a large public auditorium built in a style someone referred to as "Gothic Disneyland," with ramparts, towers, parapets, columns, and huge windows of hypermodern stained glass. Somehow the combination of traditional design and hypermodern motifs made a perfect setting for the event—a testimony to the power BUILD accumulated in its first ten years through drawing on ancient religious and cultural roots of black Baltimore, and its future-oriented and entirely pragmatic view that its real work was just beginning.

Around the walls of the Palladium hung balloons, banners, signs of individual churches: "St. Andrews BUILD—the Holy Spirit Makes Us One"; "St. Celia: Rejoice in the Lord," with a large dove; "Bethel AME, commemorating 200 years, 1787–1987: A liberating people. The motto is rejoice in thy salvation, and in the name of God we will set up our banners," from Psalm 25. A huge banner in front proclaimed "BUILD: for the 80's and 90's." A smaller sign nearby welcomed visiting delegations from IAF-affiliated groups around the country.

Promptly at 2:30 Carol Reckling, BUILD president, called the meeting to order: "This is going to be a good day," she said. "What better way to mark our tenth anniversary than in our own traditions? We will struggle and celebrate and recommit ourselves." An opening prayer followed. Then in an "accountability" roll call, each church, union, and civic group announced the numbers of its members in attendance—numbers that would later be compared with prior commitments. Greetings followed from various political figures: Paul Sarbanes, U.S. senator from Maryland; a short statement from AME bishop John Hurst Adams, a member of the IAF National Board; remarks from various IAF projects across the country. Vera Valdiviez, "representing 220,000 families of IAF organizations in Southern California," described their "all-out war to create a moral minimum wage" in that state. "We are pleased to be here to help celebrate ten years of rebuilding public life," she said, "the public life promised by our forefathers and so long denied to our fathers and mothers. We are proud to be your sisters and brothers on the other coast."

The heart of the meeting was called "Empowering the BUILD Agenda," an exchange between BUILD leaders in the four key program areas—public housing, employment, education, and neighborhood development—and public actors in the city. Their presence, more than anything said, made visible BUILD's power. Michael Middleton, executive vice president of the Maryland National Bank, spoke forcefully of the Greater Baltimore Committee's commitment to the school program, the Commonwealth. Leo Molinaro, representative of the Rouse Company, one of the nation's largest builders, made a commitment to convene business executives to discuss with BUILD a new jobs program for unemployed adults. Mary Pat Clarke, the president-elect of the City Council, and mayor-elect Kurt Schmoke both agreed to meet regularly with BUILD and in the coming months take the Baltimore City Council as a whole up to look at the

Nehemiah Project in New York City. Schmoke, the first elected black mayor in Baltimore's history, had beaten the incumbent appointee of William Schaefer, "Du" Burns, after Schaefer had gone on to become governor. And Schaefer's campaign had been waged largely around "BUILD Agenda" issues that BUILD had declared as "its candidate," garnering in the process 75,000 signatures in support. "I heard a reporter say the other day, 'I don't know which one of these guys will win,'" Schmoke recounted, "'but the real winner is the BUILD Agenda.'" In a stirring symbolic gesture, Reverend Doug Miles responded to the responses. He called for Clarke, Sarbanes, the congressmen in attendance, business executives, the school superintendent, foundation heads, and Schmoke to clasp their hands overhead. Together they pledged a "new covenant" for the future of Baltimore.

Then, running somewhat late, the convention moved to a concluding prayer service. Songs, Scripture, and prayers continued. And the Reverend Grady Yeargin brought the audience once again to its feet with an eloquent message: "One day it will be said that in the city of Baltimore in the last quarter of the twentieth century, strange and unusual things began to happen," he intoned.

> Well-known somebodies with something from someplace began to meet with little-known nobodies from noplace. The upper crust began to meet with the middle crust and with those who have no crust at all. It was a peculiar people. A strange and unusual coalition that negotiated and fought and worked together.
>
> Then stranger things began to happen. Young men started putting down their guns and started picking up their shovels to rebuild the city. Young teenage women stopped going on welfare and started going to work.
>
> Somehow the Kingdom will come in this earth. BUILD, if you are a mighty people, if you are a noble people, if you are a great people, there's forests out there. There's land to be filled. There's work to be done. Won't you be counted in the army of the Lord?

The meeting ended with cheers and applause, singing and hugs. The representative of the Rouse Company—who purportedly had never visited the black community in Baltimore before and had been worried about the trip—kept shaking his head, saying he had never seen anything so wonderful.

The event was undeniable testimony to BUILD's power. Particularly around the Commonwealth School agreement, the centerpiece of BUILD organizing over the past several years, diverse elements of the city power structure made extensive commitments. By the next February, the Commonwealth—enthusiastically endorsed by Schmoke as the centerpiece of his own administration—had become the most ambitious school incentive plan for graduates in the country.[22]

But as the convention drew to a close, IAF staff about the room from other areas of the country could be seen frowning. Cortes scowled. Chambers shook his head, in an odd counterpoint to the festive spirit. They were intimations of future arguments.

Two days later, the BUILD Action Team, the group of leaders who had put together the event, Arnie Graf, IAF supervisor for the region, and Gerald Taylor, BUILD's lead organizer, met late into the night in a stormy evaluation session. Leaders raised questions about the explicitness of several public officials' actual commitments. They challenged a number of congregations and unions for failing to meet their quotas of participants. Most problematic in their view, many pointed out that the meeting had gone a "completely unacceptable" eighteen minutes late. The issue raised the question of why there had been a prayer session at the end, and that question in turn led to a prolonged debate about whether church leaders were too dominant in the organization, whether enough attention was given to BUILD's "public" and "political" dimensions, and what public life and politics were all about. More than the convention itself, the evaluation was a window into the organizing dynamics that produced BUILD's power in general and the Baltimore Commonwealth in particular: the BUILD organization treats *every* occasion primarily as an experience from which to learn new lessons and insights into particular issues, policy questions, power dynamics, and the broader meaning of public life and politics. BUILD, like its sister organizations, sees itself as a "school for public life," and it mirrors such a theme in the projects it undertakes.[23]

BUILD had begun in 1977 with a sponsoring committee led by an ecumenical group of ministers, Vernon Dobson, Wendell Phillips, and the late Monsignor Clare O'Dwyer of the Catholic Church, and nine founding members. For three years, it worked on local neighborhood issues like police protection, arson control, and rat eradication, while churches raised an initial funding base. But the early years were not easy. Some point to supposed mistakes by an allegedly abrasive IAF organizer, no longer with the network. "The first organizer here really screwed some things up, alienated people and congregations who still haven't come back in," according to Reverend Joe Muth, priest at St. Ann's, an inner-city congregation, who sought for several years to get his congregation to join. The organization did not apparently begin to cohere into a promising project until Graf, lead organizer at San Antonio COPS after Cortes, arrived in the spring of 1980. By that time, the *need* for a new powerful citizen organization in Baltimore's black community had become widely apparent. The question was whether it could succeed.[24]

Arnie Graf, white, Jewish, soft-spoken, presents a figure decidedly different from the image of the traditional, "tough-guy" organizer out of the Alinsky mold. But Graf also conveys a keen intuition into what motivates other people, and a kind of steely strength, under a gentle humor. By the time he arrived in Baltimore, Graf had years of experience behind him: the sixties civil rights movement, two years in the Peace Corps in Sierre Leone, welfare-rights organizing in Harlan County, West Virginia. In 1971, Graf had worked in an IAF group in Milwaukee, convinced that the network included the best citizen organizing around. In 1976, he followed Ernie Cortes as the lead organizer of COPS in San Antonio. Graf's own work to encourage community leaders' exploration of their Mexican and religious cultural traditions contributed considerably to the developing IAF approach.

Graf found the Baltimore organization deeply in debt and struggling with a small group of discouraged leaders. So, despite the emphasis in IAF on slow, patient organization-building without much publicity, he urged what he called a "movement approach," tied to recruitment and training of leaders. "We didn't really have time to do a slow process of parish renewal work," Graf recounted. "The only thing I could think to save it was to start a black movement with a lot of visibility, large issues, a great deal of action and momentum." To add to the sense of activity, Graf himself conducted ten or eleven meetings each day for months, probing people's interests, seeking to motivate them and engage them in the effort.[25]

The IAF skills Graf brought with him included a thorough knowledge of targets, potential victories, and appropriate strategies that had been missing in the failed efforts of black leaders in the late 1970s. In particular, Graf knew that under existing federal and state legislation the Baltimore banks and savings and loan associations could be pressured to reveal where they were making loans and that disclosure of such information would give the organization tools to use in reaching agreements for more mortgage loans in black communities. BUILD members, taught how to do the necessary research, discovered that most banks lent only a small portion of their mortgage funds in inner-city and mainly black areas. Provident Bank, for instance, despite its self-description as a "community bank," lent $660,000 out of more than $50 million, barely one percent.[26]

In the spring of 1981, the organization launched a major campaign with a dramatic, colorful action. "Sixty or seventy of us went to Provident Bank and asked for a meeting with the vice president," remembered Gary Rodwell, a former Eagle Scout who had long waged his own private wars against discrimination he felt in Baltimore and during his college years at the U.S. Naval Academy. "We wanted to ask them to become a participating member of the Maryland Housing Investment Fund," a state program that insured mortgages in lower-income areas without cost to the lender.[27]

The bank officer refused. So the group formed long lines at the windows and asked for change into pennies. Police came. Officials panicked. And the president of the bank asked to meet with a delegation. Several meetings later, Provident agreed to invest several million dollars in low-income neighborhoods.[28]

Rodwell, who became treasurer of BUILD in 1981, felt the action was the sort of effective effort he had been waiting for all his life. "I said to myself, 'This is it. I'm finally doing something that can have impact.'" Doug Miles, whom Arnie Graf had finally enticed to the demonstration after repeated rebuffs, was similarly deeply affected. "I hadn't been involved in anything where you could get sixty people there since the antiwar movement," said Miles. "It was a magnificent feeling of excitment." He soon joined the Strategy Team, the key group of leaders who make day-to-day organizational decisions in BUILD, and saw a dramatic difference in its approach. "In the late seventies, we really never thought we would win," said Miles. "Winning was just being able to say you were on the right side; it was a moral victory. Nothing substantive came out of it."[29]

When Miles began going to BUILD meetings, he was struck by written agendas, meetings that began and ended on time, and most of all, the focus on actual accomplishment. "There was a constant teaching role about what leadership is, what power is—how power isn't a dirty word. The need for accountability. The difference between the world as it is and as it should be. The stuff was a mind-boggling change."[30]

Involvement in BUILD and other IAF groups seems almost invariably to work considerable personal change, but it varies. Marian Dixon, president of the organization in 1982, had been a teacher for many decades. Dixon conveys, when one meets her, a calm indomitability, and the stories of her encounters with city officials and other members of the power structure form a major part of the folklore of the organization—she is especially well known for insisting on respect and proper etiquette from elected politicians, not allowing them to call her by her first name in a public setting or allowing them to "get away" with evasive rhetoric. But Dixon credits this assertiveness to her experiences in BUILD and in an IAF 10 Day Training session. "BUILD taught me to demand what was right," she says. A devout church member and lay leader, Dixon thought certain facets

of Christianity had previously taught her and others the wrong lessons. "You're not supposed to have self-interest. You're not supposed
to want power. You're supposed to be meek and humble and be tram-
pled on! But we learned."

In contrast, experience taught Doug Miles a certain humility—
he realized *he* alone was not responsible for his church—and a willingness to bend and compromise where appropriate. "Back in the
seventies, we didn't believe in compromise," he explained. "So when
we couldn't get everything we wanted, we'd go off with a nice quiet
whimper into the darkness of the night."[31]

In John Gwaltney's insightful work *Drylongso,* a study of "core
black culture," one of the key figures, Hannah Nelson, recounts the
pervasive feeling of powerlessness felt by blacks in urban areas. "The
most important thing about black people is that they don't think
they can control anything except their own persons," she argues. "So
everything is very personal." Dixon agreed that blacks historically
felt considerable powerlessness, but she pointed to the *public* consequences. "Black people generally don't understand the power and
self-interest of whites. It doesn't mean you're dumb. You've just never
thought about it." When people feel completely powerless, she continued, there is a hopelessness which simply precludes attention to
the other. "There's just no need to focus on it." IAF taught a theory
of careful attention to others' self-interests. And BUILD began to
accumulate the successes that made the lessons come to life.[32]

Such practical lessons and experiences formed the background
for the campaign for the revitalization of Baltimore's public schools.
By the early 1980s, IAF groups across the country had begun to take
leading roles in policy initiation, especially around key questions of
infrastructure. "The classic approach in the seventies was to pressure
government for X, Y, or Z," said Mike Gecan, regional IAF director in
the New York City area. "But now they can't or won't do it. Nehemiah
never would have happened if we hadn't taken on responsibility." In
New York, the infrastructure crisis had become acute. "Nobody else
is taking on the big things like streets or corruption or bridges, whatever. There's a great vacuum. The political leaders don't really deal
with these issues. They see themselves as captives of the bureaucracy.
The whole productive side of government has begun to collapse."[33]

Gecan, like other IAF leaders and staff, saw pitfalls in assumption of responsibility for infrastructure programs. "If we take on the
role of government, part of the danger is they'll just do less and less."
IAF groups' goal is to revitalize the older understanding of government and elected officials as neither saviors nor enemies, but public
"servants." In the meantime, however, there were also benefits in taking on such questions: an education for members in the intricacies

of policy issues; a sense of ownership and "stake" in key elements of community life; and perhaps more intangible but crucial to the organizations' self-defined mission of recreating public life, the creation of important occasions to work with diverse elements of the larger community in a collaborative, ongoing way.[34]

In Baltimore in 1983, BUILD began to investigate the shortages and disparities in school supplies, especially in the zone or comprehensive schools. They discovered that the schools were short not only on paper products—everything from writing materials to toilet paper—but also textbooks, film projectors, typewriters, and an array of other basic resources. By that time, with victories in hand involving bank loans, auto insurance, utility rates, and other issues, the organization had accumulated a notable reputation in the city. BUILD's third convention in October the next year drew over 1,500 delegates. Unlike the convention two years before when not one elected official appeared, the audience this time included a congressman, two candidates for governor, a half dozen members of the General Assembly, the state's attorney, and a number of City Council members—although then-mayor Schaefer continued to boycott the group, after a confrontation with Dixon and others the year before. The question was what to do with such power.[35]

Graf, who had served as staff while the organization became a visible public presence in the city, saw continuing weaknesses in the organization. "We could turn people out. But I knew we were still not deep. A 'movement' style alone can feed on itself. You don't do house meetings. You don't train people carefully enough. But it can't last." Graf himself had been deeply affected by the civil rights movement and saw the same prophetic spirit in BUILD. But the civil rights movement had faded, leaving an incomplete legacy. The challenge for BUILD was how to sustain such transformative energy. "So we stopped for a while," Graf related. "We did a series of retreats about what our purposes were. We did house meetings. And we talked about what to do about the schools."[36]

The new superintendent of schools, Alice Pinderhughes, was vunerable to pressure, they knew. A Schaefer appointee, Pinderhughes lacked a graduate education and, despite her race, was viewed with skepticism in the black community. When they first approached her about supply shortages, she was doubtful about the accuracy of the charge. A simple confrontation might have forced the issue into the open in a way that BUILD would have won. But BUILD's leaders, after a careful analysis of Pinderhughes's "self-interests," concluded that whatever the precariousness of her position, she did indeed care about the schools. What she needed was some new and positive visibility. She could use allies. And a "public relationship" with Pinderhughes was important if they were to take on the broader crisis of the school system as a whole. So a delegation of BUILD leaders approached her, and together they broke the story about school shortages. It was the beginning of a new stage for BUILD.[37]

BUILD used this method of "public relationship building" throughout its schools campaign over the next several years. In BUILD's analysis, locally owned and rooted businesses—from local industry to insurance, banks, and other service providers—all had what they called "institutional self-interests" in seeing that the school system did not totally disintegrate. From the point of view of a few key business leaders as well, schools provided a perfect "neutral issue" around which to repair a badly fractured city. "BUILD had first approached us on unemployment," remembered Alan Hoblitzel—ironically, the same chief executive whose curt dismissal of Miles in the 1970s had led to the minister's near-retreat from public engagement altogether. Hoblitzel took on the presidency of the main business organization, the Greater Baltimore Committee or GBC, in 1984. "I was initially skeptical. I had read about their adversarial nature, their confrontations, thing like that. The question was whether you could sit down in a cooperative vein to deal with problems that are common." Hoblitzel further knew he would have difficulty selling anything to other business leaders that smacked of "quotas, track programs, things that seemed to invade the way people ran their businesses." But he felt there had to be some other way to get businesses "to be aware of and sensitive to the needs of minority groups." Thus, when BUILD leaders told him about the Boston Compact, an incentive program begun by Boston businesses to help secure jobs for college graduates, he was interested. "I told them this may be something we can both rally around. This would help convince youth that something was out there for them, that there would be a job. And it would assist the business community to be responsive to people's needs."[38]

The unfolding series of discussions had moments of drama. Miles, Graf, Hoblitzel, and Bob Keller all remember a crucial meeting in the fall, just before the BUILD convention, that was a turning point—although their accounts vary somewhat. Hoblitzel recalls it as the meeting he went to with an intention to reach a serious agreement. Miles tells a different story. "We had had several meetings without reaching agreement," said Miles.

> Hoblitzel kept looking at his watch, saying, "I have to catch a plane. I really don't have time to pin anything down." He said a final no. Then I looked at him and said, "Mr. Hoblitzel, you and

I stand at a very unique position, a crossroads in the life of this community. We can take the leadership of building one community, or become perpetual enemies. Wouldn't the history of Baltimore read better if a black preacher and a white businessman helped save the city rather than further divide it?" He sat there a minute. He headed for the door, put his hand on the doorknob. Then he turned around and said, "We can work this out. Put together some ideas. When I get back from this trip we'll get together more people and sit down and see what we can do."

Miles said, "It was nothing but the spirit of the Lord that saved that day." The power of BUILD likely also had a hand.[39]

Soon after the convention, when Graf became regional director of IAF projects in the midatlantic area, Gerald Taylor replaced him as lead organizer of BUILD. Taylor had already acquired a remarkable reputation as an organizer: during the civil rights movement, as head of the New York Youth Division of the NAACP, he had been the brash challenger to the organization's old guard which had joined civil rights demonstrations only with reluctance. In the 1970s, Taylor acquired a national reputation in community organizing circles for successfully building a large community group in Williamsburg-Greenpoint, a white ethnic area of Brooklyn. He had also worked for a time as a teacher in the famous Harlem Prep storefront schools, through which many black teenage dropouts acquired a high school education.

Taylor, like Ernie Cortes, combines organizing talents with an indefatigable interest in ideas. Taylor brought these distinctive talents to the negotiations. Despite opposition, for instance, he urged the BUILD organization to sign an initial agreement with GBC for considerably less than they wanted—their original proposal had been a strong job guarantee for every high school graduate with good attendance; Greater Baltimore's counter proposal was job help for those with B averages—out of his understanding of the dynamics of public life. "I felt our first challenge was establishing a public relationship," said Taylor. "I knew if we did we'd have the clout over time to realize our program." Such an approach reflected a broader theory of public life. "I'm trying to create with the leaders a way to think about the city. Politics is really the discussion and action of creating community. And an understanding of the importance of *time* and *patience* at certain points is an indispensable part of that."

Taylor also suggested the word "commonwealth" as the description of the new agreement. "I was intrigued by the word and the idea, commonwealth," said Taylor. "That's what we were about. About the *wealth* of the city that was created and produced by the people being *commonly* dealt with." Taylor had also been influenced by the economist Joan Robinson, who often used the term. Others saw the utility of the label. "I thought it was wonderful, but not for the reasons that I've come to understand," remembered Keller. "We thought, we've got to market this thing. It was a way to describe the 'neutral' issues that a lot of people can rally around—education, community stability, good jobs."[40]

For the next four years, the Commonwealth Agreement, later the Baltimore Commonwealth, traveled on two tracks: the development of the program for high school graduates soon became a national model, while less visibly, but with even more far-reaching implications, BUILD sought to use the incentive plan as a scaffolding around which to change the schools themselves and to open discussions with GBC on a range of other issues, like adult unemployment and housing.

In the first instance, the incentive plan for high school graduates continually expanded. By June 1989, city high school graduates with attendance records of 95 percent in their last two years were guaranteed three job interviews at one of the 150 members of GBC, and additional help in securing employment. If the interviews themselves did not produce a job, the city Office of Employment Training evaluated the young person and provided additional training. At the end of April 1988, BUILD, GBC, Schmoke, and a coalition of area colleges and universities announced a further element: a $25 million fund that guaranteed financial aid through college for any graduate from Baltimore schools with good attendance.

Even in the first couple of years—when the school aid packages were not as extensive, the program was not widely known, and patterns of juniors and seniors had been shaped by their many years of school experience—teachers and counselors in zone schools noted a considerable impact. "Traditionally we had two or three students go on from here to the University of Maryland," said Charlotte Brown, guidance counselor at Patterson High School."Last year, with the Commonwealth Agreement, we had between twelve and fifteen, and two students went to Loyola." When Steve Johnson, a Patterson student, got word he was accepted to Johns Hopkins—the first student in anyone's memory to go there from any of the zone schools—the news was broadcast over the public address system again and again, all day long.[41]

The second aspect of BUILD's school initiative involved efforts to change the Baltimore school system itself, in line with approaches of the Coalition for Essential Schools and school site management advocates. In the attempt, the organization used hundreds of volunteer organizers—in the spring of 1986 and again in 1988, BUILD contacted thousands of parents of high school students and held dozens of meetings on the Commonwealth Agreement and other school issues. Parent and community workshops explored the changes in schools over the last decade, bringing to the surface people's anger and dismay at the demise of a once proud system. They compared schools with churches as a "mediating institution," a form of association midway between family life and large-scale macroinstitutions, and talked about strategies for democratizing and renewing such structures. They identified problems and complaints, reasons parents had felt hesitant to become involved in school projects. They developed strategies for intensive work with twelve schools, including two high schools—Douglass and Walbrook—and a number of feeder middle and elementary schools. Douglass, formerly the premier school of Baltimore's black educational system, had radically deteriorated in recent years and was virtually without any parent involvement—the PTA had three members before BUILD's organizing. Walbrook, a member of the national Coalition for Essential Schools, served as one model for what BUILD envisions in the future.

By the fall of 1988, a collaborative discussion involving community leaders, politicians, teachers, principals, and the business community had raised ideas for a comprehensive reform of the system, leading to local site management by teams that have power over the key issues of budget, curriculum, and staff decisions; small schools; considerable teacher-student interaction; and simplified curriculum. As a complement to changes within the schools themselves, BUILD proposed that community boards called "trustees" be vested with authority for after-hours building use, allowing school facilities to once again become community resources for programs that might range from school clubs and service projects to adult education and community events. Each activity, in turn, would be evaluated in terms of how it developed "public skills," from political imagination and judgment to understanding of self-interests.[42]

In theory, the administration has expressed openness to such changes; but in practice (here as elsewhere), the encrusted nature of school-system bureaucracies tends to thwart significant shifts in power and authority. BUILD, having proven an ability to enlist large numbers of community leaders, parents, and educators in such efforts is therefore in a rare position. What marks its initiative as virtually unique in such experiments nationally is its combination of use of public pressure with extensive experience in training.[43]

Thus in Baltimore, serious structural change seems at least imaginable. The possibilities for a program of school change with far-reaching implications are further enhanced by BUILD's membership, which includes both the BTU teachers union and the organization of principals, the Public School Administrators and Supervisors Association, or PSASA. This has meant opportunities for *interaction* among school staff, community leaders, and parents. It has also allowed school professionals a continuing opportunity for extensive discussion and training in what a different sort of school system might look like. In the spring of 1988, Taylor held workshops for building representatives from all the city schools. "We looked at how our schools are structured—like a factory. People felt like workers on the assembly line, controlled by the outside. It resonates strongly," he asserted. "Teachers feel they're not treated with respect. Twenty or thirty years ago, the teacher in the black community was a role model."

The workshops explored the reason for the difficulties facing teachers' unions—a "failure of vision," Taylor argued. "We've stayed on dollars, benefits, grievances, and lost the creative side, teaching as an art or a craft."

They then explored what teachers desired: "control over the workplace, materials, the idea of master teachers who were mentors, a school day broken up to allow visitation with parents and one-on-one interactions with students." Taylor drew on his own experiences with the freewheeling, experimental, and effective storefront schools in Harlem in the 1970s, to obviously good effect. "Teachers said this was the most exciting discussion they'd had in years. They asked, 'Can we really do this?' I said, 'This is what we can do in the future. But it means you've got to want it. It means retraining, accountability, recognizing that not everybody should be teachers. Seeing teaching like a craft again'."[44]

It is still too early in the process of these efforts to evaluate the prospects for BUILD's most ambitious hopes around schools. But already, the Baltimore Commonwealth has created a series of striking new precedents and begun to explore new dimensions for the emerging debate about America's educational future.

Moreover, like the old village greens in New England towns, the Commonwealth created a new forum, both city-wide and in the tangible, localized spaces of particular schools, through which diverse elements of Baltimore could meet, identify problems, disagree, find areas of agreement, plan, work on programs together. Gerald Taylor, BUILD's lead organizer, described the creation of such forums as the move from simple protest to governance: "The first struggle for the black community, coming out of a segregated history, is the fight to be recognized. When you've been out of power so long, there's a tendency to not want to be responsible or to be held accountable. But to participate in creating history, one must move into power," he said. "Moving into power," in Taylor's view, meant being prepared "to negotiate, compromise, understand others have power and ways of viewing the world other than your own." It involved agreement "to engage with others" that eliminated violence or alienated protest as a strategy. Perhaps most notably, it served as a declaration of independence by the black community that recalls Frances Harper's Reconstruction Era image of the "commonwealth of freedom." BUILD members took on a leading role for Baltimore as a whole, signaling that they would no longer simply be objects of forces beyond their control. The Baltimore Commonwealth—like the Nehemiah Project in New York and similar efforts elsewhere—was a language of human agency that taught an important lesson: that things like school systems are human artifacts.[45]

The Baltimore Commonwealth served as a community-wide arena that reknit and created relationships that were badly frayed in some cases, virtually nonexistent in others, but which were essential for effective action. "The Commonwealth created a vehicle by which we could continue to have a dialogue about the school system and other issues in ways that I never would have expected," explained Alan Hoblitzel, chief executive of Maryland National Bank. "It's changed the thinking of a lot of businesses in the city. And it's been a way to learn about people. It's just not my normal experience to sit down with a black minister and talk about the issues we do." Kurt Schmoke, mayor of Baltimore, echoed the views of other political leaders like Henry Cisneros in San Antonio, whose contact with IAF groups has given them a different view of the role and meaning of the citizenry. "As an elected official, I can't solve all the problems," explained Schmoke.

> It's a gamble, in a sense, because if you have powerful organizations out there, when it comes to disagreements they have influence. They can battle you. But the benefits outweigh the risks.
>
> They show people what citizens can achieve without the government doing the whole project for them. They say, we have some power. We can influence policy. Let's show you how not in an abstract way, but by working together where we can around concrete issues like Commonwealth, or the Nehemiah plan.

The Baltimore Commonwealth schools effort subsequently led to a series of other initiatives around adult unemployment and other issues.[46]

In sum, the sort of collaboration pioneered by BUILD—parallelled as it is by a number of continuing struggles and confrontations with establishment interests in Baltimore around other questions—furnishes a paradigmatic example of a particular understanding of "public life." For BUILD, public life is a contested, turbulent arena that mixes values, interests, and differences with common purposes. It aims at an understanding of what democracy is and can become that is far different from conventional definitions, but which has old roots in the commonwealth tradition of citizen politics.

The Larger Lessons
of Community Initiative

*I*n American history, a reinvigoration of our democracy has regularly come from outside the "mainstream" of white, middle-class politics and culture. So too, today, groups like COPS, BUILD, and Valley Interfaith have a prophetic relevance for the whole of American society. They help show how ideas like citizenship and public life can have substantive meaning in our time and circumstances. Especially they highlight the importance of the themes of disciplined and constructive anger, relational power, and citizen group autonomy for a theory of citizen politics and the commonwealth adequate to our age.

The network of organizations like BUILD in Baltimore and the "guild" of organizers that compose the Industrial Areas Foundation, like everything in human affairs, are marked by their cultures and histories. Saul Alinsky came from an Orthodox Jewish background; despite his strident agnosticism as an adult, he fiercely kept his Jewish cultural identity. The Eastern European Catholic values of Back of the Yards—a strong emphasis on ethnic heritage, religious traditionalism, family, community, hard work, patriotism—find echoes today in the vocabulary and values of IAF groups that draw their main strength from those whom organizers call the "core moderates" in urban minority and ethnic communities generally, and mainline religious congregations specifically. The IAF organizations' vocabularies and basic constituencies are far different from the worlds of professionals, intellectuals, high school and college students, or suburban neighborhoods on the one hand, or rural areas and small towns on

the other. IAF organizing is at the forefront of the society in addressing certain key issues—drugs, for instance, or education, or housing.
But around others—from AIDS to most environmental issues to comparable worth or child care or disability rights or foreign policy questions—their groups have to date had little to say.

With the exception of the campaign to "organize the middle
class" heralded by Alinsky just before his death, and taken up mainly
by other forms of citizen activism, IAF organizing strategy has until
recently been content to concentrate on deepening its roots among
its bases. Even in the aftermath of its strategic revisions of the
1970s that concluded with the need for metropolitanwide, multieth-
nic, and ecumenical organizations, IAF has fashioned its organizing
around its analysis of local power struggles, not broader change. Following an old adage of Alinsky himself, it has held that the skillful
organization of only a relatively small percentage of the population
is sufficient to achieve significant reforms and win major victories
for poorer and minority populations. This has meant, in practice, a
curious bifurcation in political language. The political culture *within*
IAF groups like COPS, BUILD, or EBC is full of multilayered reflection and discussion of the meaning of politics, democratic values,
theological questions. Yet in the world "outside"—when leaders or
delegates go to a city council meeting on their issues, for instance—
their discussion tends to be much thinner and issue-specific. Even
political figures with whom such groups have worked for many years,
like Henry Cisneros, the former mayor of San Antonio, give little evidence of having picked up central IAF distinctions and concepts, like
the difference between public and private arenas or their understanding of power.

The entrance of many IAF organizations into what they call the
"multiverse" (conveying a more pluralist sense of "universe") of
open public space, especially in relation to infrastructural issues like
education, transportation, economic development requirements, or
water supply and treatment, has in the recent past brought them into
regular contact with a great variety of interests, political viewpoints,
and perspectives. IAF organizers and leaders now freely speculate
about the environments in which their approach might work and
other cultural contexts where it probably would not. And they have
begun to consider how their core concepts might be generalized and
taught to other audiences, like seminarians or politicians.[1]

Their network, in sum—already a powerful presence in several
areas of the country—could well expand its direct impact in the coming years. But there also seem clear limits to IAF's organizing efforts
for the foreseeable future. IAF groups depend for their initial development on organizers with an extraordinary degree of training and
skill. Moreover, they have the most success where there are deeply

rooted, relatively dense religious networks to build upon with interest in ecumenical action. And their sharply confrontational style and emphasis on intense organizational commitments seem most likely to succeed in drawing in "community moderates" in poor, minority, and low-income neighborhoods; it is hard to imagine their suburban counterparts.[2]

But if the IAF network's particular approaches to organizing are of limited applicability in a country as diverse as the United States, its understanding of politics has a relevance far beyond its specific organizations. Put simply, the IAF melds several strands of political language and culture—populism, republicanism, and religious concerns for social justice—in a distinctive mix that helps revive the commonwealth tradition of pragmatic citizen politics, a tradition that forms a practical antidote to the abstract and idealized discussions about public life, civic virtue, and citizenship widespread today. Citizen politics, in this sense, begins to furnish a language and set of themes with potential appeal in many different settings.[3]

For leaders in BUILD, as in the IAF network generally, "public life" has dramatic appeal. They like to recall the root Greek meaning of "idiot," someone who has only a private existence. When Vera Valdiviez declared to the BUILD convention, "We are pleased to be here to help celebrate ten years of rebuilding public life, promised by our forefathers and so long denied to our fathers and mothers," she got thunderous applause.

What BUILD activists *mean* by "public life" requires a deeper exploration and a contrast with conventional understandings of citizenship and public action. The concept, as they develop it in practice, recalls American traditions of active citizen involvement in public affairs. But BUILD's understanding of public life is considerably different from the classic republican tradition, grounded in small face-to-face communities, as well as from most recent neorepublican arguments. In BUILD's terms, public life is an open and dynamic process initiated by diverse self-interests and disciplined anger, animated by an interactive, "relational" conception of power, sustained by autonomous popular organizations, and cultivated by an active and skillful process of listening in public relationships to others of far different backgrounds and values.

Several decades or so ago, "public life" continued to mean something more than government, or arenas in which most people were spectators. But it was a slippery definition. "The outstanding problem of the Public," wrote John Dewey in 1928, "is discovery and identification of itself."[4]

Discovery and identification of the public is reappearing as a

problem in our contemporary society, in the evening of our unques-
tioning reliance on experts, technicians, and professionals to manage the world of larger systems. But the participatory, community-
based view of public identified by Dewey and urged by a number of
writers and leaders today is insufficient.

IAF is not entirely clear about its own tradition and its dynamics. Part of the problem lies in the language of the foundation
itself. IAF makes a sharp distinction between "the world as it is"
(what public life is like now) and "the world as it should be" (what it
would be like if it expressed our full ideals). This follows the customary view, where the term "public," like "politics," either conjures up
something corrupt, degraded, and far removed from the lives of ordinary citizens, or else is idealized as the active arena of the self-
sacrificing citizenry, the *polis,* the "human" world which the ancient
Greeks distinguished from the "animal" world of the *oikos,* the household. To IAF leaders, however, "public life" in practice means something different: an arena *between* the ideal and the real, constructed out
of the tension between the two. This blending of populist concerns for
self-interest and power with an understanding of the sense of public
life characteristic of republican thought results in the creation of a
balance that is highly unusual.[5]

In the twentieth century, most neorepublican efforts to revive
an activist conception of public life have continued to carry idealized
overtones of public activity that especially neglect themes of difference and hetereogeneity, as well as the operation of power. John
Dewey's strategy for public revitalization, drawing on a tradition
which stemmed from thinkers like Rousseau, saw public life in this
fashion. For him, participation in local community affairs was a kind
of political therapy for the discontents and alienations of the modern world. "Evils which are uncritically and indiscriminately laid at
the door of industrialism and democracy might, with greater intelligence, be referred to the dislocation and unsettlement of local communities," he wrote in *The Public and Its Problems.* "Vital and thorough
attachments are bred only in the intimacy of an intercourse which is
of necessity restricted in range. . . . Democracy must begin at home,
and its home is the neighborly community." A decade later, Dewey
added that local participation forms a kind of counterforce, or "balance wheel," to the immense institutions and impersonal forces of
the modern world. "Local agencies of communication and cooperation, creating stable local attachments . . . militate against the centri-
fugal forces of present culture, while at the same time they are of a
kind to respond flexibly to the demands of the larger unseen and
indefinite public." Dewey recognized that the world of the twentieth
century was far different from that of the nineteenth. But he offered

no advance on the kinds of skills and values that were taught by localized, community involvement.[6]

Dewey's arguments clearly anticipated the current "neorepublican" discussions of citizenship mentioned in Chapter One. And they find resonance in contemporary, smaller-scale local initiatives—neighborhood associations, development organizations, small cooperatives and others of many kinds that seek to restore a sense of mutuality, neighborliness, and local cooperation. The benefits of local involvement remain important, for all the reasons that Dewey and contemporary republicans articulate. But taken as the main form of public life, they are simply too marginal to convey the strong sense of power over the commonwealth at the center of citizen politics.[7]

As an illustration of the problem, neorepublican writers about citizenship and public life thus dismiss "self-interests" as antithetical to a healthy public practice. But in the real world of vast cultural differences and distinctions, combined with economic inequities, budget balancing, drugs, job worries, gangs, and toxic wastes, an understanding of public life without close attention to "self-interests"—understood as the various identities, loyalties, and histories that propel people into a public world—offers too little cultural *space* for individual differences, turmoil, conflict, and power.[8]

To succeed today, citizen politics needs an understanding and practice of public life that conveys a more turbulent, angry, dynamic, diverse, and power-laced sense than is suggested by the vocabulary of community and participation alone. Here, IAF's understandings are especially helpful. In their terms, constructive expressions of anger become a central principle of action on the basis of self-interests, in a public realm shaped by the themes of relational power and citizen autonomy.

———

For the IAF, learning a healthy direction for anger is the beginning of a new political culture where citizens once again become the agents. It is the motivational force, in the first instance, for changing the terms of the relationship between political leadership and citizenry.

"What Valley Interfaith tries to do is redo the political culture," explained Christine Stephens, directing the IAF effort in the vast Rio Grande Valley. Stephens described the *educational* process she sees at the heart of any serious empowerment of ordinary citizens. "In any community you have people who set themselves up as the brokers. When you form an organization like Valley Interfaith, you're really saying there's no one person in the community who brokers that community." A "change in culture," according to Stephens, means a twofold change. "You're trying to change both sides of the political culture." In the first instance, ordinary citizens need to learn to redefine "politics" in a more activist way, "so that they will be involved in the political process on a much more regular basis, not just voting."

Secondly, change in political culture involves a reeducation of politicians so they will learn to deal with the citizenry in a "respectful" and collaborative fashion. "Politicians still come to me and ask, 'Will you support me?'" said Carmen Anaya, a former "broker" of the Mexican community who is now a leader in Valley Interfaith. "I tell them the story has changed. Now I belong to this organization. We would like to have a dialogue with you about our needs, but not in the way we have done it in the past. Now we will present issues to you, and if you are willing to work with us on those issues, we are willing to work with you." Anaya's previous brokering of votes for promises was a constant frustration, because politicians rarely honored what they had said before the election. During many years of political leadership in the valley, she had never bothered to become a citizen or vote. Since 1983, Anaya has helped Valley Interfaith win a number of victories for the desperately poor communities of the valley from local and state officials, from new drainage and business development to the statewide Texas campaigns for public schools and health care. Through her involvement, her view of politics—and citizenship—underwent a basic change.[9]

Key to such reeducation, at least in the poorer communities that form IAF groups' base, is the ability of leaders like Anaya to express anger. As Ernesto Cortes put it, "We try to get people in touch with their own anger. Anger that comes out of a concern for people, that is disciplined and mature." In "classic" republican thought, anger and public life are not only rarely put together, they are also frequently seen as opposed. Anger (like power and self-interest) conveys the imagery of disruption, selfishness, and individualism that were what "citizens" supposedly put aside when they acted in "public" for the "common good." But anger and public life together point toward a different basis for politics that reintegrates the sharp divisions between "the world as it is" and "the world as it should be," everyday life-worlds and the arena of politics, by creating a field between, shaped by the commitments that actually move most people to action.[10]

The etymological roots of anger, from the Old Norse word *angr*, suggest grief—the sense that grows from separation, deep loss, failure to attain fundamental goals. And anger today, understood in these terms, is a widespread reaction to worsening social problems.

The question is whether anger can be disciplined and directed in constructive, positive fashion or whether it becomes "rage," leading to violence, disruption, and social disintegration.[11]

For the IAF, public anger is not seen to be selfishly motivated. As Cortes put it, "What we mean by anger is being your brother's keeper." But it does grow out of "self-interests," complexly understood to mean one's primary ties, sources of identity, basic commitments. Indeed, for groups based in minority and ethnic communities across the country, a constitutive element in "leadership" is a strong sense of self and identity, based on a respect for one's heritage and roots.[12]

The IAF Black Caucus document *Tent of the Presence* made the point with some eloquence:

> Anger and grief are rooted in our most passionate memories and dreams—a father whose spirit has been broken by demeaning work or no work, a brother or sister lost to violence or alcohol or drugs, a church burned down by an arsonist, a college career sabotaged by a substandard high school, a neighborhood of shops and families and affections and relationships ripped apart because banks wouldn't lend to it, because insurance companies wouldn't insure it, because city officials wouldn't service it, because youth wouldn't respect it, or because teachers wouldn't teach in it. Anger sits precariously between two dangerous extremes. One extreme is hatred, the breeding ground of violence. The other extreme is passivity and apathy, the breeding ground of despair and living death. Anger that is focused and deep and rooted in grief is a key element in the organizing of black churches in the 1980s.[13]

When anger is given discipline and form by skillful public action, it is the mechanism through which private values and self-interests become a passion for change in the immediate and justice in the longer term. When public action and disciplined anger are understood in this way, moreover, it shifts the dynamic interplay of public and private, and suggests a different way of understanding political culture that stresses its *rootedness* in everyday life-worlds as well as its specificity as public and long-term.

The tradition of practical political theory portrayed by writers like Machiavelli, Tocqueville, and, in our day, Arendt conveys this turbulent, diverse, variegated understanding of the public as an arena with its own specific dynamics, distinct from those of personal life. In the present, writers such as Bernard Crick (whose book *In Defense of Politics* is a favorite of IAF staff and organizational leaders) and Hannah Pitkin have, especially, continued to urge a sense of the turbulent, distinctive nature of public life and politics as mingling different self-interests, values, backgrounds, and projects.[14]

Such arguments about self-interest, difference, and constructive expressions of anger suggest an old and broad (if neglected) tradition of political theorizing in which IAF is clearly located. They also set the stage for understanding two other key themes of public life. To summarize, the most effective citizen efforts of recent years, like those of the IAF, point to new dimensions to the meanings and actual practice of *power* and to concepts of *autonomy* in politics.

Power, in the IAF practice, is the animus of action, "the ability both to produce and to undergo an effect." But the dual, *relational* nature of power suggested by the simultaneous stress on "producing" and "undergoing" an effect marks its approach as an innovative and detailed elaboration in practice of the dynamic view of power which has heretofore been eclipsed by both mainstream empirical political science and most of its critics on the left, who also see power solely as the ability to *produce* an effect.

For much of political theory, power is seen as a one-dimensional operation and participation is scarcely viewed as a problem. Robert Dahl's early work furnished classic definitions that still largely operate. "My intuitive idea of power is something like this," Dahl argued in the late 1960s. "A has power over B to the extent that he can get B to do something that B would not otherwise do." In these terms, participants are those who feel intensely about an issue. "The political system is easily penetrated," wrote Dahl in his classic book *Who Governs?* published in 1961. "The independence, penetratibility and heterogeneity of the various segments of the political stratum all but guarantee that any dissatisfied group will find a spokesman." From such a perspective, the operation of power is observable in visible political processes.[15]

A more critical vein of theory about power has long charged pluralist and empiricist writers with an inattentiveness to the ways large groups are excluded from active participation, and certain questions are neglected or suppressed by the dominant political discussion. Air pollution, segregation, corporate tax rates, discrimination against women, plant closings—to name a sampling of issues that seemed to come "from nowhere" in the last generation—have, at various earlier times, been absent from conventional discourse not because they were of no concern to significant groups but because the "rules" of what is discussed and how discussion takes place show systematic "mobilization of bias" in favor of those with the most power, access, and knowledge.[16]

The problem with such perspectives on power is that they tend to operate from a distance that views "the people" in a monochromatic fashion, as victims of a unidirectional operation of power. Such a perspective ironically reproduces the idea of mainstream theorists: power is seen as getting "B to do something that B would not otherwise do."

The view of the people as simply victims creates an alternating despair and romanticism. Thus, by way of contrast with the wild fantasies of two decades ago (or, variously, the determined democratic aspirations in the more arduous circumstances of the Soviet bloc today) in the loose, open environment of Western democracies—and the United States in particular—a mood of near-hopelessness about democratic prospects pervades intellectual culture.[17]

Only when one enters the dense and dynamic world of power-contested-in-practice, what can be called "relational power," can one hope to develop broader principles about why democratic action fails or is sustained, and how democratic possibilities can emerge from settings that seem to be on the face of it tranquil or complacent. Constructive statements about politics that argue, from practical reference, what might be done to accomplish democratic change are out of intellectual fashion. But the dominant view of power as inexorably controlling and one-directional in its operation is as wrong as it is widespread today. In particular, such an understanding of power overlooks the constant interplay between "actor," or "power wielder," and those "acted upon." And it flattens what is in fact a densely textured, lumpy, and contradictory landscape of power relations in modern societies: if power relationships, in many settings, are vastly unequal (producing such experiences as "politics as spectacle") they also are always contested and mutually transformative. One never simply "acts on" another—any process of action always has reciprocal moments, changing both partners in the drama.

Groups of people in society are never simply "powerless": there are always resources, strategems, and social and cultural maneuvers available to and used by even those who seem at first most unambiguously victimized. Out of the density and complexity of power dynamics and in ways that have rarely been explored, relatively autonomous popular activity—what can be called "free spaces"—can be sustained over long periods. These, in turn, form the invisible seedbeds for renewed moments of public freedom.[18]

IAF has, at least intuitively, a clear understanding of the democratic possibilities to be found in almost any setting. In workshops on power, when IAF workshop leaders ask for associations with the term, participants almost invariably list negatives associated with a one-directional understanding of power: corruption, evil, "Power corrupts," Hitler, Napoleon. Such associations correspond to the apparent context of people's daily lives, in which their experiences are overwhelmingly those of feeling *acted upon*. And when IAF discusses the "context of organizing," their simple framework is a classic populist analysis: a few elite institutions, mainly corporations, have the dominant power in communities; politicians (and to some extent other professionals) occupy intermediate "power positions"; and most citizens have little voice or say. The only serious counter to "money power," in IAF's stick-figure rendition, is organized "people power": citizens who form strong, artful organizations through which they can assemble numbers and resources.

But the IAF further refines these terms. In the Western tradition and in most theology, they argue, power is defined in radically incomplete ways, as the "ability to produce an effect." It is that experience of power which produces people's negative associations, and the desire to counter it produces the first impulse to create "people power" in the effort to create countereffects. This is what IAF terms "unilateral power." A unilateral view of power, however, is based on a greatly impoverished view of the self, as formed and to be understood *prior* to and ultimately apart from relationships and experiences. And it can be demonic in its consequences, aiming at the reconstruction or manipulation of the world around one in ways that treat others as simply means or problems or obstacles.[19]

Power exercised in a unilateral fashion is, further, abstract: it views others not in their whole and complex concreteness and difference but rather in terms of their usefulness to the given ends. Political power has been conceived primarily in this fashion in the modern "world as it is." IAF trainers develop a typology of power, a mapping of different sorts of power operation, that reflect different versions of one-directional action. There is coercion, or power wielded with threat and overt force. There is expertise, power based on claims of superior knowledge, customarily drawn from a supposedly scientific method. There is authority, power accorded a person through moral or traditional sanction. There is "habit," the unthinking acquiescence in "the way things are" that comes from privatist withdrawal from public affairs. Echoing Hannah Arendt's observation about the "banality of evil" under the Nazi regime, they argue that habit often produces the greatest injustices.

The IAF trainers contrast these sorts of one-directional power with the sort of reconstructed power dynamic they see as their aim, based on "informed consent" and "relational" interactions. A relational view of power changes the dynamics of one-way operations. It recognizes the constant transformation of *self* as well as "other" in any power exchange, an insight that has undergirded the remarkable process of evaluation and reflection that IAF groups constantly undertake.

The BUILD and IAF theory of the relational nature of power was illustrated by the kinds of questions leaders explored as part of the evaluation of the BUILD convention in 1987, questions they had posed and thought about in advance: "What are our feelings about what happened?"—the rationale for which was that one's first instinctive, emotional reaction is crucial raw data. "What about time?"—a question that teaches respect for the drama itself and practices of accountability. "Is there a new political reality?"—a way to explore the reactions of other public actors outside the organization and how their reactions have changed over the last year. "Was there an exchange of power?"—an analysis of what public acknowledgments and exchange of visibility occurred as a part of the event. "Is there a different way of operating?"—looking at the texture and dynamic of BUILD's unfolding relations for the future. "Is it a drama?"—involving a specific evaluation of the event as an exciting, inspiring public activity.

All of these questions aim at an analysis not only of the concrete and immediate *results* of the event, but also at the impact of such a process on BUILD and its members. A relational understanding of power, in this view, also entails the assumption of responsibility for action. It means an unsettling willingness to shake up and challenge assumptions for the sake of developing an enlarged understanding, a "civic common sense," or judgment, that takes account of the views of others. And it involves a certain "leap of faith" that dynamic public relationships themselves are the essence of power relations, if well understood. It was this sort of insight, for instance, that led Gerald Taylor to argue for the importance of "time" and "patience" in the early negotiations with Baltimore businesses. Consent based on relational power is dependent on what the IAF organizers term "informed judgment," an active process that weighs conflicting values, looks at the broader contexts of actions, acknowledges fears, anxieties, and difficulties, and rests on a strong sense of ownership. "Judgment is a public activity and an art," Ernie Cortes argued. As he sees it, judgment is different from opinion: it requires explication and discussion; it is based on evaluation of evidence, recognition of context, codes, community traditions, and rules. But it also requires some measure of disinterestedness, a conscious act of partially suspending one's biases. Judgment takes place, for instance, when one chooses one's leaders with a view not just toward one's own immediate interests but also toward the longer-run needs of the community as a whole.[20]

For a continuing consciousness of such relational dynamics to
be sustained also requires a strong sense of independence and autonomy—"ownership" of both one's own actions and the collective in-
strumentalities through which one acts—sufficient to feel like an
actor as well as a recipient of action. Autonomy is the second key
element in public life.

In classical republican theory, property was never an end in itself, a view that strongly shaped the American revolutionary generation. Property was important in this understanding because it
created a foundation for independence that allowed citizens to be
free from unwarranted pressures and threats as they participated in
public affairs. In the best and most thoughtful forms of political theory, property was also, optimally, associated with a distinctive vantage point from which to *see* the common world, the world of public
life. The interaction among different perspectives creates a more
multidimensional view.[21]

Citizens, of course, were a restricted class, made up largely of
white middle- and upper-class males who owned property. But
throughout American history, the linkage between the preconditions
of independence and the ideal of full participation in the life of the
community has formed a potent axis for popular movements, as
those initially left out of the definition mounted struggles that demanded not only formal "rights" to inclusion but the material bases
for autonomy as well. In the present, for instance, such an implicit
link continues to strengthen the public appeal of feminist issues like
comparable worth and programs to help women establish small businesses or other sources of economic independence.

Property or other foundations for independent participation in
community affairs (like a secure job, or an education) concern especially the *individual* citizen's capacity for action. Out of exploration
of Americans' variegated voluntary traditions and their central role
in democratic movements has also come some historical attention—
though as yet little notice in political theory—to the importance of
group autonomy for effective, powerful public action and the sustenance of a vital public life. Voluntary groups with a strong open,
public dimension create "free spaces."[22]

Free spaces are occasioned by voluntary associations with roots
in everyday life-worlds that sustain an important measure of independence from large-scale systems and institutions of government,
on the one hand, and that have public dimensions where a relational
practice of power among different interests develops, on the other.
Churches or synagogues, civic groups, voluntary educational or recreational societies, moral or political reform organizations—all have
functioned at different times as occasions for a free public life.

In the first sense, free spaces have a resemblance to communal structures championed by a long line of conservative writers, from Edmund Burke to contemporary theorists like Peter Berger and John Neuhaus, who have called them "mediating institutions."

Dating from writers like Burke—who championed "little platoons" of daily life like the church, club, and family against the force of the modern age—conservatives have argued that communal institutions are the bulwark of liberty against large institutions, preeminently government. Robert Nisbet described how totalitarianism in Germany depended upon precisely the destruction of such communal institutions:

> All autonomous organizations were destroyed and made illegal: professions, service clubs, voluntary mutual aid groups, fraternal associations, even philatelist and musical societies. Such groups were regarded, and correctly, by the totalitarian government as potential sources of future resistance, if only because in them people were brought together for purposes, however innocent, that did not reflect those of the central government.[23]

In a similar vein, Berger and Neuhaus described how modern government, justified by principles like equality, justice, and the public good, "aspires to an all comprehending jurisdiction." But the state expands at terrible cost: "a growing trend toward legally enforced symbolic sterility in public space"; the systematic weakening of communal and small group connections; the widening intrusion of experts and professionals into the most private realms of life; and, accompanying these processes, the erosion of those buffers that protect the individual against the "megastructures" of modern society. The IAF finds the language of "mediating institutions" a useful vocabulary to describe the churches, synagogues, and other local community institutions on which they build their organizations.[24]

Critics on the left often remark that conservatives have been far less alert to the ways that business institutions and the marketplace also constantly undermine mediating or community institutions. But what conservative critics and their opponents share is the tendency to lump communal institutions together in a way that obscures the vast differences among them, especially along the axis of cultural and social homogeneity versus difference: communities can be "private" or homogeneous in character, or they can be "public" and diverse.

In fact, community places with an independence from dominant power, but also with an open, public face that allows the mingling of different perspectives, cultures, and ideas, are highly dynamic. They form the seedbeds of democratic action and, at moments, broad democratic movements. The black church, for instance, historically has played this role as an occasion for free space. Since the days of slavery in the South, it created a place which the black community itself "owned" and about which whites knew little. But it was also a place outside the family, strengthened and enriched by different perspectives and ideas and a relatively free intellectual life where a far more relational practice of power operated than in other settings. In the black church, people could socialize, dream of freedom, discover in biblical stories and Christian traditions (taught by slaveowners as an ideological "program of pacification") subversive themes, and develop public skills of action and organization.

More sophisticated elites—spanning the range from the eighteenth-century Southern planter Whitemarsh Seabrook, who said anyone who let blacks read the whole Bible by themselves should be consigned to an insane asylum, to Communist party opponents of Gorbachev's *glasnost* today—have understood the unsettling possibilities that free spaces introduce into politics. "Who knows what they would pray for, if left alone?" argued one Southern preacher in the nineteenth century upon refusing a request for a women's prayer group. Although the IAF has not developed a theory to differentiate sorts of communal structures, in fact its practice dramatically suggests the democratic disturbances that autonomy connected to public life can generate.[25]

Indeed, the IAF has raised the concept of autonomy on both individual and collective levels to a constitutive part of citizen politics. Leaders and organizers regularly use the republican argument about the material bases for full citizenship as a part of their rationale for decent education and good jobs, and one can see strong echoes of the classic commonwealth notions of property in something like the Nehemiah Project to spread home ownership. Inside organizations, moreover, the central theme of autonomy translates into IAF's "iron rule": "Never do anything for someone that they can do for themselves." Such a principle extends to small things: training sessions, for instance, do not include name tags, as a prod to participants to ask each others' names directly. For the IAF, the concept of individual autonomy is akin to the principles that infuse self-help groups. Indeed, IAF workshops often compare addictions like chemical dependency with the dependency of those who look to others to solve their problems in public life. "When one takes on another's problems they can solve themselves, you take away both their freedom and their responsibility," argued Chambers.[26]

Further, the concept of group autonomy is basic to what the IAF calls "mass-based organizations" of the kind they help organize, which they distinguish from both "civic" and "service" organizations—

dependent on government or other sources of funds—and "social movements," which they argue are typically "owned" too much by charismatic leaders and large donors. They place a strong central importance on the idea of financial self-sufficiency in "people's organizations," and spend a great deal of time trying to demystify "money," in the same way that they demystify self-interest and power. "The development of dues in the Citizens Action Program in Chicago in the 1970s turned out to be a real key to our whole approach," argued Larry McNeil. "The organization wasn't dependent on government funds, or foundation money, or corporations. Members raised funds themselves" through activities ranging from bake sales to congregationwide donations. In the IAF view, money "tests" commitment whereas fund-raising produces a practice of measurable accountability. Self-sufficiency, moreover, creates the ability to determine organizational objectives and actions free of feelings of contingency, even on the IAF itself. Staff are suggested for IAF-affiliated citizen organizations, but the groups themselves hire and fire the staff, and are free to make their own decisions about whether to take or reject any staff suggestions. Such groups decline large grants from sources like corporations and foundations; most funds come from members, like religious congregations, unions, or civic groups, and from an annual campaign in which they produce a book about the group, filled with advertisements from businesses and others. IAF itself functions like a guild of organizers, with which affiliated groups contract for specific services (consultation, training, and the like) and from which lead organizers are typically hired. Although groups are in principle free to choose lead organizers from outside the IAF, in practice it has never been done. Yet there are many instances of local groups disagreeing strenuously and rejecting proposals from people like Chambers.

It should be noted that IAF groups' typical budgets are very small compared to their size and power: most run about $120,000 a year, almost all for staff. Their intensive process of leadership education means that most of the functions taken on by staff in voluntary groups are undertaken by leaders, including most of the training; San Antonio COPS, for instance, has periodically functioned without a lead organizer.[27]

As with any structure in the real world, the autonomy of IAF organizations has limits and cultural meanings: within individual congregations, for instance, particular theological traditions operate. In the kinds of lower-class and minority Catholic parishes or Protestant congregations that typically form their base, a gendered "God language" that uses a masculine construction ("He") is common. But IAF's attentiveness to the "public" dimensions of autonomy in community institutions leads to a stress on the regular encounter with difference that constantly works democratizing changes within such organizations. Thus, for instance, Marian Dixon described the way BUILD had taught her and others to challenge the tendency toward deference she had learned in Christianity. Beatrice Cortez of San Antonio COPS said that the organization's redefinition of leadership and "public and private" had "created a revolution" in women's roles in the Mexican community of the city and many other Texas towns besides. And writing the Vision Glorious paper, a visionary statement of the Black Clergy group in BUILD, proved an occasion for a discussion of gender issues in biblical and religious language. The result, for the paper, was the deletion of masculine references to God.

IAF groups in practice thus suggest the fashion in which free spaces are kept open by concerns, interests, directions, and projects that reach beyond particular communities' internal life, toward a larger world outside. In recent years as the groups have grown, maintained themselves over long periods, and developed collaborative relations with other elements of their areas as well as state and national institutions, IAF practice has illustrated the multidimensional schooling in civic knowledge conveyed by such activity, summed up by the concept of commonwealth.

Commonwealth in
the Information Age

When citizen groups take the initiative in the public debate, assuming a responsibility for public goods in which everyone has a stake, they may link their own concerns and interests with those of the broader society in ways that have a transformative effect. Here, the language and practice of the Baltimore Commonwealth find parallels in the most effective citizen initiatives elsewhere in the nation. All, in various ways, give citizens a schooling in democracy, which involves not only information about the issues, but also the skills and concepts and public value discussions that turn "information" and "issues" back into human products, under human control.

The first populists felt a pervasive sense of crisis. "The air of our beloved America has been heavy for many years with the weary footfalls of the people," wrote Henry Demarest Lloyd, describing working people "tramping around, to find no doors open for them in the palaces of industry they built"; farmers "surrendering [farms] to market riggers and usurers"; and "clerks, the salesmen, the skilled organizers of business set adrift." In his view, the foundations of independence and virtue were at stake. The People's party, he argued, "is the only party that stands against the division ... of the property of the people among the billionaires." The issues they addressed—credit, marketing, land, common-law rights, transportation—were tools to use, in their view, for self-organization: "The millions who have espoused these principles will not stop until they have become incorporated into the constitution of the government and the framework of society."[1]

The movement never resolved the daunting problems of credit and distribution facing its organizational base in the cooperatives, which experienced ferocious opposition from banks; nor did populism overcome the entrenched two-party system. But its fundamental thrust, in which issues, platforms, and party documents were less the goal in themselves than the means to the "self-organization of the people," drew on a many-sided tradition of public life and politics in the nineteenth century and adapted it to the emerging modern world. Such a tradition was summed up in the language of the "cooperative commonwealth," adding a visionary and mythic dimension to the first populist crusade expressed in their songs, stories, and imaginings of a future. One can find counterparts in recent years, but they are rare.[2]

In the public television series taped shortly before his death, Joseph Campbell, dean of the field of comparative mythology, distinguished between myths linking the person to the natural world and mythology connecting one to a society, a group, a people. "Mythology is the song of the imagination," Campbell said to journalist Bill Moyers. Compared to the intricate popular myth-making Campbell described at the nation's founding, he pointed out that Americans today mostly have a dessicated store of myths with which to explain our origins and purposes.[3]

Myths tell a story of how a people "came to be." In populist movements and prophetic utterance, they also take on a utopian dimension, drawing on the reservoir of common cultural symbols and images in the service of a "critique of the present." They challenge the present in the name of certain fundamental themes and values which, it is argued, are being violated. They also point toward an alternative future. The wellspring of such prophetic myth is a sense of human agency and culture. And the reason for our impoverished mythical storehouse is clear-cut: although many, perhaps most, Americans experience a sense of crisis that bears a resemblance to that of the first populists, we have largely lost our perception of human control over the larger forces that shape our lives as we have lost confidence in our capacity to understand their functioning.[4]

Today, the "eerie" sense of independent reality that Karl Marx once attached to machines and the industrial work process has become characteristic of the large-scale systems of the modern world generally—from the skyscraper canyons we walk through in big cities to the incomprehensibly complex global financial markets that shape our lives, to the seemingly inexorably collapsing public school systems. The language of commonwealth—conveying a strong sense of citizen responsibility for the foundations of our lives—has all but disappeared. "Politics" has come to mean a world where technocracy reigns almost unchallenged.

This implies a view of the citizenry as simply an object to be manipulated. Gerald Taylor calls it the "commodification of politics." He refers to "the proliferation on both left and right of electoral and single issue organizing tied to 'membership markets,' worked for money and volunteers—political action committees, the National Rifle Association, the Rainbow Coalition, public interest groups and others." Specialists in polling, media imagery, canvassing, and campaign management, he asserts, guide our elections. "The public" are passive groups of consumers, to be appealed to in different ways.[5]

But other currents have been at work, drawing upon the older tradition of citizen politics. When these combine effective organizing with a broader commonwealth vision of change, it can have a transformative impact on large populations.

In the 1920s, Terry Pettus and his wife, Berta, moved to Seattle, Washington, where he became a newspaperman and well-known writer. Over the next two decades Pettus was a leading figure in many popular movements: the fight for public power and rural electrification; the battle for popular initiative and referendum; the effort to win industrial-accident insurance and old-age pensions. At the heart of each, in his view, was the notion of the whole, "the common good—the people versus the special interests." In the mid-1930s, labor unions, farmers, neighborhood groups, and others came together during the Great Depression in a new political movement to press their own interests. They called themselves the Washington Commonwealth Federation, drawing on old currents of indigenous radicalism. Organizing by precincts, the federation in the late 1930s and '40s became the dominant force in the state Democratic party, sending many congressmen to Washington, at times controlling the state legislature.

However, in the early 1950s, the mood of the country changed sharply as rancorous charges of "communism" were leveled against radicals and reformers of all kinds. Pettus, target of FBI investigations, was convicted under the Smith Act and spent six months in jail before his conviction was overturned. Free, he decided to retire after a generation as a journalist and activist. He wrote mystery novels. Retirement lasted a decade.

In 1933, Pettus and Berta had purchased and moved into a houseboat on Seattle's Lake Union. At that time, more than a thousand houseboats were moored along the lake near the center of town, close together, paying dirt-cheap rents for moorage. The houseboat community was a freewheeling mix of sailors, students, boatyard workers, bohemians, poor folks, retired radicals—all wanting cheap quarters and space for peculiar life-styles.

City officials had long looked skeptically at the floating community as a "health hazard," while real estate and development interests had long coveted the lakeshore. In 1962, the powers-that-be moved vigorously to evict the boaters, acquire the land, and erect apartment and other large projects along the lakefront. Pettus got an eviction notice in April. That galvanized him into his "second political career."

Most thought the iconoclastic individualists of Lake Union could never be organized, but Pettus knew they could. "People will fight for their existence, if not for abstractions," he explained. He and others formed the Floating Homes Association to solidify the houseboat community. And they redefined the issue, tying their fate to the future of the city as a whole. "We knew we could never win if the issue was simply the survival of the houseboats," said Pettus. Drawing on the commonwealth legacy which had shaped his language and politics for decades, Pettus and his neighbors created a broader vision of Lake Union as the common wealth of the people of Seattle—"a gift to us from the Ice Age," as he put it.

A major complaint against the houseboats was sewage pollution on the lake. Few knew that in fact the city of Seattle itself dumped raw sewage into Lake Union through thirteen sewer lines. The boaters' contribution was minuscule—something like one half of one percent of the total. But again Pettus knew the association could never win by debating percentages, or claiming "less responsibility" than others. So they turned the issue on its head. Houseboaters, to the consternation of the city, demanded that they be permitted to pay for sewer lines to their boats. The association held workshops on how to weld pipes and how to hook up sewer lines. And they found new allies, like the city's Health Department.

The association made the issue Lake Union and its ties to the city as a whole. Constantly seeking to embed their efforts in a call for public control over the future of the entire city and its environment, they put the issue and their arguments before the public in a variety of ways: historic tours of the lake, articles in local magazines, parties, festivals, broadsides, speeches to organizations throughout Seattle. "The simple fact is that we were organized and could focus attention," said Pettus. As the campaign developed, they connected the idea of the lake as an environmental resource with the concept of it as an integrated human community whose multiple uses—recreation, commerce, residence—were linked.

The effect was dramatic. By late 1963 the city, responding to the association's remarkable popular support, issued a study that called for protection of the lake. With such a statement, the association was able to block industrial use of a large area, press the city to acquire twenty-three acres to create a public park, and inspire the state legislature to pass one of the strongest shoreline management control acts on new development in the nation. Terry Pettus helped write the legislation.[6]

By the early 1970s, the spirit of the houseboaters' victory had energized a number of other citizen efforts. The historic Pike Place Market was saved from the developers when a local architect and friend of Pettus, Victor Steinbrueck, framed the fight in similarly broad terms, touting the market as an irreplaceable part of the city's heritage. At the decade's end, Seattle had achieved national notice as a pioneer in a number of neighborhood-based programs and participatory civic initiatives, most of which could trace their roots to the Lake Union fight and drew directly on the commonwealth vision that Terry Pettus had reinvigorated. Even establishment figures who battled community activists acknowledged the benefits. "Seattle had a major era of citizen participation," said James Ellis of the prestigious firm of Preston, Thorgrimson, Ellis and Holman, a man sometimes called the informal leader of the city's elite. As a result, he believed, "there was an incredible flowering in the city."[7]

The efforts of Pettus and the houseboaters, like those of the IAF, went against the grain of the times. Although the city of Seattle had declared an official "Terry Pettus Day" before he died in 1985, by the latter years of the eighties new development projects again threatened the city shoreline, while much of the vibrant energy of the 1970s neighborhood activism had eroded. No democratic initiative continues forever—and the problem with powerful citizen initiatives like Pettus's in recent decades has been the absence of ways to reflect self-consciously upon their lessons. Against this background, IAF's greatest contribution may ultimately prove to be the constant process of self-reflection and evaluation of its efforts which takes place throughout its network. Such activity creates an approach to knowledge that dramatically contrasts with politics-as-technique: it generates a sustained process of collective memory and learning from which many citizen efforts can benefit.

From stories like Pettus's and the IAF projects, it is possible to generalize several basic principles. Specifically, the themes of these renewals in the commonwealth tradition highlight the ways citizens are reenfranchised through a process of education for public life that teaches new and more communal ways of looking at information about issues, that conveys a series of skills specific to a dynamic public arena, and that reembeds the objects of struggle and action once again in culture and a sense of human agency. The three vital components of such citizen education might be called information, knowledge, and wisdom.

———

What are known as "facts" make up the *information* flow of the modern world. Information can be considered as discrete bits of data: the "yes" or "no" coding of a computer, the color of a flower—or something as complex as the vote of a legislator or the place to go to get health care, when detailed in isolation from a broader framework of knowledge and action. But the pretenses of positivism aside, there is no such thing as strictly "neutral" information: *what* one observes always is connected to a scheme of interpretation, shaped by the perspective, values, and history of the observer.

IAF activists have pioneered in the systematic formulation of a public "virtue" that makes this clear in politics. They view sustained public action as depending on a close connection to everyday life-worlds and the interests they generate. At the heart of the IAF organization building, campaigns, and public relationships is the art of "listening," expressed in the activity of face-to-face meetings. Listening, for organizers or leaders, aims at exploring the self-interests of individuals that grow out of their actual life-world commitments, worries, angers, and loyalties. But the listening process involves definite intention, not a pose of neutrality: people's concerns for health care or education, for instance, are framed not simply as individual goods that each is encouraged to pursue singly; they are translated into goals on which people can act together. The result is an educational process about the *commons.*

The idea of commons requires historical retrieval against the grain of the interpretative scheme of modern social science. In his famous piece "The Tragedy of the Commons," Garrett Hardin articulated the conventional interpretation of commons as a "free resource," open to all, that inevitably eroded as increasing numbers of people took advantage of it. But Hardin's analysis depends on an individualist, rational-choice model of motivation:

> As a rational being, each herdman seeks to maximize his
> gain . . . he asks, "What is the utility *to me* of adding one more
> animal to my herd." [Thus] each man is locked into a system
> that compels him to increase his herd without limit in a world
> that is limited. Ruin is the destination toward which all men
> rush, each pursuing his own best interest in a society that
> believes in the freedom of the commons.

Hardin's "scientific" language hides his own, superimposed theory about motivation, which bears little resemblance to the way medieval villagers, for example, understood the world. In their villages, "freedom of the commons" was defined mainly in terms of the well-being of the community, not individual gain. The commons represented *collective resources,* not free goods, whose use entailed clearly defined responsibilities. There is considerable evidence, in fact, that commons developed *because* of population pressures that required a more careful tending of such resources. In New England, those commons which survived were those seen to be in the *community's* self-interest, and for which people took responsibility as a result.[8]

This kind of communalization of interest involves the rebuilding of community relations as a critical source of power. Terry Pettus knew the houseboaters' direct interests were at stake and could visibly be addressed only by treating them as common goods, but he had to make the connection explicit. When the boaters sought out information about such issues as sewage and development patterns, they acted together, recognizing their common fate. IAF groups often operate in a less urgent setting, but they stress cooperation. Through "listening," tied to the formulation of possibilities for common action, they reemphasize the dimensions of a series of "goods," from transportation, education, and health care to housing or small business development, whose communal aspects have been rendered increasingly invisible by the erosion of public vocabulary. Such a process is the beginning of effective citizen politics.[9]

Information is made up of facts, or data, that seem on the surface to be divided into isolated bits. *Knowledge* is information that is made *usable* through skills, methods, connections to other information. In effective, sustained citizen action, people learn the skills of public life with which to act effectively. "Commons," or the common wealth—the public goods that are objects of sustainable public action—become not only occasions for collaboration but invaluable sources of citizen education in their own right because they are the occasions for learning such skills.

Lake Union's Houseboat Association found itself in the midst of a series of ongoing relationships as a result of its assumption of responsibility for "the gift from the Ice Age." As an indispensable aspect of their efforts, the boaters learned how to make their information usable in many contexts, developing skills of public relations, bargaining, research, organization, and coalition building. Their story is paralleled in the rediscovery of a wider public world by other effective citizen efforts today.

Organizations like BUILD in Baltimore, COPS and Valley Interfaith in Texas, UNO in East Los Angeles, or EBC in New York have pioneered in the revival of public life and the creation of public space that depends on common projects, occasions of public life. In this sense, the commonwealth theme addresses the current widespread worry that America is suffering from a potentially debilitating loss of a sense of collective political will.[10]

Increasingly, we witness the proliferation of what sociologist Robert Bellah and his colleagues called "lifestyle enclaves," segmented groups whose creation celebrates "the narcissism of similarity" and which "explicitly involves a contrast with others who 'do not share one's lifestyle.'"[11]

Against this background, commonwealth ends that occasion active public life in a sense of diverse interests, values, groups, and cultures are especially important because they teach the skills of public life in a complex, heterogeneous world.

In the first instance, commons for effective citizen groups are generally infrastructural dimensions of the community, those foundational elements whose sustenance or repair commands a potentially broad public agreement. Here, the lessons of citizen organizing suggest practices of "public relationships," the need for a relational understanding of power, the crucial importance of autonomous "free spaces," voluntary instruments of action that diverse groups of citizens "own" and control. All these can contribute to a reawakened sense of collaboration and conflict around those ends which communities can agree are essential, in some sense, for survival. And they result in an ongoing schooling of the citizenry for action.[12]

The view of citizen sovereignty as depending upon a widespread civic education process does not dictate constant or broad citizen involvement in every infrastructural issue—and the types, styles, and extent of ongoing citizen involvement vary from issue to issue and community to community. In general, for instance, schools, or housing development patterns, or health care and crime prevention, are clearly potentially accessible to more direct and continual citizen input than, say, drainage systems. But the ideal of a transformed "political culture" where citizens once again are the main actors suggests the need for a practice of openness and accountability by public officials around *any* important issue, new forums for active intervention by citizens when problems or controversies arise, and new information sources and ways to learn public skills. For COPS, for instance, the first battle was to be heard, and taken seriously, on the issue of drainage.[13]

Public life depends upon an array of different skills and arts. "If we think of public life as the exercise of power around self-interest," said Arnie Graf, "the art of organizing is figuring out how to get public relationships with people when you want something." The normal method, he continued, is to approach someone with requests, or demands—with a given agenda. "But that is not conducive to deeper public life." He continued with the story of the first time BUILD leaders met with Paul Sarbanes, senior U.S. senator from Maryland. When the group came in the door, Sarbanes smiled, took out a notebook, and asked, "What can I do for you?" "Nothing," replied the leaders, "we're here to get to know you. We want to know why *you're* here, what are your interests and concerns. We think that will help us develop a working relationship over time." An extension of the old IAF principle of the virtue of listening, this practice of face-to-face individual meetings has become a pivotal centerpiece of IAF organizational practice, both within groups and outside. "It's the way to understand the other in their specificity, to break down stereotypes, to find out who the other person is," concluded Graf.[14]

To clarify and situate the practice of face-to-face meetings, BUILD has conducted a number of workshops on the differences between "publics." There is for example the sort of public one finds within citizen organizations like BUILD. It involves a particular range of groups and interests, but is far from the broad community as a whole. And it generates "virtues" like membership loyalty and friendship that are not necessarily appropriate for the broader public world.

The public space beyond such groups comprises conflicting belief systems, heritages, and interests. "It is what we call 'multiverse,'" explained Gary Rodwell, contrasting the word with "universe." "There, things are less 'fixed' and predictable. Relational power operates by exchange, compromise, listening. This is an arena of eternal struggle and change." IAF argues that in the broad "multiverse," there are no permanent allies—or permanent enemies. Gerald Taylor used the biblical story of Job to bring home the point of unpredictability and constant "testing." Relevant public skills and virtues in such an arena are not mainly "getting out the vote" or presenting one's own viewpoint, but rather listening, negotiating, creating public drama and exchange, holding officials accountable.[15]

Finally, common wealths teach more than public skills and methods. In this regard, the themes of the commonwealth tradition prompt a visionary strand of action clearly different from the pragmatism and attention to "self-interest" with which Alinsky-style organizing is usually associated. IAF groups have most visibly helped to revive the commonwealth tradition as they have discovered how to infuse their activity with a rich sense of values, purposes, and long-range democratic aspirations.

Commonwealth ideals encourage the voicing of aspirations and needs that may well be suppressed or dismissed as "impractical" in conventional public forums, but which nonetheless can prompt not

only the defense of community and public, but also their reimagin-
ing. In the process, they teach a crucial lesson of citizen politics:
large-scale systems need to be reembedded in human values and a
sense of human agency. They need to be guided by wisdom.

———

Information is relatively segmented pieces of data; knowledge
is information made usable. *Wisdom* adds more: knowledge that has
meaning added, structured, guided, and informed by an evolving
value and conceptual framework.

Terry Pettus and the houseboaters held a kind of protracted
workshop on Seattle's public values that at least for a period of time
tamed and guided the headlong rush of the city toward unbridled
high-tech development. IAF leaders and organizers effect a similar
transformation in political culture when they develop a language
and vision that reembeds "issues" and institutions in human agency.
BUILD's "commonwealth" has counterparts in the rich imagery of
transformation associated with projects like Nehemiah or the Genesis efforts of groups in Southern California.[16]

Lake Union's campaign impacted on the entire political culture
of Seattle in the 1970s. BUILD fleshed out its Commonwealth Agreement with a "vision glorious" for Baltimore. The Baltimore Commonwealth began with the creation of a "commons." It was not a
blueprint for a new society, nor a prescription for any other issues
beyond schools, nor even—despite its members' hopes—initially
much of a specific plan for the rebuilding of the schools. The program was more an open-ended *process*.

But interestingly, BUILD leaders generalized its language into a
set of associations with a theme much like the utopian-edged uses
of "commonwealth" in older popular movements in America—the
nineteenth-century Knights of Labor, woman suffragists, populist
farmers; twentieth-century movements like the Industrial Workers of
the World or the farmer-labor coalitions of the Great Depression.
"Money power is like Pharaoh in Egypt. Unless it exists in a creative
struggle and tension with the power of the people, it's Godless; it's
destructive," said Vernon Dobson, explaining "commonwealth" in
ways that recalled the historic use of the commonwealth ideal to op-
pose commercial civilization and overweening power beyond the
possibility of popular control. Doug Miles described the commonwealth as the vision of "whole community, where there are no left-
outs, where everybody feels a part and is respected for their person-
hood." For Miles, commonwealth is inclusive. "It looks at the common wealth of Baltimore which we claim as our Jerusalem to make
new."[17]

For BUILD, the combination of a new forum with a rich set of historical and political associations strengthened the desire and design for substantive change. Indeed, it prompted BUILD members to elaborate their vision in the paper "Reclaiming the Vision Glorious," written six months after the Commonwealth Agreement, a vision which then combined with early experiences and the "public process" to spur BUILD to undertake other aggressive organizing efforts around issues as diverse as drugs, neighborhood renewal, jobs, nursing home care, and gun control.

This kind of democratic practice, forging a politics out of the tension between the world-as-it-is and the world-as-it-should-be, deepens both immediate capacities for practical reform and the visionary imagination. In doing so, citizen efforts suggest how "commonwealth" *ends* of public life can create both occasions for action and sources of inspiration.[18]

A sense of an unfolding of possibilities within the existing world prompts such citizen groups to pose new issues and questions in terms of an expansion of the parameters of the commons, understood as the basic goods widely recognized and affirmed by the community. Thus after the school program in Baltimore was well underway, BUILD undertook a controversial campaign to unionize nursing home workers in collaboration with Hospital Workers Union District 1199. But they framed it differently from the conventional approach to unionization. Instead of concentrating on signing up prospective members—an approach that immediately casts a campaign as a "labor" issue—BUILD and the union began with a research project that unearthed often scandalous conditions. And they sponsored a series of strategy sessions and workshops that looked at the role and function of nursing homes in the community, what stake other BUILD members had in the issue, how senior citizens in the homes might regain a sense of dignity and "citizenship," and what nursing home workers themselves wanted out of their jobs. That involved making the condition and function of nursing home care a major public issue, rather than simply the plight of the workers themselves.[19]

A commonwealth vision has no detailed blueprint implicit within it. BUILD's actions do not presuppose answers to Middle East conflicts or what to do about Social Security or what a good society would look like. Citizen politics is a dynamic process. It suggests key principles, values, redefinitions, and projects that have a wide applicability. It also has a growing audience.

In a glitzy, high-tech age of media consultants and airbrushed personalities, public life usually seems to most citizens a far-distant spectacle. We watch *others* on the political stage—making decisions, deliberating current events. During the 1988 presidential election,

Jesse Jackson challenged the notion of politics-as-spectacle. Most pundits—even, at times, Jackson himself—in labeling his essential message as "liberal" failed to understand how his campaign cut across traditional political divisions in ways that had widespread appeal.[20]

IAF activists tend to be very critical of *any* electoral campaign, including Jesse Jackson's. They fault him for failing to "share the spirit" of power and leadership after the fashion suggested in their document *Tent of the Presence.* In their view, Jackson continued to reflect a "charismatic" sixties style of black church leadership. Moreover, they saw his definition of "public" and "politics" as relatively superficial. But despite such criticisms, Jackson's campaign suggested the growing responsiveness of a wide and diverse audience to core commonwealth themes of citizen power and citizen responsibility which the IAF, in different terms, is reviving.[21]

Jesse Jackson appealed to many who did not especially like his "politics," narrowly defined. White factory workers, farmers, small businesspeople, and many conservatives remarked that he seemed like a "human being," not a corporate spokesman. Polling after the Democratic primary in Wisconsin found that 22 percent of self-described conservative whites had voted for Jackson.[22]

Jackson's view of the American dream envisioned an ongoing struggle—what he called "the ancient and endless cause." It included a legacy of those before—"the blood and sweat of innocents." And it entailed a future, a challenge for listeners to make themselves part of the action. This kind of challenge formed the background for the candidate's visionary theme, the call for "common ground," the title of his speech to the Democratic Convention in Atlanta.

It was not an appeal for Americans to "come and reason together." Rather, Jackson's call involved conflict, anger, and difference. One hundred years before, populist farmers struggling to keep their lands had challenged railroad barons and industrial tycoons— "the masses against the classes." Jackson portrayed the 1980s as a huge party given for the affluent, a party that left the rich richer and the poor behind, conjuring up a strategy as old as that of the Israelites in Egypt: if we don't pull together, we'll be defeated separately. This renewed populism spoke to widespread unease. "I think he captures the essence of America," said Nick Vukovich, a bricklayer in Flint, Michigan, after hearing Jackson talk. "He's people. He's not a corporate front. Four years ago, some people saw him as a threat. I think of him as being the essence of this country."[23]

As with older commonwealth traditions, Jackson's protest went to the heart of what America *stands for* as a society, but in a way that conveyed a sense of difference, not a "melting pot" of cultural or political homogeneity. Indeed, images of the strength that comes from diversity were constitutive of his message. "America is not a blanket, woven from one thread, one color, one cloth. . . . Now, Democrats, we must weave a quilt," he told the convention on July 19, 1988, talking about his grandmother:

> Blacks and Hispanics, when we fight for civil rights, we are right—but our patch is not big enough. Gays and lesbians, when you fight against discrimination . . . you are right—but your patch is not big enough. Conservatives and progressives, when you fight for what you believe, right wing, left wing, hawk, dove, you are right from your point of view, but your point of view is not enough.
>
> But don't despair. Be as wise as my grandmother. Pull the patches and the pieces together, bound by a common thread. When we form a great quilt of unity and common ground, we'll have the power to bring about health care and housing and jobs and education and hope. . . . We the people can win.[24]

Jackson's challenge to the violence of drugs and unemployment was reinforced by the nature of his campaign, a low-budget "people's alternative" to politics as the marketing of slickly packaged personalities. When Jackson said his victories represented "flesh and blood" winning out over "money and computers," he not only connected with people who felt economically left behind by the Reagan years. His message also resonated with millions who worried that local communities and ordinary citizens were endangered by a barren, depersonalized technocracy that idolized the rich and famous.[25]

Further, Jackson—like the first populists but notably unlike demagogues who have claimed the mantle of populism and used it to fuel racial and other prejudices—was not a simple protest candidate, nor did he only promise what *he* would do if elected. Although his concepts of citizen action were thin compared to those of the IAF, at the heart of Jackson's campaign was the call for renewed civic responsibility. In the face of a good deal of initial resistance from some black groups, Jackson in 1988 preached that the preeminent issue was not racism but economic justice that calls for corporations to be accountable for actions that affect workers and the community welfare. And he called upon black and white youths to take positive action against problems like drugs and teenage pregnancy. "Hold your head high. Stick your chest out. You can make it," he declared. Moreover, Jackson emphasized not only the need for an increased sense of personal responsibility but also the need for renewed collective responsibility for basic public goods as well, those things essential to the welfare and survival of the community as a whole.[26]

Thus, Jesse Jackson developed imagery of a public world created through struggle that cut across divisions of class. "We're all in the same boat now," he said, whether children of former slaves brought to America against their will or former immigrants seeking freedom and opportunity. The lion and the lamb, in his account, are both threatened by acid rain, drugs, and decaying bridges. Jackson was the only candidate to talk about the ways in which roads and waste facilities and waterways and other public goods have been jeopardized in recent years by neglect.[27]

In many ways, those pundits who debated endlessly the "electability" of Jackson missed the point. Jackson was not a typical "candidate": his campaign is best seen as the resurfacing of older strands and themes of citizen politics that showed their growing appeal. Ideas such as common ground, citizen responsibility, and the "American Dream" as a constant struggle are put into practice in experiences like Lake Union's, or, in different terms, Baltimore BUILD's.

This commonwealth tradition of citizen politics creates an expansive, dynamic vision: Once renewed, with the power, rootedness, and process of citizen learning needed to make the themes of commonwealth again *believable* in a world of massive institutions and expertise, the sense of politics as an ongoing activity among equals begins to illumine and reframe a series of other questions as well. And it adapts an old understanding to the modern "information age." "Knowledge will forever govern ignorance," wrote James Madison at the nation's birth. "A people that means to be their own governors must arm themselves with the power that knowledge brings." Whatever its effect two hundred years ago, Madison's insight today has a prophetic ring. Democracy, if it is to have any serious meaning at all in the technological, changing world which lies ahead of us, will require a dynamic process of education.

IAF's description of its organizations as "schools for public life" contains a crucial insight for our time. It highlights the disenfranchisement of the citizenry from the foundations of public knowledge, from information to skills to concepts essential for coping effectively with a fast-changing world, and the need to create ways to address the problem. A dynamic education for democracy and citizenship must take place in many settings in our society, and not simply in formal educational institutions or large-scale citizen groups. In the coming years we need to experiment with a variety of new public forums, instruments, civic resource centers, and community commons through which the basic concepts and arts of public life can be relearned by the citizenry.

A wider perspective on commonwealth and commons should draw attention to issues largely unaddressed by low-income groups in the IAF network but that nonetheless get at core issues facing the society as a whole, such as the ecological crisis, the nature of technology, the "built environment"—the quality, heritage, and nature of physical spaces; modern communications media; the quality and nature of labor and work. But in each case, the lessons of recent citizen organizing suggest the need to ground action in an ongoing conversation among citizens—not simply one-way efforts to "mobilize constituencies" around a previously worked-out "program" or "platform." Moreover, citizen politics needs to show how any questions are connected to everyday life experiences in tangible ways; how such issues, defined as major "problems," can be broken down into manageable pieces; and how particular campaigns are tied to the community as a whole.[28]

Citizen efforts that take responsibility for the projects of commonwealth are both means and ends. They illustrate how themes of a challenge to concentrated patterns of power and wealth need to be reintegrated into living contexts, not imagined abstractly. They suggest how our ideas and aspirations for democracy can be refreshed by examination of the actual experiences of citizen action over the past fifty years and more. And they remind us once again that America is a vast laboratory of democratic experiments. Even as we lament the loss of public life, it reappears in a myriad of forms, with intimations of a citizen politics for the future.

Notes

Preface and Acknowledgments

1. From a conservative point of view, for instance, George Will has pointed to the new inequalities and disruptions threatened by the "information society." Using the examples of drug abuse, AIDS, and other hazards, Will quoted James Q. Wilson: "What began as a clever experiment for affluent Americans quickly became a living nightmare for disadvantaged Americans." Will argued,

> It is axiomatic that the rich get richer. They have money to put to work making more money. However, there is a more encompassing axiom: In this information age, the advantaged become more so, and the disadvantaged fall from the back.... Life is increasingly regressive because the benefits of information are distributed disproportionately to those already favored by many advantages. The more certain kinds of information matter, the more unequal society—life—becomes.

See George Will, "In the Modern World, Knowledge Matters as Much as Money," *Minneapolis Tribune*, January 8, 1989.

2. For mainstream views see, for instance, Robert A. Dahl, *Preface to Democratic Theory* (Chicago: University of Chicago Press, 1956); and Giovanni Sartori, *Democratic Theory* (Detroit: Wayne State University Press, 1962). Republican theorists are discussed in chapters 1 and 8 *CommonWealth*. For a sampling of writers in the republican vein in the twentieth century, see Henry S. Kariel, ed., *Frontiers of Democratic Theory* (New York: Random House, 1970).

Quentin Skinner sketches both empirical and normative traditions and offers his own critique in "The Empirical Theorists of Democracy and Their Critics: A Plague on Both Their Houses," *Political Theory*, 1:3 (1973), pp. 277–306; for a criticism of liberal empiricist and socialist traditions, see Norbeto Babbio, *The Future of Democracy* (Minneapolis: University of Minnesota Press, 1987).

3. Alasdair MacIntyre, *After Virtue* (Notre Dame, Ind.: University of Notre Dame Press, 1981).

4. A striking fact about contemporary political theory, across most theoretical positions, is its detachment from those everyday life worlds of communal practice invoked in the abstract. It is as if the history of Africa were being written by historians who not only never visited the continent but also rarely read any of the reports of those who had.

   For a pioneering discussion of the need for feminism to develop a specific theory of *politics,* see Mary G. Dietz, "Learning about Women: Gender, Politics and Power," *Daedalus,* 116:4 (1987), pp. 1–24; for a critique of the ways in which most contemporary political theory eclipses politics itself, see Benjamin Barber, *The Conquest of Politics: Liberal Philosophy in Democratic Times* Princeton: Princeton University Press, 1988).

5. The themes of these thinkers are well described in James T. Kloppenberg, *Uncertain Victory: Social Democracy and Progressivism in European and American Thought, 1870–1920* (New York: Oxford University Press, 1986).

6. Richard Bernstein, *Beyond Objectivism and Relativism: Science, Hermeneutics and Praxis* (Philadelphia: University of Pennsylvania, 1983), p. 229.

7. For instance, Harry C. Boyte, *The Backyard Revolution: Understanding the New Citizen Movement* (Philadelphia: Temple University Press, 1980); Harry C. Boyte, *Community is Possible: Repairing America's Roots* (New York: Harper & Row, 1984); Sara M. Evans and Harry C. Boyte, *Free Spaces: The Sources of Democratic Change in America* (New York: Harper & Row, 1986); Harry C. Boyte, Heather Booth, and Steve Max, *Citizen Action and the New American Populism* (Philadelphia: Temple University Press, 1986); and the collection edited by Boyte and Frank Riessman, *The New Populism: The Politics of Empowerment* (Philadelphia: Temple University Press, 1986). For a discussion of the invisibility of local citizen activism in the seventies, see, for instance, *Christian Science Monitor* articles on "the invisible story" of the decade, December 23 and 26, 1977.

8. See, for instance, Robert Fisher, "Organizing in Search of a Vision," *Commonweal,* May 31, 1985.

Chapter 1
Civic Life and the American Dilemma

1. On the National Civic League's index of civic infrastructure see *Civic Index Workbook* (Boston: National Conference on Civic Renewal, 1987); David Mathews, *The Promise of Democracy* (Dayton: Kettering Foundation, 1988); George Bush, "I Seek the Presidency to Build a Better America," *New York Times,* August 19, 1988.

2. On voting levels, *The Vanishing Voter and the Crisis in American Democracy* (Washington, D.C.: People for the American Way, 1988), and Steve Berg, "Voters Turn Backs on Political Process," *Minneapolis Tribune,* November 13, 1988; E. J. Dionne, "New Poll Shows Attacks by Bush Are Building

Lead: Still, Voters See Campaign as Negative and Dislike the Choice of Nominees," *New York Times*, October 26, 1988; Hunter quoted and polls cited from "The Smear Campaign," *Newsweek*, October 31, 1988; Dionne, "Voters Fault Selection of Presidents," *New York Times*, November 22, 1988; Robert Berke, "Voter Turnout Is 64 Year Low," *New York Times*, December 18, 1988; Gallup poll on preference for neither candidate, *Minneapolis Tribune*, November 19, 1988.

3. On voter turnout, David Glass, Peverill Squire, and Raymond Wolfinger, "Voter Turnout: An International Comparision," *Public Opinion* 6:6 (1984), pp. 49–57; John Sullivan, Michel Shamir, Nigel S. Roberts, and Patrick Walsh, "Political Intolerance and the Structure of Mass Attitudes: A Study of the U.S., Israel, and New Zealand," *Comparative Political Studies*, 17:3 (1984), pp. 319–44; John Sullivan, James Pierkeson, and George Marcus, "An Alternative Conceptualization of Political Tolerance: Illusory Increases, 1950s–1970s," *American Political Science Review*, 73:3 (1979), pp. 781–94; on the rise of racial violence, see for instance the series by Larry Batson in the *Minneapolis Tribune*, "Fear and Fanaticism in the U.S.," beginning December 28, 1986; "Mean Streets in Howard Beach" and "A Chilling Wave of Racism," *Newsweek*, January 5, 1987, and January 25, 1988; Allan Gold, "Educators Seek Answers as Bias on Campus Rises," *New York Times*, January 25, 1988; board game described in Lena Williams, "It Was a Year When Civility Really Took It on the Chin," *New York Times*, December 18, 1988.

4. Paul M. Weyrich, *Cultural Conservatism: Toward a New National Agenda* (Washington, D.C.: Free Congress Research and Education Foundation, 1987), p. 6; see also E. J. Dionne, "Conservative Call for Compassion," *New York Times*, November 20, 1987; Robert Bellah et al., *Habits of the Heart: Individualism and Commitment in the American Experience* (Berkeley: University of California Press, 1985).

5. National Council on Public Works Improvement, *Fragile Foundations* (Washington, D.C.: U.S. Government Printing Office, 1988), pp. 2, 11, 17. See also George Will, "Listen to the Bridges," *Newsweek*, April 25, 1988; Bill Clinton, "America Is Buckling and Leaking," *New York Times*, June 25, 1988; "Study Sees Harm in Reagan's Plan to Shift Services to the Private Sector," *Los Angeles Times*, November 28, 1988.

6. On dropout rates, see U.S. Department of Education, *Dealing With Dropouts: The Urban Superintendents Respond*, cited in Rona Wilensky, "Renewing Urban Schools" (Denver: Education Commission of the States, 1988), p. 1; on students who graduate, Michelle Fine and Pearl Rosenberg, "Dropping Out of High School: The Ideology of School and Work," *Journal of Education*, 165 (1983), pp. 257–72; on the patterns contributing to widespread school failure, especially for minority students, John Goodlad, *A Place Called School* (New York: McGraw Hill), 1984.

7. Carnegie Forum on Education and the Economy, Report of the Task Force on Teaching as Profession, *A Nation Prepared: Teachers for the 21st Century* (New York, 1986); also Henry M. Levin and Russell W. Rumberger, "Educational Requirements for New Technologies: Visions, Pos-

sibilities and Current Realities," *Educational Policy,* 1:3 (1987); on issues of political will, see Wilensky, "Renewing Urban Schools."

8. "Commonwealth Coalitions" of community, consumer, rural, and other groups have developed in both Kentucky and Massachusetts. On the differences among information, knowledge, and wisdom, see T. S. Eliot, "The Rock," *Collected Poems* (New York: Harcourt Brace Jovanovich, 1955).

9. Daniel Kemmis, "Barn Building: Cooperation and the Economy of the West," *Kettering Review* (Summer 1988), pp. 6–14; quotes from 6, 7, 8.

10. Thomas Jefferson quoted from Bruce Johansen, *Forgotten Founders: Benjamin Franklin, the Iroquois and the Rationale for the American Revolution* (Ipswich: Gambit, 1982), p. 102, 112; Madison from James Kloppenberg, "The Virtues of Liberalism: Christianity, Republicanism and Ethics in Early American Political Discourse," *Journal of American History,* 74:1 (June 1987), p. 27.

11. For classic twentieth-century views that reflect a thin or largely "liberal" view of politics, see for instance Joseph Schumpeter, *Capitalism, Socialism and Democracy* (London: George Allen and Unwin, 1943); Robert A. Dahl, *Preface to Democratic Theory* (Chicago: Chicago University Press, 1956); and Giovanni Sartori, *Democratic Theory* (Detroit: Wayne State University Press, 1962). For alternative and more participatory, communitarian writings, see for instance John Dewey, *The Public and Its Problems* (Athens, Ohio: Swallow Press, 1954); Alasdair MacIntyre, *After Virtue* (Notre Dame: University of Notre Dame Press 1981); Fred Dallmayr, *Polis and Praxis: Exercises in Contemporary Political Theory* (Cambridge, Mass.: M.I.T. Press, 1984). For contrasts, see also Henry S. Kariel, ed., *Frontiers of Democratic Theory* (New York: Random House, 1970); Kariel's collection illustrates both the "thinning" of conventional understandings of politics to a narrowly electoral view and, in my opinion, the idealized quality of alternative participatory democratic political theory in the twentieth century. Quentin Skinner sketches both empirical and normative traditions and offers his own critique in "The Empirical Theorists of Democracy and Their Critics: A Plague on Both Their Houses," *Political Theory,* 1:3 (1973), pp. 287–306; for a good brief sketch of the narrowness of conventional political science treatments of "politics," see also Barbara Nelson, "Women's Poverty, Women's Citizenship: The Political Consequences of Economic Marginality," *Signs,* 10:2 (1984), pp. 209–31. For a criticism of both liberal empiricist and socialist traditions, see Norberto Bobbio, *The Future of Democracy* (Minneapolis: University of Minnesota Press, 1987).

For a useful critique of the ways conventional left theory sees politics as largely derivative and instrumental (in a fashion with certain parallels to liberalism), see Gareth Stedman Jones, *Languages of Class: Studies in English Working Class History, 1832–1982* (Cambridge: Cambridge University Press, 1983). In particular, Jones's recent essay in this collection, "Rethinking Chartism," conveys a sense of the specificity and constitutive quality of politics and political language, and shows the fruitful new lines of inquiry that are opened up with such an approach; Joan

Scott, "Gender: A Useful Category of Historical Analysis," *American Historical Review*, 91:5 (1986), pp. 1053–75, is similarly suggestive.

Michel Sandel, in *Liberalism and the Limits of Justice* (Cambridge: Cambridge University Press, 1982), describes this tradition as a classic liberal approach, concerned with what he calls "the unencumbered individual" that is imagined to be ontologically prior to any social or historical context. For a thoughtful critique of the foundations of the mainstream liberal theory of politics from a feminist perspective, see Mary G. Dietz, "Learning About Women: Gender, Politics and Power," *Daedalus*, 116: 4 (Fall 1987), pp. 1–24; for a powerful analysis and critique of the epistemological assumptions of liberalism and most contemporary political theory, see Benjamin Barber, *The Conquest of Politics* (Princeton: Princeton University Press, 1988).

12. William M. Sullivan, *Reconstructing Public Philosophy* (Berkeley: University of California Press, 1986), pp. 159, 157, 163, 215.

13. So far the very existence of widespread populist citizen activism has rarely been acknowledged in either the national media or the modern academy. The extent of such efforts is described in more detail in chapter 5, especially note 27. See also Harry C. Boyte, *The Backyard Revolution: Understanding the New Citizen Movement* (Philadelphia: Temple University Press, 1980); Carl Boggs, *Social Movements in the West* (Philadelphia: Temple, 1986).

14. Daniel Bell, *The Coming of Post-Industrial Society: A Venture in Social Forecasting* (New York: Basic Books, 1973); Kenneth Boulding, *Meaning of the Twentieth Century: The Great Transition* (New York: Harper & Row, 1964); Harlan Cleveland, *The Knowledge Executive* (New York: E. P. Dutton, 1985), p. 20. For critical perspectives, see Peter N. Stearns, "Is There a Post-Industrial Society?" reprinted in Leigh Estabrook, *Libraries in Post-Industrial Society* (Phoenix: Oryx, 1977), pp. 8–18; and Michael Harrington, "Post-Industrial Society and the Welfare State," Eastabrook, *Libraries*, pp. 18–29.

15. The concept of the twentieth century as a "managerial era" is developed well in Robert Reich, *The Next Frontier: A Provocative Program for Economic Renewal* (New York: Penguin Books, 1983); for a discussion of the hypothetico-deductive model, see Bernstein, *Beyond Objectivism*, and Donald W. Fiske, and Richard A. Shweder, *Metatheory in Social Science: Pluralisms and Subjectivities* (Chicago: University of Chicago Press, 1986.

16. On the clientization of the citizenry, see for instance Barton Bledstein, *The Culture of Professionalism: The Middle Class and the Development of Higher Education in America* (New York: W. W. Norton, 1976); Christopher Lasch, *Haven in a Heartless World: The Family Besieged* (New York: Basic Books, 1977); and Joseph Tussman, "Obligation and the Body Politic," in Kariel, *Frontiers of Democratic Theory*, pp. 18–21. This is developed further in Chapter Three.

17. For instance, Joan C. Durrance in her book *Armed for Action: Library Response to Citizen Information Needs* (New York: Neal Schuman, 1984) studied a cross-section of citizen activists and found that almost all success-

ful leaders were sophisticated consumers and users of information, skilled in knowing where to find out what they needed to know.

18. Milan Kundera, *The Book of Laughter and Forgetting* (New York: Penguin Books, 1981), p. 3; Zuboff quoted in Garry Emmons interview with Zuboff, "Smart Machines and Learning People," *Harvard Magazine,* November-December 1988, p. 60; see also Shoshana Zuboff, *In the Age of the Smart Machine* (New York: Basic Books, 1988).

19. For a discussion about the ways "knowledge" differs as a resource from things like capital or raw materials, see Cleveland, *Knowledge Executive,* especially pp. 29–35.

Chapter 2
The Populist Commonwealth

1. On the collapse of faith in communism and Marxism around the world, see the poignant three part-series by Serge Schemann, "Communism Now: What Is It?" *New York Times,* January 22–24, 1989; for a sampling of discussion of global resources as commonwealth, see reports from an international symposium on governance, edited by Harlan Cleveland and Lea Burdette, *The Global Commons* (Minneapolis: Humphrey Institute, 1988).

2. Sombart himself ascribed the absence of a socialist movement comparable to Germany's to Americans' relative affluence—"all socialist utopias have foundered upon roast beef and apple pie"—although he thought the condition a temporary one.

  For excellent summaries of debates over the question, see Richard Oestreicher, "Urban Working-Class Political Behavior and Theories of American Electoral Politics, 1870–1940," *Journal of American History,* 74:4 (March 1988), pp. 1257–86; Michael Harrington, *Socialism* (New York: Bantam Books, 1972); and Eric Foner's remarkable essay "Why Is There No Socialism in the United States?" *History Workshop,* 17 (Spring, 1984) pp. 57–80.

  James T. Kloppenberg in his recent, fine study, *Uncertain Victory: Social Democracy and Progressivism in European and American Thought, 1870–1920* (New York: Oxford University Press, 1986), also summarizes the argument. Kloppenberg establishes that the welfare state as it came to embody technocratic themes was different from—and far less democratic than—the views of many of the late-nineteenth- and early-twentieth-century theorists who are seen as its architects.

  Harrington's argument about America's "invisible social democratic movement"—the labor unions and their civil rights, intellectual, and other allies who increasingly shaped Democratic party policies in directions similar to European socialist programs—is found in *Socialism.* Harrington here echoes the views of Richard Hofstadter and, more recently, J. David Greenstone. See Seymour Martin Lipset, "Americans Sneer at Liberalism. Why?" *New York Times,* October 28, 1988; Greenstone, *Labor in American Politics* (New York: Alfred A. Knopf, 1969).

3. Foner has been almost a unique voice in pointing out that the relative absence of a strong socialist or social democratic party in the twentieth century did not signal a void, but rather the presence of something else. "Pre-capitalist culture, it appears, was the incubator of resistance to capitalist development in the United States," wrote Foner:

> The world of the artisan and small farmer persisted in some parts of the United States into the twentieth century, and powerfully influenced American radical movements. . . . These movements inherited an older republican tradition hostile to large accumulations of property, but viewing small property as the foundation of economic and civic autonomy. . . . Not the *absence* of non-liberal ideas, but the *persistence* of a radical vision resting on small property inhibited the rise of socialist ideologies. ("Why Is There No Socialism," p. 63).

4. For a discussion of the strong liberal focus on redistributive justice that has developed in contemporary American political theory—much the same as Harrington's emphasis on the "invisible" social democratic quality of American liberalism—see Michel Sandel, *Liberalism and the Limits of Justice* (Cambridge: Cambridge University Press, 1982).

5. For discussions of the importance of understanding language in context, see for instance Eugene Nida, *Toward a Science of Translating* (Leiden: E. J. Brill, 1964); also Michael Stubbs, *Discourse Analysis* (Chicago: University of Chicago Press, 1983); see also Quentin Skinner, "The Empirical Theorists of Democracy and Their Critics: A Plague on Both Their Houses," *Political Theory*, 1:3 (August 1973), pp. 287–306; Skinner, "Some Problems in the Analysis of Political Thought and Action," *Political Theory*, 2:3 (August 1974), pp. 277–303; and rejoinders, Jonathan Wiener, "Quentin Skinner's Hobbes," *Political Theory* 2:3 (August 1974), pp. 251–60, and Gordon Schochet, "Quentin Skinner's Method," *Political Theory*, 2:3 (August 1974), p. 261–75.

   For a summary of the methodological literature and its impact on intellectual history, see also James T. Kloppenberg, "The Virtues of Liberalism: Christianity, Republicanism and Ethics in Early American Political Discourse," *Journal of American History* 74:1 (June 1987), pp. 9–33.

6. Pendleton quoted from Gordon Wood, *Creation of the American Republic: 1776–1787* (Chapel Hill, University of North Carolina Press, 1969), p. 56. This conception of government dedicated to the general welfare included a challenge to "private" interests, when necessary, that led to expanded governmental policing of large economic interests even in the early years of the republic. Such themes of the commonwealth were clearly illustrated in the career of Lemuel Shaw, who from 1830 to 1860 served as Chief Justice of the Supreme Court of Massachusetts. As Leonard W. Levy put it in his biography of Shaw.

> The commonwealth idea precluded the laissez-faire state whose function was simply to keep peace and order. . . . The people of Massachusetts expected their Commonwealth to participate actively

in their economic affairs.... Shaw taught that "all property ... is derived directly or indirectly from the government, and held subject to those general regulations, which are necessary to the common good and general welfare."

Such a view of government, in turn, rested on a theory of "men as by nature social," as Shaw put it, and a political theory

> that all power resides originally in the whole people as a social community, that all political power is derived from them, is designed to be exercised solely for the general good, and limited to the accomplishment of that object.

Leonard W. Levy, *The Law of the Commonwealth and Chief Justice Shaw* (New York: Oxford University Press, 1957), pp. 306, 309, Shaw quoted from p. 306.

7. Early English uses from *Oxford English Dictionary (OED)*; Cicero from "Common Good" entry, *New Catholic Encyclopedia (NCE)* (Washington, D.C.: Catholic University Press, 1967).

8. Cicero from "Common Good" entry, *NCE.*

9. Parliamentary act quoted from *OED*; for a treatment of the related concept of common good in Christian, especially Catholic, thought, see the entry under "Common Good," *NCE*, 1967 edition, and Alan Brinkley, *Voices of Protest* (New York: Alfred A. Knopf, 1982), pp. 76–77; James Harrington, *The Political Writings of*, edited with an Introduction by Charles Blitzner (New York: Liberal Arts Press, 1955), p. 45; Mark Goldie has a useful discussion of the ways in which contemporary theorists have slighted the religious themes that also find expression in Harrington's *Oceana,* in "The Civil Religion of James Harrington," in Anthony Pagden, ed., *Ideas in Context: The Languages of Political Theory in Early-Modern Europe* (Cambridge: Cambridge University Press, 1987).

10. Adams from Oscar and Mary Flug Handlin, *Commonwealth: A Study of the Role of Government in the American Economy: Massachusetts, 1774–1861* (Cambridge, Mass.: Harvard University Press, 1969), pp. 29–30. Adams drew very directly on the writings of Harrington, especially for his theories of property and of balanced government. For the most elaborate treatment of Harrington's thought and its influence in the "country" tradition of opposition to the Crown, see J. G. A. Pocock, *The Machiavellian Moment: Florentine Political Thought and the Atlantic Republic Tradition* (Princeton: Princeton University Press, 1975); for an alternative view, see John P. Diggins, *The Lost Soul of American Politics: Virtue, Self-Interest and the Foundations of Liberalism* (New York: Basic Books, 1984).

11. Quotes from Wood, *Creation of the Republic*, pp. 32, 55.

12. Ibid., pp. 55, 54.

13. Quotes on male virtues and public life from ibid., p. 52.

14. The account of Adams's *Dissertation* and the deletion of the section on property is from Gary B. Nash, *The Urban Crucible: The Northern Seaports*

and the Origins of the American Revolution (Cambridge, Mass.: Harvard University Press, 1976), p. 223; Adams on rabble quoted in Wood, *Creation,* p. 62.

15. Adams quoted in Wood, *Creation,* p. 574; Hamilton in Vernon Louis Parrington, *Main Currents in American Thought: An Interpretation of American Literature from the Beginnings to 1920,* vol. 1, 1620–1800 (New York: Harcourt, Brace, 1927), p. 298 (italics in original).

16. As historians Oscar and Mary Handlin described the resonances of commonwealth in Massachusetts, for instance:

> For the farmers and seamen, for the fishermen, artisans and new merchants, commonwealth repeated the lessons they knew from the organization of churches and towns, and it embodied the wisdom of a people many decades in the wilderness . . . the value of common action. . . . The Revolution was, at once, evidence of their power when united, and the repository of hopes for which . . . they had endured hardships and sacrifices (*Commonwealth,* p. 30, 16).

Such a background provided the most distinctive American innovation in political theory and practice: the concept of popular derivation of governments—that governments are created by and beholden to *the people.* As Thomas Paine put it, "A constitution is not the act of a government, but of a people constituting a government"; quoted in Hannah Arendt, *On Revolution* (New York: Penguin Books, 1963), p. 145. The voluntary foundations of a particular strand of American public life are well described in David Mathews, "The Independent Sector and the Political Responsibilities of the Public," keynote address to the Spring Research Forum, Independent Sector, Washington, D.C., March 19, 1987.

Kammerer is quoted from Russel L. Hanson, " 'Commons' and 'Commonwealth' at the American Founding," paper presented to the Conference on Conceptual Change and the Constitution of the U.S., Conference for the Study of Political Thought, Washington, D.C., April 15, 1987, p. 36.

17. Gary B. Nash, *Race, Class and Politics: Essays on American Colonial and Revolutionary Society* (Urbana: University of Illinois Press, 1986); also Gary Kulik, "Dams, Fish and Farmers: The Defense of Public Rights in Eighteenth-Century Rhode Island," in Steven Hahn and Jonathan Prude, *The Countryside in the Age of Capitalist Transformation* (Chapel Hill: University of North Carolina Press, 1985), pp. 25–50.

18. "Common Good" entry, *NCE*; for a discussion of Aquinas's theory of property and his role in the Renaissance, see Quentin Skinner, *The Foundations of Modern Political Thought,* vol. 1: *The Renaissance* (Cambridge: Cambridge University Press, 1978).

There has been very little discussion to date of the Jubilee tradition which runs as a dramatic commonwealth thread through the Old and New Testaments. One exception is found in Robert Sloan, Jr., *The Favorable Year of the Lord: A Study of Jubilary Theology in the Gospel of Luke* (Ph.D.

dissertation, University of Basel, Austin, Texas, 1977). There is evidence that this tradition comes from premonarchical, Israelite history, during which, according to some modern scholars, a loose egalitarian confederacy of antiimperial groups emerged to challenge the power of urban city-state empires. See for instance Norman Gottwald, *The Tribes of Yahweh: A Sociology of the Religion of Liberated Israel, 1250–1050 B.C.E.* (New York: Orbis, 1979).

19. Franklin quoted from Bruce Johansen, *Forgotten Founders: Benjamin Franklin, the Iroquois and the Rationale for the American Revolution* (Ipswich, Mass.: Gambit, 1982), pp. 85, 88, 104–5.

20. Richard Lingeman, *Small Town America: A Narrative History 1620 to the Present* (Boston: Houghton Mifflin, 1980), p. 29.

    "Commons," as Ivan Illich has described, bears close resemblance to the German terms *Allmende* and *Gemeinheit* and the Italian *gli usi civici*. Illich defines the commons as

    > that part of the environment which lay beyond the person's own threshold and outside his own possession, but to which, however, that person had a recognized claim of usage—not to produce commodities but to provide for the subsistence of kin. Neither wilderness nor home is commons, but that part of the environment for which customary law exacts specific forms of community respect

    Illich conveys the nonprivate nature of the commons, and concepts of stakeholding and responsibility, but he neglects the public and power dimensions. See chaps. 8 and 9 of *CommonWealth*. Ivan Illich, *Gender* (New York: Pantheon Books, 1982), pp. 17–18.

21. For a detailed discussion of New England commons, see John Stilgoe, "Town Common and Village Green in New England: 1620 to 1981," in Ronald Lee Fleming and Lauri A. Halderman, *On Common Ground: Caring for Shared Land from Town Common to Urban Park* (Cambridge, Mass.: Harvard Common Press, 1982). One little explored but fascinating question is the cross-cultural interaction of conceptions of commons in American history. North American Indians, for instance, had a view of all land and material goods, outside personal possessions, as commons, but in a somewhat different sense, endowed with living spirit; to date, no evidence that I am aware of has surfaced of early European immigrants' having consciously reflected upon Indian meanings of the term, although eighteenth-century discussions of Indian conceptions of property were frequent in both North America and Europe. See, for instance, Bruce Johansen, *Forgotten Founders*. In the Southwest, *mexicanos'* struggles to maintain traditional common land use led to the formation of El Partido del Pueblo Unido in 1890, which forged alliances with the Populist party around issues like land and workers' rights. Billy Pope, "Down on the Farm: The Agrarian Revolt in American History," *Radical America*, 16:1 & 2 (1982), pp. 139–47.

    For centuries the theme of common grazing lands, footpaths, waterways, and other public property—and especially the struggle against their enclosure by commercially minded interests—had given a radical, popular edge to the language of commonwealth. Thomas More's sixteenth-century *Utopia,* for instance, can clearly be seen as part furious protest against enclosures of commons by sheep-farming interests. "Look in what parts of the realm doth grow the finest and therefore dearest wood," More had his mythical visitor to England, Raphael Hythloday, pronounce.

> [T]here noblemen and gentlemen, yea and certain abbots . . . much annoying the public weal, leave no ground for tillage, they inclose all in pastures; they tear down houses; they pluck down towns, and leave nothing standing, but only the church to make of it a sheephouse . . . the unreasonable covetousness of a few hath turned that thing to the utter undoing of your island, in the which thing the chief felicity of your realm did consist.

Sir Thomas More, *Utopia: The First Book of the Communication of Raphael Hythloday, Concerning the Best State of a Commonwealth* (New York: P. F. Collier, Harvard Classic Series edited by Charles W. Eliot, 1910).

In English history, deliberation by villagers about the exercise of the rights and upkeep of common lands, footpaths, food lands, and fishing areas, as well as maintenance of common buildings like the village church, gave to middle-level peasantry a constant, daily schooling in rough democracy. As historians Edward Miller and John Hatcher described the common pattern, sometimes village communities collaborated with lords, sometimes they engaged in bitter struggle with them, but there was customarily space for regular consultation: "There is . . . a good deal of evidence for the corporate action of village communities, especially where the interests of its members interlocked in the communal routines of open-field agriculture and common pastures." Male villagers regularly promulgated laws, sometimes in joint consultation with lords, over "such things as gleaning after harvest, exercises of rights of common and the grazing of village paths and ways." Churches—the village site of feats and celebrations, public deliberation, courts, storage, refuge from raids, dances, marketplace, sometimes even theater for pagan plays, banquets, and drinking bouts—were another kind of commons involving not only rights to use but clear responsibilities. Parishioners "were called on to keep the nave in repair, the churchyard in good order, to provide many items of equipment including . . . bells for the steeple, a pyx, a Lenten veil, a font, a bier for the dea, a vessel for holy water and certain other items of equipment" as well as taxes and tithes of corn, garden produce, and livestock. On the traditions of open-field agriculture in England, see Trevor Rowley, ed., *The Origins of Open-Field Agriculture* (London: Croom Helm, 1981); Edward Miller and John Hatcher, *Medieval England: Rural Society and Economic Change, 1086–1348* (London: Longman, 1978); Warren Ortman Ault, *Open-Field Farming in Medieval England: A Study of Village By-Laws* (London: Allen and Unwin, 1972); on the effects of the English Civil War, Christopher Hill, *The Cen-*

tury of Revolution: 1603–1714 (New York: W. W. Norton, 1961), pp. 148–
49, also Miller and Hatcher, *Medieval England,* pp. 105, 106, 108–9.

The threat to the commons gave rise to popular radical groups like
the Levellers and Diggers during the English Civil War period, while,
ironically, the conversion of lands held by the king (who generally held
formal title of commons) to unconditional ownership by the large land-
holders in 1660 opened the way for enclosures on a vast scale in the
eighteenth century.

22. Nash, *Race, Class and Politics,* p. 249.

23. As Gary Kulik put it: "Farmers saw their rights to fish threatened by
powerful ironmasters closely tied to the colony's political leadership.
They drew upon a common sensibility—distrust of corrupt and arbitrary power." Kulik, "Dams, Fish and Farmers" pp. 36–41.

24. *Federalist* 57, quoted in Wood, *Creation,* p. 477; Bryan in Herbert J. Storing, *What the Anti-Federalists Were For: The Political Thought of the Opponents
of the Constitution* (Chicago: University of Chicago Press, 1981), p. 115.

25. Sean Wilentz, "Artisan Republican Festivals and the Rise of Class Conflict," in Michael H. Frisch and Daniel J. Walkowitz, eds., *Working Class
America: Essays on Labor, Community and American Society* (Urbana: University of Illinois Press, 1983); quote from p. 61.

26. Working Men's Committee quoted in Leadership Program Selections,
Humphrey Institute Leadership Program Essays, p. 305.

Similarly, parks were proposed by advocates like Frederick Law Olm-
sted partially to "inspire communal feelings among all urban classes,
muting resentments over disparities of wealth and fashion." Parks were
often called "the commons" or "common," yet they soon became objects of conflict over upkeep, usage, and differing cultural norms. "Our
wealthy citizens live in elegant homes on all the hills of Worcester,"
protested a letter to the working-class newspaper *Worcester Sunday Tele-
gram:*

> They have unrestricted fresh air and perfect sewage, their streets
> are well cleaned and lighted, the sidewalks are everywhere, and
> Elm Park, that little dream of beauty, is conveniently near. The
> toilers live on the lowlands, their houses are close together, the
> hills restrict the fresh air, huge chimneys pour out volumes of
> smoke, the marshy places give out offensiveness and poison the air,
> the canal remains uncovered, the streets are different. . . .

Quoted from Roy Rosenzweig, "Middle-Class Parks and Working-Class
Play: The Struggle over Recreational Space in Worcester, Massachusetts,
1870–1910," in Herbert G. Gutman and Donald H. Bell, eds., *The New
England Working Class and the New Labor History* (Urbana: University of
Illinois Press, 1987), pp. 214, 221.

27. On early nineteenth-century popular republicanism based among artisans, see Sean Wilenz, *Chants Democratic: New York City and the Rise of the
American Working Class, 1788–1859* (New York: Oxford University Press,

1984). Harper quoted in Philip Foner, *The Voice of Black America* (New York: Simon & Schuster, 1972), p. 431. On the maternal commonwealth, see Sara M. Evans, *Born for Liberty: A History of Women in America* (New York: Free Press, 1989); on labor organizations—especially the Knights of Labor, the largest nineteenth-century workers' organization—see Leon Fink, *Workingmen's Democracy: The Knights of Labor and American Politics* (Urbana: University of Illinois Press, 1983). Also Foner, *Reconstruction: America's Unfinished Revolution, 1863–1877* (New York: Harper & Row, 1988).

28. Homestead workers quoted in Oestreicher, "Urban Working-Class Political Behavior," p. 1259; strike described in Robert Reich, *The Next Frontier: A Provocative Program for Economic Renewal* (New York: Penguin Books, 1983), p. 37.

   The emergence of working-class, women's, and black forms of popular struggle and the ways they gave a distinctive cast to American insurgent civic traditions are described in detail in Sara M. Evans and Harry C. Boyte, *Free Spaces: The Sources of Democratic Change in America* (New York: Harper & Row, 1986).

29. See Gianna Pomata, "A Common Heritage: The Historical Memory of Populism in Europe and the United States," in Harry C. Boyte and Frank Riessman, eds., *The New Populism: The Politics of Empowerment* (Philadelphia: Temple University Press, 1986), pp. 30–50. For similar currents in European and American populist movements, see also Steven Hahn, *Roots of Southern Populism: Yeoman Farmers and the Transformation of the Georgia Upcountry, 1850–1890* (New York: Oxford University Press, 1983). For a close examination of populist themes and their differences from Marxism in twentieth-century Third World movements and industrial societies alike, see Vladimir G. Khoros, *Populism: Its Past, Present and Future* (Moscow: Progress Publishers, 1984). This book by Khoros, a senior Soviet scholar, is fascinating on a number of counts, not least because of the way it clearly challenged Marxist orthodoxy and anticipated *glasnost* and the *perestroika* movement under Gorbachev.

30. Richard Darman, "Historic Tax Reform: The Populist Correction," speech to the Institute for Research on Economics of Taxation, Washington, D.C., April 15, 1985; Tom Harkin, interview with Harry Boyte, Washington, April 30, 1985. For a description of the "left" and "right" populist debate, see Michael Kazin, "Populism: The Perilous Promise," *Socialist Review* 89 (1986), pp. 99–106, which describes a conference pitting figures like Darman and Newt Gingrich against Harkin, Jim Hightower, and others with a progressive perspective. For a description of populist themes in the 1988 election, see Paul Taylor, "Democrats Against the 'Establishment,'" *Washington Post,* January 6, 1988; E. J. Dionne, "Twin Messages of Protest," *New York Times,* April 10, 1988; and Robert Kuttner, *The Life of the Party: Democratic Prospects in 1988 and Beyond* (New York: Penguin Books, 1988). On the election aftermath, see for instance David Shribman and David Rogers, "Democrats' Troubles in Winning Presidency Are Likely to Persist," *Wall Street Journal,* November 15, 1988.

Critics have argued that politically different populist appeals use an apparently similar vocabulary, made up of terms like "community," "family," "local empowerment," and "the people." Thus, for instance, Ronald Reagan achieved much of his success through populist-sounding appeals. During the fight for the 1980 Republican nomination, the polls conducted by the *Washington Post* found that "in sharp contrast to other Republicans, Reagan does substantially better with rank and file Republicans who seem skeptical of big business." Instead of posing as the candidate of big business—those he called "the country club set"—Reagan titled himself the candidate of the blue-collar worker and the small businessman. He rhetorically championed those hometown institutions and commitments that seemed to many Americans at risk, calling for "a shift of power away from Washington." As George Will put it, in the elections of both 1980 and 1984 Reagan spoke "the language of the small republic renaissance." He called for "an end to giantism" and for "a return to the human scale . . . that human beings can understand and cope with; the scale of the local fraternal lodge, the church organization, the block club, the farm bureau." Hedrick Smith, "Reagan's Populist Coalition," *New York Times,* March 6, 1980; Reagan quote from William A. Schambra, *The Quest for Community and the Quest for a New Public Philosophy* (Washington: American Enterprise Institute, 1983), pp. 32–33; George Will, "The Real Campaign of 1984," *Newsweek,* September 2, 1985.

31. This was the central argument, for instance, in Seymour Martin Lipset's often overlooked early work on the populist farmers' movement in Saskatchewan, *Agrarian Socialism* (Berkeley: University of California Press, 1950). See also Lawrence Goodwyn, *Democratic Promise: The Populist Movement in America* (New York: Oxford University Press, 1976); Hahn, *Roots of Southern Populism.* Alan Brinkley's book *Voices of Protest* (New York: Alfred A. Knopf, 1982) suggests the consequences of the absence of such experience in his examination of the movements of Huey Long and Father Coughlin in the 1930s, a subject taken up in chap. 3.

32. Jones quoted in Hahn, *Roots,* p. 239; quote on "plain people" from the Preamble to the Populist Party Platform of 1892, which read in more detail:

> Corruption dominates the ballot box, the legislatures, the Congress and touches even the ermine of the bench. Assembled on the anniversary of the birth of the illustrious general who led the first great revolution on this continent against oppression, filled with the sentiments which actuated that grand generation, we seek to restore government of the republic to the hands of the "plain people," with whom it originated. (Goodwyn, *Democratic Promise,* p. 265).

33. These descriptions of America's transformation are taken from Reich, *The Next Frontier,* pp. 30–32.

34. Recent historical analysis has accented the ways in which republican *utopian* themes of the nineteenth century seemed idealized and ethereal

in the world of modern industry, urbanization, mass communications, and large government. According to historian John Kasson, the late nineteenth-century utopian literature of American writers like William Dean Howells—imagining a "commonwealth" of small, egalitarian, participatory communities bound together by inexpensive transportation systems, dedicated to craft and beauty, to replace the depredations of rising capitalism—seemed largely an "ethical tonic . . . sweetened with Christian molasses and laced with a reproving sulphur." Howells, dean of American letters during the later years of the last century, seemed to convey a nostalgia, between whose ideals and the emerging industrial world "yawned an immense gulf." John Kasson, *Civilizing the Machine* (New York: Penguin Books, 1976), p. 234; Brinkley, *Voices of Protest,* p. 166.

35. Hahn, *Roots,* pp. 251–53.

36. "The freedom to which [agrarian radicals referred] was not merely that founded upon ownership of one's person and exchange in the marketplace," as one historian of the Georgia movement, Steven Hahn, summarized. It was a freedom "founded upon control over productive resources, labor time and subsistence which, in turn, could be realized only through membership in the commonwealth of producers." Ibid., p. 254.

37. Doster quoted from Norman Pollack, ed., *The Populist Mind* (Indianapolis: Bobbs Merrill, 1967), pp. 12–13.

38. On criticisms of populism, see for instance Bruce Palmer, *Man Over Money: The Southern Populist Critique of American Capitalism* (Chapel Hill: University of North Carolina Press, 1980); Jeff Lustig, "Community and Social Class," *democracy* 1:2 (Spring 1981), pp. 96–108; Jim Green, "Culture, Politics and Workers' Response to Industrialization in the US," *Radical America* 16:1 & 2 (January-April 1982), pp. 101–28; Carl Boggs, *Social Movements in the West* (Philadelphia: Temple University Press, 1987); Ernesto Laclau, *Politics and Ideology in Marxist Theory: Capitalism, Fascism, Populism* (London: Verso, 1977); Robert Fisher, *Let the People Decide: Neighborhood Organizing in America* (Boston: G. K. Hall, 1984).

39. Martin Luther King, Jr., *Why We Can't Wait* (New York: Harper & Row, 1963), p. 99.

40. As social-movement theorist Richard Flacks described the pattern of the origin of social protest in resistance: "Most commonly, popular movements arise as efforts to resist threats to established patterns of everyday life. Movements are particularly apt to occur when these threats are seen as the fault of those in authority." Flacks, "Making History vs. Making Life," *Working Papers for a New Society,* Summer 1974, p. 60; this argument is expanded in Flacks, *Making History* (New York: Columbia University Press, 1988).

41. Expanding somewhat on a typology of social movement once suggested by Barrington Moore, "democratic" movement here embraces both the struggle by a self-conscious group for control over its destiny within a given setting and the notion of free and cooperative participation. As

such, it can be contrasted with forms of authoritarian communal movements, or with "libertarian" movements resting on a marketplace,
highly individualistic model of human beings. This definition is developed in Evans and Boyte, *Free Spaces.*

42. See Goodwyn, *Democratic Promise;* also Hahn, *Roots;* for a rich and fascinating view of the Knights of Labor's republican themes in this vein,
see Fink, *Workingmen's Democracy;* for a detailed discussion of the Populist party platform, Palmer, *Man Over Money;* for a discussiono of populism's relative democracy, Walter K. Nugent, *The Tolerant Populists: Kansas Populism and Nativism* (Chicago: University of Chicago Press, 1963).

    Rowland Bertoff has a fascinating discussion of the social founda-
tions for the continuing resonance of republican themes in the experiences of immigrants, as well as native-born Americans, in his piece
"Peasant and Artisans, Puritans and Republicans," *Journal of American
History* 69:3 (1982), pp. 579–98. He argues that Americans' original
dream of rough communal equality, sustained by an independent citizenry, was nourished by wave after wave of ethnic groups hoping to
recreate communities of self-sufficient, self-governing freeholders. Such
aspirations fit common patterns in the areas immigrants came from.
Typically, they were "middle peasants," whose families had worked
mainly for themselves, handing over only a small portion of their produce to the nobility. They had considerable experience in a range of
cooperative activities, such as open plowing and harvesting. Their land,
by custom and sometimes law, was handed down over generations, with
considerable security of tenure. With others of similar rank—the bulk
of male adults in many villages—they had had considerable practice in
a rough self-government concerning day-to-day affairs. Values included
hard work, rough equality, self-government, independence, frugality—
all bound by a strong sense of life in common. Values and aspirations
were similar among immigrants from urban areas, who often retained
older rural traditions and sustained communal participation through
an array of craft, fraternal, sororal, and mutual-aid associations. John
Bodnar's extensive studies of immigrants largely reinforces this por-
trait; see Bodnar, *The Transplanted: A History of Immigrants in Urban America* (Bloomington: Indiana University Press, 1985).

43. See for instance C. Vann Woodward, *Tom Watson: Agrarian Rebel* (New
York: Oxford University Press, 1963).

Chapter 3
The Eclipse of the Citizen

1. For a vivid view of populism's ardent embrace of science and technology, see Bruce Palmer, *Man Over Money: The Southern Populist Critique of
American Capitalism* (Chapel Hill: University of North Carolina Press,
1980); for a discussion of the excessive reliance of early twentieth-
century participatory democrats like Dewey on scientific epistemology,
see William Sullivan, *Reconstruction Public Philosophy* (Berkeley: University of California Press, 1985).

In defending democratic philosophers, progressives, and social democrats like Thomas Hill Green, Henry Sidgwich, Alfred Fouillee, Richard Ely, Walter Rauschenbusch, John Dewey, and Beatrice and Sidney Webb against charges that they were positivists, James T. Kloppenberg inadvertently describes well the flaw that would feed welfare state structures whose authoritarianism most of these individuals would have found abhorrent. Kloppenberg admits such figures were, by and large, enamored of the scientific method. And he argues, correctly, that true science is not dogmatic; it is by its best ideals always open ended and experimental—constantly engaged in a process of evaluation and debate. But from a democratic perspective on knowledge about human society and politics, dogmatic claims of truth are not really the problem with scientific methodology; the model of detachment from engagement with living, ongoing communities of ordinary citizens that appears in the scientific ideal is by far science's most problematic feature when reproduced as the standard of judgment for politics. See James T. Kloppenberg, *Uncertain Victory: Social Democracy and Progressivism in European and American Thought, 1870–1920* (New York: Oxford University Press, 1986).

2. For a brief history of usages and concepts of class, see Raymond Williams, *Keywords: A Vocabulary of Culture and Society* (New York: Oxford University Press, 1976), pp. 51–59.

3. *Communist Manifesto* in Lewis Feuer, ed., *Marx and Engels: Basic Writings on Politics and Philosophy* (Garden City, N.Y.: Doubleday, 1959), pp. 1–41; Karl Marx, *18th Brumaire of Louis Bonaparte* (New York: International Publishers, 1963), pp. 123–24; Friedrich Engels, *The Housing Question* (Moscow: Progress, 1970), p. 29.

4. Marx is here quoted from Lucio Colletti, *From Rousseau to Lenin: Studies in Ideology and Society* (New York: Monthly Review Press, 1972), p. 86–88.

5. Marx's comments from the *Critique* quoted from David McClellan, *Karl Marx: His Life and Thought* (New York: Harper & Row, 1973), p. 96; Karl Marx, *The Holy Family* (Moscow: Foreign Language Publishers, 1956), pp. 52–53; Friedrich Engels, "On Historical Materialism," in Feuer, *Marx and Engels,* p. 66.

6. Quoted in McClellan, *Karl Marx,* p. 6.

7. Daniel Bell, *The End of Ideology: On the Exhaustion of Political Ideas in the Fifties* (New York: Free Press, 1960), chap. 16, includes a good discussion of Marxist theories of rationality and science as the basis for modern radicalism, and Lenin's reliance on Karl Kautsky's theories in particular. Trotsky describes the Bolsheviks as a "moral medium" in *The Russian Revolution* (Garden City, N.Y.: Doubleday, 1959), p. 303. Michael Harrington, *The Twilight of Capitalism* (New York: Simon & Schuster, 1976), p. 291; Ralph Miliband, *Marxism and Politics* (New York: Oxford University Press, 1977), p. 44; Stanley Aronowitz, "The Working Class: A Break with the Past," in Colin Greer, ed., *Divided Society: The Ethnic Experiences in America* (New York: Basic Books, 1974), p. 44. Miliband describes clearly the Marxist theory of agency and program for the fu-

ture: in the Marxist view, old relations of civil society will be replaced by a classless association, created by the working class (p. 11). To accomplish such a transformation, the working class must absorb all particularities into its abstract universalism. Miliband's very sophistication about "traditions" and culture makes the theory the more striking:

> Traditional is not a monolith. On the contrary, it always consists of a large and diverse accumulation of customary ways of thought and action ... there is in most societies a tradition of dissent as well as a tradition of conformity.... But from a Marxist point of view, this "polymorphous" nature of tradition is not particularly helpful ... the Marxist notion of a "most radical rupture" with traditional ideas ... signifies a break with all forms of tradition, and must expect to encounter the latter not as friend but as foe (p. 44).

Many left-wing thinkers like Aronowitz who explicitly identified with the Marxist tradition in the 1970s have now come to embrace a postmodernist stance that is not nearly so explicitly hostile to traditional relations and communities. For instance, in his recent piece "Postmodernism and Politics" in Andrew Ross, ed., *Universal Abandon: The Politics of Postmodernism* (Minneapolis: University of Minnesota, 1989), pp. 46–62, Aronowitz shows a new attentiveness to "local communities" across the world as the foundation for politics. The problem with postmodernism is its view of power as one-directional; power, for Aronowitz (and here he is emblematic of the genre of postmodern theorists), is something to be simply "resisted." Indeed, the slogan of postmodernism might well be "To Resist the Leviathan." See chap. 8 of *CommonWealth,* especially note 17.

8. Eric Hobsbawm's observation that irreligious fervor has been far more typically a characteristic of socialist-movement intellectuals and core activists—those most socialized into the "moral medium" of the movement—than of the broader socialist, working-class base in Europe is noteworthy in this regard. He describes movements that have had generations of secular and rational "education" and still have not "outgrown" their "backwaters of superstition." The recent religious revivals in Eastern Europe and the Soviet Union, feeding into working-class movements like Polish Solidarity and the intellectual ferment around *glasnost* and *perestroika,* are other striking cases in point. Eric Hobsbawm, "Religion and the Rise of Socialism," *Marxist Perspectives,* 1 (1978), p. 26. For a discussion of the ways in which popular memory and traditions are always social and political constructions, see David Thelen, "Memory and American History," *Journal of American History* 75, 4 (1989), pp. 1117–29.

9. On the history of "socialism," see Williams, *Keywords,* pp. 238–43; on socialist programs, see Michael Harrington, *Socialism* (New York: Bantam Books, 1972), and his *Twilight of Capitalism.*

10. For a skillful description of the contradictions between populist and modernizing egalitarian themes in one African struggle, see Allen Isaac-

man and Barbara Isaacman, *Mozambique: From Colonialism to Revolution, 1900–1982* (Boulder, Colo.: Westview Press, 1983). Milan Kundera's work brilliantly depicts this inner contradiction of socialism; see, for instance, his *The Book of Laughter and Forgetting* (New York: Penguin Books, 1981).

11. James Kloppenberg's treatment of the similarities between European and American philosophers and activists at the turn of the century here obscures their differences. For instance, he notes that European social-ists were far more enamored of nationalization of industry than were Americans like Walter Rauschenbusch, Richard Ely, Herbert Croly, and Walter Lippmann, who pursued various strategies of control and reg-ulation through government. But Kloppenberg, neglecting the distinc-tive commonwealth tradition that had always seen government as ide-ally an instrument of popular power over concentrated economic interests, credits Americans' preference for regulation as simply a sign of political backwardness. In fact such preference is better seen as an indication of American progressives' more central preoccupation with popular *power,* in particular, their more extensive theorization of volun-tary associations (such as religious groups) as foundations for action. These voluntary associations' independence from state and corporate systems into the twentieth century made popular control over large sys-tems seem at least imaginable. See Kloppenberg, *Uncertain Victory,* espe-cially chapters 8–10.

12. Nicholas Salvatore, *Eugene v. Debs: Citizen and Socialist* (Urbana: Univer-sity of Illinois Press, 1982), p. 151, 171.

13. "Theodore Roosevelt's New Nationalism," in Sidney Hyman, ed., *Law, Justice and the Common Good: Reading for Leadership Program* (Minneapolis: Humphrey Institute, 1981), pp. 334–35.

14. Herbert Croly, *The Promise of American Life* (New York: Macmillan, 1909, pp. 139, 453; Lippmann quoted in William A. Schambra, *The Quest for Community and the Quest for a New Public Philosophy* (Washington, D.C.: American Enterprise Institute, 1983), p. 5.

15. Harrington makes this argument about "America's invisible social dem-ocratic movement" in *Socialism;* Louis Harz, *The Liberal Tradition in Amer-ica* (New York: Harcourt, Brace, 1955), p. 62; See also Kloppenberg, *Un-certain Victory.*

16. Douglas quoted in Howard Zinn, "Middle Class America Refurbished," in Allen Davis and Harold Woodman, eds., *Conflict and Consensus in Amer-ican History* (Lexington, Mass.: D.C. Heath, 1972), p. 310; government programs that facilitated and supported civic initiatives are described in Harry C. Boyte, "Ronald Reagan and America's Neighborhoods," in Alan Gartner, Colin Greer, and Frank Pressman, eds., *What Reagan Is Doing to Us* (New York: Harper & Row, 1982).

17. Shannon quoted in Samuel Hays, "The Politics of Reform in Munici-pal Government in the Progressive Era," in Stanley Katz and Stanley Kutler, eds., *New Perspectives on the American Past* (Boston: Little, Brown, 1969), p. 146.

18. See for instance Burton Bledstein, *The Culture of Professionalism: The Middle Class and the Development of Higher Education in America* (New York: W. W. Norton, 1976); Thorstein Veblen, *The Engineers and the Price System* (New York: Viking Press, 1932); Robert Wiebe, *The Search for Order, 1877–1920* (New York: Hill and Wang, 1967); James Weinstein, *The Corporate Ideal in the Liberal State, 1900–1918* (Boston: Beacon Press, 1968); Raymond E. Callahan, *Education and the Cult of Efficiency* (Chicago: University of Chicago Press, 1962); Michael B. Katz, *In the Shadow of the Poorhouse: A Social History of Welfare in America* (New York: Basic Books, 1986); and John Kenneth Galbraith, *The New Industrial State* (New York: Signet Books, 1967), p. 326.

19. Guidance counselors quoted from Christopher Lasch, *Haven in a Heartless World: The Family Besieged* (New York: Basic Books, 1977), p. 18; on domestic science, see Laura Shapiro, *Perfection Salad: Women and Cooking at the Turn of the Century* (New York: Farrar, Straus & Giroux, 1987), pp. 91–95; Evans quoted from Sara M. Evans, *Born for Liberty: A History of Women in America* (New York: Free Press, 1989), p. 163.

20. Arnold quoted in Zinn, "Middle Class America," p. 306; Toynbee in John Kenneth Galbraith, *New Industrial State*, p. 109; Myrdal, in Jeffrey Galper, *The Politics of Social Services* (Englewood Cliffs, N.J.: Prentice-Hall, 1975), p. 113.

21. Lipset and Stevenson quoted from William E. Leuchtenburg, *A Troubled Feast: American Society Since 1949* (Boston: Little, Brown, 1973), pp. 4, 11. It is noteworthy that Lipset continued to call himself a social democrat through this period, as did other technocratically minded thinkers like Galbraith and Daniel Bell.

22. J. David Greenstone, *Labor in American Politics* (New York: Alfred A. Knopf, 1969), pp. 16, 351. This is also the central argument of Michael Harrington in his 1972 work *Socialism*; see especially chap. 11, "The Invisible Mass Movement."

Chapter 4
The Politics of Everyday Life

1. Leon Fink, *Workingmen's Democracy: The Knights of Labor and American Politics* (Urbana: University of Illinois Press, 1983), p. 34; a central and often overlooked theme in the thinking of Progressives was the way to give working people and citizens new forms of "property rights" in the emerging industrial economy. As Henry Adams put it in his presidential address to the American Economic Association in 1896, "Property is essential to liberty," defined as "personal independence and self-realization." In the new era, new forms of "industrial property" must be developed for liberty to have any meaning. Indeed, this remained the central concern of writers like Charles Horton Cooley, Albion Small, founding editor of the *American Journal of Sociology*, and John Commons. Adams quoted in Stephen Eric Barton, "Property Rights and Democracy," Ph.D. dissertation, University of California at Berkeley, 1985, p. 45.

2. Thucydides, *The Peloponnesian War,* chap. 7, (IAF handout), pp. 1–6.

3. Ed Chambers, Alinsky's closest associate and current executive director of IAF, turned the reading into the first part of the training program when the group of organizers established the IAF Training Institute in 1969 to systematize and spread the lessons of their experiences in grass-roots action to larger numbers of organizers (and today, legions of civic leaders as well). The IAF still uses the account of the Athenians and Melians as their basic entree into the world of public affairs, politics, and organizing; most students still take several days to work through the implications of the story. Chambers, the IAF director, and others on the staff say, however, that there has been a change in tone since students came infused with the stronger "movement spirit" of the 1970s, when the full ten days would often be taken up by debates about whether the Melians should have done anything different. Firsthand observations, IAF 10 Day Training session, Baltimore, November 1987.

4. *Time* Essay, March 2, 1980; Charles E. Silberman, *Crisis in Black and White* (New York: Vintage Books, 1964), p. 318.

5. Silberman, *Crisis in Black and White,* pp. 314–15.

6. Telephone interview with Chambers, May 2, 1988.

7. "Sordid raiment" quote from Alinsky's "Citizen Participation" speech, p. 5; on his theory of power and avoidance of the concept, see Dan Dodson, "The Church, Power and Saul Alinsky," reprint from *Religion in Life,* Spring 1967, p. 2.

   Alinsky's approach to "truth" and language bore on the face of it a striking resemblance to the emphasis that has emerged from poststructuralist and deconstructionist strains of thought in recent years, especially his stress on the radical dependence of any utterance or action on the social context for its meaning. See for instance Kenneth J. Gergen, Correspondence Versus Autonomy," in Donald Fiske and Richard Shweder, *Metatheory in Social Science: Pluralisms and Subjectivities* (Chicago: University of Chicago Press, 1976), p. 143; see also Richard Bernstein, *Beyond Objectivism and Relativism: Science, Hermeneutics and Praxis* (Philadelphia: University of Pennsylvania Press, 1985).

   Yet Alinsky's "disruptions" of conventional conceptions of truth and epistemology, even at their most ideologically denuded, always had an objective of providing tools for the powerless to use in struggle with the powerful—what Jim Scott has called the "weapons of the weak"—that is not nearly as explicit or developed in deconstructionist and poststructuralist thought.

8. Saul David Alinsky, *Reveille for Radicals* (New York: Vintage Books, 1946), pp. 13–14.

   The significant omission from Alinsky's long list are suffragists and women's rights crusaders. Alinsky's brusque chauvinism was legendary, although it strikingly violated his constantly professed allegiance to all who were powerless. On another level, it created an ironic line of tension which has continued to plague the organizing tradition, pitting the "tough guy" persona of the organizer against the complex interpersonal challenges of the task—a challenge heightened by the female leadership that customarily emerges in community organizing contexts. IAF's gendered imagery of organizing has been considerably tempered in recent years, both by the strong female leaders and organizers who have emerged and by the evolving dynamics of the organizing method itself, with its deepening attentiveness to virtues like listening and accountability. Transcript of Alinsky's "Priests Class," April 28, 1964, in author's possession.

9. Jim Green, *The World of the Worker: Labor in Twentieth Century America* (New York: Hill & Wang, 1980).

10. Ibid., pp. 28–31.

11. Vorse quoted in ibid., p. 163.

12. John S. McGrath and James J. Delmont, *Floyd Bjornsterne Olson: Minnesota's Greatest Liberal Governor, A Memorial Volume* (Minneapolis: McGrath and Delmont, 1939), p. 13.

13. See David Brody, "The Emergence of Mass Production Unionism," in John Braeman, Robert H. Bremner, and Everett Walters, eds., *Change and Continuity in Twentieth-Century America* (Columbus: Ohio State University Press, 1964), pp. 221–64; on communist neighborhood approaches, Robert Fisher, *Let the People Decide: Neighborhood Organizing in America* (Boston: G. K. Hall, 1984), pp. 34–46 (Nelson quoted p. 38); on communist use of democratic themes, Irving Howe and Lewis Coser, *The American Communist Party: A Critical History* (New York: Praeger, 1962); Pettus from interview with author, Seattle, March 14, 1983.

14. Richard Flacks summarized the contradiction that existed throughout the Communist party's experience between local members, who were often skilled in organizing, and the demands of the party structure.

> From the beginnings, the relationship between the Communist Party and its activist members was fundamentally contradictory. The Party was socializing its members to seek effective leadership roles in everyday work and community situations and become creative initiators of popular protest and organization, while it was demanding from these members total fidelity to policies and "lines" promulgated by a top-down, centralized leadership.

Flacks, *Making History: The Radical Tradition in American Life* (New York: Columbia University Press, 1988), p. 149.

15. Ibid., pp. 92–99, for an account of earlier organizing campaigns.

16. Statement quoted in Robert A. Slayton, *Back of the Yards: The Making of a Local Democracy* (Chicago: University of Chicago Press, 1986), 203; see also Fisher, *Let the People Decide,* pp. 54–56.

17. Alinsky, *Reveille for Radicals,* pp. 76–79.

18. Along with a few other major voices in the first half of the twentieth century (the French theorist Simone Weil, for instance, whose book *The Need for Roots* is a classic statement of the wellsprings of popular radicalism), Alinsky developed a political method which challenged the hierar-

chies of power in the modern world and the value systems that masked and legitimated such power, using a language and categories that did not simply mirror the uprootedness of capitalist civilization itself. For a remarkable treatment of Weil's political theory, see Mary G. Dietz, *Between the Human and the Divine: The Political Thought of Simone Weil* (Totowa, N.J.: Rowman and Littlefield, 1988).

Other intellectual traditions and methods paralleled Alinsky's efforts to connect analysis to everyday life-worlds and experiences. For instance, the phenomenological investigations of Alfred Schutz called strong attention to the common life-worlds of everyday experience and common sense: "the world of cultural objects and social institutions into which we are all born, within which we have to find our bearings and with which we have to come to terms." Alfred Schutz, *Collected Papers,* vol. 1, edited by Maurice Natanson (The Hague: Martinus Nijhoff, 1962), p. 53; see also Peter L. Berger and Thomas Luckmann, *The Social Construction of Reality: A Treatise in the Sociology of Knowledge* (London: Penguin Press, 1967).

Such approaches to everyday life-worlds pointed to lived experiences of the sort that Alinsky's "listening" attuned one to. But in their theoretical formulations, intellectual disciplines like phenomenology and its offshoot, ethnomethodology, tended to suggest a static quality to experience. They gave little attention to mechanisms of change, nor did they suggest ways of separating out the historically and culturally given from those which express broader human "predicaments" reaching across time and location. See Bernstein, *The Restructuring of Social and Political Theory* (New York: Harcourt Brace Jovanovich, 1976), p. 168. For a discussion of the conservative consequences, see, for instance, Harry Boyte, *The Backyard Revolution: Understanding the New Citizen Movement* (Philadelphia: Temple University Press, 1980).

19. March quoted in Slayton, *Back of the Yards,* which given a masterful account of Alinsky's background, drawn in part from discussions with Sanford Horwitt, who is writing an Alinsky biography. Alinsky, *Reveille,* pp. 174–75.

20. Chambers, sent by Alinsky to Rochester after a group of ministers asked for help in 1965 to organize the black community organization called Rochester FIGHT, made the point that "outside of Back of the Yards, the only organization Saul organized, all the others were in combination with us. Saul talked and wrote about our work. He spent about five and a half days in Rochester." Interview with Ed Chambers, May 2, 1988.

There are vague references throughout the accumulated Alinsky legends about his projects here and abroad—from Kansas City to Italy, where it is rumored he spent time in the 1950s organizing anticommunist labor unions. But in fact, and adding considerably to other evidence that Alinsky's real talent was as a practical theorist, not an organizer, Alinsky himself seems to have organized no group after Back of the Yards that lasted any significant period of time or had any noteworthy public successes: *every one* of the subsequent organizing projects associated with his name—the Community Service Organization in California, The Woodlawn Organization in Chicago, FIGHT in Rochester, and Citizens Action Program in Chicago—was primarily organized and staffed by associates, not Alinsky himself. It all suggests strongly that the mythology surrounding Saul Alinsky has concealed, at least as much as it has clarified, the man, his work, and his contributions.

21. For a candid description of some of the problems in ACORN, by one of its chief theoreticians, see Gary Delgado, *Organizing the Movement: The Roots and Growth of ACORN* (Philadelphia: Temple University Press, 1986); see also Boyte, *Backyard Revolution,* for a detailed description of the differences in organizing methods.

22. *Playboy* interview, March 1972.

23. For a good summary of this strategy, see John McKnight and John Kretz-mann, "Toward a Post-Alinsky Agenda," *Social Policy,* Winter 1984, pp. 15–18; for a description of the traditional Alinsky method, see, for instance, Boyte, *Backyard Revolution,* and *Community Is Possible: Repairing America's Roots* (New York: Harper & Row, 1984); also Robert Fisher, *People.*

24. Comments on dogma from Alinsky's Introduction to a new edition of *Reveille,* unpublished, in author's possession; on highway of life, Alinsky, "Citizen Participation and Community Organization in Planning and Urban Renewal," IAF publication, Chicago, 1962.

25. "The Professional Radical: Conversations with Saul Alinsky," *Harper's* reprint, June and July 1965, p. 9; interview with Father John Egan, South Bend, August 2, 1980.

26. Saul Alinsky, "Is There Life After Birth?" Speech to the Centennial Meeting of the Episcopal Theological School, Cambridge, Mass., June 7, 1967 (Chicago: IAF reprint), pp. 12–13.

27. See Fisher, *People.*

Chapter 5
The Rise and Fall of Participatory Democracy

1. Alinsky quoted from Robert Fisher and Joseph M. Kling, "Leading the People: Two Approaches to the Role of Ideology in Community Organizing," *Radical America,* Spring 1988, p. 39.

2. On the local community bases of civil rights, see Aldon Morris, *The Origins of the Civil Rights Movement: Black Communities Organizing for Change* (New York: Free Press, 1984); on the republican roots of the New Left, James Miller, *Democracy Is in the Streets: From Port Huron to the Siege of Chicago* (New York: Simon & Schuster, 1986).

3. On economic and social changes in the south, see Anthony Oberschall, *Social Conflict and Social Movements* (Englewood Cliffs, N.J.: Prentice-Hall, 1973), especially pp. 205–11; and Morris, *Origins of Civil Rights,* pp. 7–9, 79–80.

4. On the background and dynamics of the boycott, see Stephen B. Oates, *Let the Trumpet Sound: The Life of Martin Luther King, Jr.* (New York: Harper & Row, 1982), pp. 63–69; also Morris, *Origins,* pp. 43–44.

5. King's social and political thought is discussed in Oates, *Let the Trumpet Sound*, 25–41; one evening in August 1964 in St. Augustine, Florida, King discussed with me at some length his identification with the Southern populist tradition.

6. King's speech quoted from Oates, *Trumpet*, p. 71; "Letter from a Birmingham Jail" from Martin Luther King, Jr., *Why We Can't Wait* (New York: Harper & Row, 1963), p. 99.

7. The creation of SCLC, Baker's role, and the Citizenship Schools are described in Morris, *Origins*, pp. 82–99, 149–57, 236–37; Cotton quoted p. 239; on the point of the movement, see Pat Watters and Reese Cleghorn, *Climbing Jacob's Ladder: The Arrival of Negroes in Southern Politics* (New York: Harcourt, Brace and World, 1967), p. 6.

8. Janitor quoted in Oates, *Trumpet*, p. 112; research team study by Frederick Soloman et al., "Civil Rights Activity and Reduction of Crime Among Negroes," *Archives of General Psychiatry* 12 (March 1965), pp. 227–36.

9. My father, as special assistant to King in 1963–67, would often recount these exchanges about the "lack of serious organizing that would last." For a time he headed an SCLC program area, "Operation Dialogue," designed to try to build lasting community organizations, but it, too, suffered from the absence of any connection to older organizing wisdom and traditions. When I worked on the SCLC staff in 1964 and 1965, I often took part in such discussions myself. Account of SCLC organizers come from an interview with Chambers, May 1, 1988.

10. Ginsberg and Kerouac quoted from Todd Gitlin, *The Sixties: Years of Hope, Days of Rage* (New York: Bantom Books, 1988), pp. 44, 47; for a marvelous depiction of these dissenting cultural strands of the fifties, see chaps. 2 and 3.

11. Burry and MSM statement from Sara M. Evans, *Personal Politics: The Roots of Women's Liberation in the Civil Rights Movement and the New Left* (New York: Alfred A. Knopf, 1979), pp. 30, 31; Evans has an extensive discussion of Y and campus center networks.

12. For a description of such ties see Evans, *Personal Politics;* Gitlin, *The Sixties;* and Doug McAdam, *Mississippi Summer* (New York: Oxford University Press, 1988).

13. Quotes from Appendix of Miller, *Democracy Is in the Streets*, pp. 330, 333, 336.

14. For a discussion of the difference between prophecy and social criticism, see Michael Walzer, *Interpretation and Social Criticism* (Cambridge, Mass.: Harvard University Press, 1987), and Harry C. Boyte and Sara M. Evans, "Response," *Tikkun*, 2:3 (1987), pp. 73–74.

15. This version of commonwealth can be seen as the great limitation of the New Left's appeal to a broader audience. See Miller, *Democracy,* pp. 170–71.

16. Ibid., pp. 329, 360, 354, 330.

17. Alinsky quoted from Fisher and Kling, "Leading the People," p. 39.

18. *Port Huron* from Miller, *Democracy,* pp. 332; Gitlin, *Sixties,* pp. 200–1; Dylan from ibid., p. 200.

19. Interview with Susan Cobin, Minneapolis, March 11, 1983.

20. Interview with Martha Ballou, St. Paul, September 16, 1977; with Miles Rapoport, Boston, April 18, 1977; with Bill Thompson, Boston, April 18, 1977.

21. Interview with Heather Booth, Chapel Hill, North Carolina, February 14, 1976.

22. Saul D. Alinsky, *Rules for Radicals: A Pragmatic Primer for Realistic Radicals* (New York: Random House, 1971), 14.

23. Leon Fink, *The Radical Vision of Saul Alinsky* (Mahway, N.J.: Paulist Press, 1984), discusses Alinsky's personal crises and traumas.

24. All of these themes came together in the early 1970s when, as his final strategic plan, Alinsky laid plans for a major organizing drive among the middle class—those he called the "have-some, want-mores" who he believed were increasingly discontented with mounting economic and social changes.

Alinsky's depiction of the situation of "the Silent Majority" was more sympathetic than that of "New Politics" liberals or New Left activists, who wrote off these constituencies as inherently conservative. "Conservative? That's a crock of crap," he told the *Playboy* reporter. "Right now they're nowhere. But they can and will go either of two ways in the coming years—to a native American fascism or toward radical social change." The right, in his view, had a simple strategy: "Give them scape-goats for their misery—blacks, hippies, Communists." He painted the alternatives in apocalyptic, if humorous, terms: "If [the right wing] wins, this country will become the first totalitarian state with a national an-them celebrating 'the land of the free and the home of the brave.' "

But his descriptions of the concerns, motivations, lives, and fears of the Silent Majority resembled those of pop sociology, while his views on the dynamics of organization and action had a formative impact on the entire sociological approach to social movement theory known as "resource mobilization." Missing was any treatment of the complex voices and cultures underneath the veneer of America's consumer culture; Alinsky took the stereotypes at face value. In his view, Americans were consumer-oriented and mindless:

> Right now, they're frozen, festering in apathy. . . . Their personal
> lives are generally unfulfilling, their jobs unsatisfying, they've
> succumbed to tranquilizers and pep pills, they drown their
> anxieties in alcohol, they feel trapped in long-term endurance
> marriages or escape into guilt-ridden divorces. . . . They're
> alienated, depersonalized, without any feeling of participation.

One ironic result of Alinsky's impact on theory about social move-ments was the obliteration of any distinction between democratic and authoritarian forms of protest, a typological mapping that could still be found in earlier literature. For examples of the new resource mobilization approaches, see Oberschall, *Social Conflict;* and the overviews of the field: Craig Jenkins, "Resource Mobilization Theory and the Study of Social Movements," *Annual Review of Sociology* 9 (1983), and Jo Freeman, "On the Origins of Social Movements," in Jo Freeman, ed., *The Social Movements of the Sixties and Seventies* (New York: Longman, 1983); Frances Fox Piven and Richard Cloward also reflect these Alinskyite emphases in *Poor People's Movements: Why They Succeed, How They Fail* (New York: Pantheon Books, 1977). The loss of a theory of specifically *democratic* movements is described in Sara M. Evans and Harry C. Boyte, *Free Spaces: The Sources of Democratic Change in America* (New York: Harper & Row, 1986).

Finally, out of such analysis, Alinsky's strategy for organizing focused on those *issues* around which he believed Middle America could be mobilized—"taxes, jobs, consumer problems, pollution." From there, he envisioned a progression toward larger issues: "pollution in the Pentagon and the Congress and the board rooms of the megacorporations. Once you organize people, they'll keep advancing from issue to issue toward the ultimate objective: people power." Alinsky quote from Saul Alinsky, "Is There Life After Birth?" Speech to the Centennial Meeting of the Episcopal Theological School, Cambridge, Mass., June 7, 1967 (Chicago: IAF reprint), p. 12; *Playboy* interview, March 1972.

25. Bert DeLeeuw, interview, Washington, D.C., May 3, 1977.

26. Wade Rathke, "ACORN: Its Philosophy of Organizing," a paper on organizing by Rathke in the author's possession, written about 1977.

27. On the detachment of trade unions from their communal roots, see for instance Evans and Boyte, *Free Spaces*.

By the end of the 1970s, journalists, policymakers, social scientists, and politicians had begun to discover that "neighborhood movements" and more general networks of "citizen activism" formed an invisible underside of the decade, below the antics of presidents, rock stars, and football heroes. On the simplest level, spontaneously organized neighborhood groups had exploded in number. In New York City alone several thousand block clubs appeared, addressing issues from rents to health care and crime control. The National Commission on Neighborhoods compiled a list of more than 8,000 sizable community groups in the nation, almost all organized in the 1970s. A *Christian Science Monitor* poll of communities with populations over 50,000—concluding a series that labeled neighborhoods "the politics of the 1970s"—found one third claiming to have already taken part in some kind of neighborhood improvement effort or protest.

Moreover, a growing number of large, enduring coalitions and citizen groups appeared, speaking the characteristic languages of multiissue organizing, self-interest, and power. In addition to ACORN, national coalitions like the National People's Action and the National Association of Neighborhoods gave community efforts a presence on the national level, while Citizen Action brought together five statewide citizen groups in 1980 in a coalition which was to grow to twenty-five state affiliates by the decade's end. See, for instance, National Commission on Neighborhoods, *People Building Neighborhoods: Final Report* (Washington: U.S. Government Printing Office, 1979); John Herbers, "Activist Neighborhood Groups Are Becoming a New Political Force," *New York Times,* June 18, 1979; *Christian Science Monitor* poll, December 23, 1977. The impact of Saul Alinsky and the development of activist community, citizen, consumer, environmental, and other networks in the 1970s is described in detail in Harry C. Boyte, *The Backyard Revolution: Understanding the New Citizen Movement* (Philadelphia: Temple University Press, 1980); the ironies of Reagan policy toward the neighborhoods and developments in community organizing are found in Boyte, "Ronald Reagan and America's Neighborhoods," in Alan Gartner, Colin Greer, and Frank Riessman, eds., *What Reagan Is Doing to Us* (New York: Harper & Row, 1982), pp. 109–24, and Boyte, *Community Is Possible: Repairing America's Roots* (New York: Harper & Row, 1984); development of the Citizen Action network of organizations and its main campaigns are described in Boyte, Heather Booth, and Steve Max, *Citizen Action and the New American Populism* (Philadelphia: Temple University Press, 1986).

28. Reagan speech quoted in Schambra, *The Quest for Community and the Quest for a New Public Philosophy* (Washington, D.C.: American Enterprise Institute, 1983), p. 30; see also Hedrick Smith, "Reagan's Populist Coalition," *New York Times,* March 6, 1980; for sophisticated treatments of the welfare state from conservative viewpoints, see, for example, Peter Berger, *Facing Up to Modernity: Excursions in Society, Politics and Religion* (New York: Basic Books, 1977); Berger and Richard John Neuhaus, *To Empower People: The Role of Mediating Institutions in Public Policy* (Washington, D.C.: American Enterprise Institute, 1977); Robert A. Nisbet, *The Quest for Community* (New York: Harper, 1954).

29. The deep crisis of faith in scientific thinking as a kind of "political culture" was well described by Sheldon Wolin in his paper "Hobbes and the Culture of Despotism," presented to the Lippincott Symposium on Political Theory, University of Minnesota, April 20, 1988; see also Richard Bernstein, *Beyond Objectivism and Relativism: Science, Hermeneutics and Praxis* (Philadelphia: University of Pennsylvania Press, 1985).

A vacuum requires something to fill it. For further discussion of capital flow and the ways in which the banking and credit systems ravage local communities today, as at the end of the nineteenth century, see William Greiger's work in *Rolling Stone* and elsewhere in the 1980s; on some of the issues that citizen action has raised to national visibility in the decade, see Boyte et al., *Citizen Action.*

30. See Boyte, "Reagan and Neighborhoods," for a detailed sketch of these ironies. Tom Pauken, the Reagan apointee to head the VISTA program—whose mandate actually was to dismantle it—declared repeatedly the administration's hostility to "organizing" and his intention to "get" any citizen or community groups engaged in such activity. "Don't you see the irony here?" asked Katie Montcastle, a Connecticut philanthropist who heard Pauken describe his plans. "These groups, which

Mr. Pauken calls pro-leftist, are mostly community organizations working for such controversial matters as clean neighborhoods. They are the very type of self-help groups the Reagan administration says it needs and wants to save." But Montcastle—like commentators on administrative urban policy generally—missed the real story. What Reagan appointees were seeking to dismantle, with every instrument at their disposal, was any vehicle or instrument of popular empowerment. Montcastle quoted in *Kansas City Star,* January 3, 1982; Pauken's plans for dismantling "activist organizations" were detailed in a meeting with conservative organizations, June 18–19, 1981; notes in author's possession.

31. The connection between Madison Avenue and politics on the right was formalized in the 1984 campaign and continued to pattern strategy through 1988. "It worked for President Reagan in 1984: reinforcing the political image makers with the advertising executives who promoted Alka-Seltzer and Puppy Chow," read the *New York Times* piece "Ad Man for Schrafft's Gets Ready to Sell Bush," May 8, 1988. "Four years later, Vice President Bush, who has generally tried to stick close to Mr. Reagan, is also turning to Madison Avenue to help give him a new, improved look, in his case to the folks who figure out how to sell Schrafft's Ice Cream and Sparks automobile tuneup centers."

   Jesse Jackson's political campaign on the Democratic side may well have marked a beginning reintegration of older, richer populist themes with political action, and it is noteworthy that his local efforts across the country typically drew on more than a decade's organizing activity. While Jackson called attention to the infrastructure as the fundamental, neglected communal responsibility of the society, in other ways his campaign still failed to go beyond conventional understandings of "politics" as electoral action, or point to a more multidimensional understanding of citizenship. IAF affiliated groups, from my discussions with leaders and organizers, generally saw support for Jackson as a heartening sign, but few felt close identification with it as an expression of their own politics.

Chapter 6
Reconnecting Power and Vision

1. Interview with Wade Goodwyn on Chambers's "relational" quality, Baltimore, November 8, 1987; on COPS depictions, interviews with Beatrice Cortez, San Antonio, July 8, and Christine Stephens and Ernie Cortes, San Antonio, July 4, 1983. Cortes was the first to begin describing COPS (see later in chapter) as a "university of public life." See also Peter Skerry, "Neighborhood COPS," *New Republic,* February 6, 1984, p. 23.

2. An exchange with Ed Chambers, Alinsky's successor as head of the IAF Training Institute, illustrated their epistemology. Chambers, describing the emphasis that IAF organizing has come to place on disen-

tangling of "public" and "private" realms, remarked that people lose
the "public" side of "mediating institutions," associations between the
individual and the state or large-scale systems. "They think of things
like churches simply as private, so they make all sorts of inappropriate
demands," he argued. I replied that the very concept of mediating institutions (seeing them as private) maintains a narrow view of public life.

"I've seen the response to this in hundreds of meetings across the
country over ten years now," he continued. "It strikes home. People
come up, sometimes with tears in their eyes, priests, women religious,
lay leaders, saying, 'I wish I'd known this years ago.' " Interview in Baltimore, November 6, 1987.

The exchange illustrated IAF's feedback process. What it calls "universals" of organizing are always contextualized, provisional, and aimed
at the particular *problems* they encounter in their work. As Ernie Cortes,
a key figure in their network, pointed out, the IAF methodology resembles the "critical method" of Karl Popper, philosopher of science, who
argued for a view of "truth" not as positive assertion, but as theories
formulated out of practice and aimed at problem solving that had not
yet been refuted. See for instance, Popper's selections in Glyn Adey and
David Frisby, trans., *The Positivist Dispute in German Sociology* (London:
Heinemann, 1976).

IAF's epistemology combines "qualitative" and "quantative" methods—a process of detailed information gathering about particular individuals, cultures, and settings combined with a rigorous analysis of the
economic dimensions of issues, rare in practice today. But it is in keep-
ing with what Michael Patton, a leading theorist in the field of evaluation, has called the growing consensus about what *should* be done:
"Pragmatism, methodological tolerance, flexibility and concern for ap-
propriateness rather than orthodoxy now characterize the practice, literature and discussions of evaluation." Michael Quinn Patton, *Utilization-
Focused Evaluation* (London: Sage, 1986), p. 210.

3. Interview with Mike Gecan, Brooklyn, N.Y., November 14, 1984; with
   Ed Chambers, New York, February 22, 1983; Youngblood and Jamieson
   quoted from Jim Sleeper, "East Brooklyn's Second Rising," *City Limits,*
   December 1982, p. 13.

4. These trends are documented in Harry C. Boyte, *The Future of America's
   Neighborhoods* (Flint, Mich.: Mott Foundation, 1986); for a discussion of
   the flight of the black middle class, see for instance Nicholas Lemann,
   "The Origins of the Underclass," *Atlantic Monthly,* June 1986, pp. 31–55.

5. *U.S. News and World Report,* quoted from David A. Roozen, William Mc-
   Kinney, and Jackson W. Carroll, *Varieties of Religious Presence* (New York:
   Pilgrim Press, 1984), p. 5, which also has a good sketch of the sources
   of increasing poverty in inner-city communities.

6. Figures on merger from Gar Alperowitz and Jeff Faux, *Rebuilding America: A Blueprint for the New Economy* (New York: Pantheon Books, 1984),
   p. 34; see also Robert Reich and Ira Magaziner, *Minding America's Business: The Decline and Rise of the American Economy* (New York: Harcourt
   Brace Jovanovich, 1982).

7. Interview with Ed Chambers, Chicago, April 29, 1977.

In a memo to other staff members at the United Church of Christ Board of Homeland Ministers dated July 18, 1977, John Moyer reported on extensive conversations with organizers Chambers and Dick Harmon in which they stressed the developing IAF view that organizing had classically *used* religious congregations to build community organizations, but it needed to take more "seriously" religious congregations and religious language. In particular, although they continued to try to enlist Jewish synagogues as well, this meant an emphasis on the sorts of mainstream, ecumenically inclined Catholic and Protestant church groups which normally proved most responsive. Moyer argued that

> IAF has made a radical shift in direction since Alinsky times: namely to view the Church as the one institution in society with the potential to work positively for the empowerment of people. In both San Antonio and East Los Angeles, the churches have been the basic organizing units and the leadership has come directly from parishes and congregations. . . . Training sessions for leaders and organizers emphasize the relationship between theology and the dynamics of power relationships.

Memorandum to Paul Sherry, Wes Hotchkiss, Herb White, Bob Strommen, from John Moyer, "Re: IAF," July 18, 1977, in author's possession.

8. Benke quoted in Jim Gittings, "Churches in Communities: A Place to Stand," *Christianity & Crisis,* February 2, 1987, p. 6.

9. For all of that, the five most senior organizers—what the IAF calls its "cabinet"—continue to be men: Chambers, Cortes, Gecan, Larry McNeil, who directs the Southern California staff, and Arnie Graf, in charge of oversight of Midatlantic organizers. Cabinet membership, according to Chambers, who decides, means an especially intensive, ongoing process of political discussion and training intended to challenge, develop, and mature their thinking. It depends mainly on seniority, he claims—although there has seemed to be controversy about cabinet makeup, and several others would appear to have a strong claim. When asked, Cortes told me that the IAF still has far too few strong women organizers, and too few black and Hispanic ones as well. Organizing, for IAF, has all the seriousness and craft of a highly skilled guild—with something of their weaknesses (of "handed down" traditions and leadership) as well as their strengths. Only about one-half of those who intern with IAF projects make it through the rigorous training and evaluation process. The network's most pressing, constantly invoked need is for more beginners.

10. The trainee was Wade Goodwyn; conversation, Baltimore, November 8, 1987.

11. Interview with Ernesto Cortes, San Antonio, July 4, 1983.

12. Interview with Sister Margaret Snipe, Baltimore, November 6, 1987.

13. Interview with Cortes, San Antonio, July 3, 1983.

"Latino Activists Travel Separate Paths: Traditional Politics Versus Community Organizations," *Los Angeles Times,* July 29, 1983; Michael Ollove, "Md. Organizer Helps Poor in Memphis Seek Power," *Baltimore Sun,* February 7, 1988; and especially the special issue of *Christianity & Crisis,* February 1987, on community organizing in America.

IAF affiliated projects by 1988 included East Brooklyn Churches (EBC), Queens Citizen Organization (QCO), South Bronx Churches (SBC), and the Interfaith Community Organization (ICO) of Jersey City in the New York–New Jersey area; Baltimoreans United for Leadership Development (BUILD) in Baltimore, Interfaith Action Communities (IAC) of Prince George's County, Maryland, and the Interfaith Sponsoring Committee (ISC) of Memphis in the Midatlantic region; San Antonio's Communities Organized for Public Service (COPS), the Metropolitan Congregational Alliance (MCA) and the East Side Alliance (ESA), The Metropolitan Organization (TMO) of Houston, Allied Communities of Tarrant (ACT) in Fort Worth, El Paso Interreligious Sponsoring Organization (EPISO), Valley Interfaith of the River Grande Valley, all in Texas; and United Neighborhoods Organization (UNO), the South Central Community Organization (SCCO), the East Valleys Organization (EVO), and the new San Fernando Sponsoring Committee (SFSC) in Southern California, along with several other fledgling efforts.

28. Chambers quoted from Ollove, "Md. Organizer."

29. "I had to argue with COPS leaders like hell to get them to have a principle of a two-year presidency," said Chambers. "And we started a principle of two and a half years for a staff to direct an organization, and then out. If you stay in one place and you're creative, it will be too much your organization." The network also came to accent the importance of a broad, hetereogeneous base. "We realized the strength of organizations came from their diversity, as well as their roots. So we don't organize commmunities. It's not defined by neighborhood. It's pluralist and nongeographic, defined by a mix of interests and values and power." Telephone interview with Ed Chambers, May 2, 1988, and New York, February 22, 1983.

30. Stephens interviews July 6, 4, 1983.

31. Chambers interview, February 22.

32. Gerald Taylor interview, Baltimore, November 12, 1987; observations of Arnie Graf, IAF 10 Day Training, Baltimore, November 5, 1987. Different IAF organizers and teachers, it is interesting to note, place significantly different emphases on the relative degree of "publicness" of churches, for instance.

33. Interview with Douglas I. Miles, Baltimore, November 14, 1987.

34. Interview with Beatrice Cortez, July 8, 1983.

35. "The notion of a city naturally precedes that of a family or an individual, for the whole must necessarily be prior to the parts; for if you take away the whole man, you cannot say a foot or a hand remains." Aris-

totle, *Politics* (New York: Prometheus Books, 1986), p. 4; see also Jean
Bethke Elstain, *Public Man, Private Woman* (Princeton: Princeton University Press, 1981) for a description of the Greek privileging of "public
life."

Chapter 7
Repairing the Commons

1. Petition quoted from Richard Kluger, *Simple Justice: The History of Brown
   v. Board of Education and Black America's Struggle for Equality* (New York:
   Vintage Books, 1977), p. 1.

2. Rush and Jefferson quoted from People's Bicentennial Commission,
   Voices of the American Revolution (New York: Bantam Books, 1974), pp.
   175–76.

3. Bernard Bailyn, *Education in the Forming of American Society* (New York:
   Vintage Books, 1960); Franklin's plan for the Philadelphia Academy in
   Colin Greer, *The Great School Legend" A Revisionist Interpretation of Ameri-
   can Public Education* (New York: Basic Books, 1972), p. 15.

4. Greer, *Great School Legend,* p. 15.

5. Ibid., p. 29, and chap. 4, "Liberal Rhetoric for Conservative Goals."
   The educator Horace Mann, despite his democratic ideals, found
   himself faced with the political necessity to justify enlarged public
   schools to business groups through the argument that education functioned as a "balance wheel" protecting the existing order. "Finally, in
   regard to those who possess the largest shares in the stock of worldly
   goods," he wrote, "could there, in your opinion, be any police so vigi-
   lant and effective, for the protection of all rights of person, property
   and character, as such a sound and comprehensive education and training as our system of common schools could be made to impart?"
   Quoted in Greer, *School Legend,* pp. 74–75.
   Interestingly, conservative opponents of the public school movement
   were often the most penetrating critics, observing that the reformers'
   chief goals—measures like centralized administration, graded schools,
   and formal teacher training—represented a significant expansion of
   state power over the lives of individuals and the values of communities.

6. Petition quoted in Peter J. Rachleff, *Black Labor in the South: Richmond,
   Virginia, 1865–1890* (Philadelphia: Temple University Press, 1984), p.
   14; Eric Foner, *Reconstruction: America's Unfinished Revolution, 1863–1877*
   (New York: Harper & Row, 1988), p. 290; Allen quoted in ibid., p. 287;
   Washington quoted in Kluger, *Simple Justice,* p. 51.

7. Kluger, *Justice,* p. 51; figures on expenditures from Gunnar Myrdal, *An
   American Dilemma: The Negro Problem and Modern Democracy,* vol. 1 (New
   York: Harper & Brothers, 1942), p. 339.
   In the years immediately following the demise of the Freedmen's Bu-
   reau schools, most education for blacks was provided by Northern phi-
   lanthropy, but it brought with it distinctive burdens as well. The 5,000

Northern teachers flooding the South looked upon black culture with often unmitigated horror and contempt. "At one of their prayer-meetings, which we attended last night, we saw a painful exhibition of their barbarism," wrote Lucy Chase to her New England family about her early experiences in Craney Island, Virginia. Northern teachers saw their mission largely as reacculturating blacks into the dominant cultural idiom. As one teacher put it, "Our work is just as much a missionary work as if we were in India or China." Historian Lawrence Levine summarized the ethos by pointing to the regional difference between white Southerns and Northern educators: "Where southern whites generally were perfectly content to allow the blacks to stew in their own cultural juices, the northerners pined to wipe them clean and participate as midwives at a rebirth." Blacks sought to preserve and sustain their own culture and learn the tools of the white world by developing a dual language. "In the classroom we all learned past participles, but in the streets and in our homes the Blacks learned to drop *s*'s from plurals and suffixes from past tense verbs," said the writer Maya Angleou. "We learned to slide out of one language and into another without being conscious of the effort." Chase and missionary quoted in Lawrence W. Levine, *Black Culture and Black Consciousness: Afro-American Folk Thought from Slavery to Freedom* (New York: Oxford University Press, 1977), p. 141; Levine, 143; Angelou, 154.

8. Greer, *School Legend,* p. 89; for a look at the wellsprings of democratic educational approaches in America—including the kind of practical "citizenship education" programs found in labor, civil rights, and other social movements—see Ruth Dropkin and Arthur Tobier, eds., *Roots of Open Education in America: Reminiscences and Reflections* (New York: City College Workshop Center, 1976).

9. For a description of elite views, see Clarence J. Karier, "Elite Views on American Education," in James J. Shields, Jr., and Colin Greer, eds., *Foundations of Education: Dissenting Views* (New York: John Wiley & Sons, 1975), pp. 44–53; on the consequences for working-class children, essays by Peter Schrag, S. M. Miller and Pamela Roby, and Brian Jackson and Denis Marsden in the same collection; also Norman Fruchter, "A History of Community Education Movements," presentation at Union Graduate School "Democratic Education" seminar, Shelter Island, N.Y., May 20, 1988. For a depiction of the patterns of a growing two-track system of education, increasing violence, and impersonality, see also Arthur Powell, et al., *Shopping Mall High School* (Boston: Houghton Mifflin, 1985).

10. The strategy flowing from the *Nation at Risk* approach is well detailed in Ann Bastien, et al., *Choosing Equality: The Case for Democratic Schooling* (Philadelphia: Temple University Press, 1986); also well sketched by Fruchter in his Shelter Island presentation; see also "Yes, Our Schools Can Be Saved," *Newsweek* Special Report, May 2, 1988, for a description of Effective School strategy.

11. Sizer, Meier, and other educators formed an outspoken network called

the Coalition for Essential Schools, including a member of high schools designed around such ideas, to press their case. For a description of core Essential School principles, see_ *Horace,* the publication of the Coalition, especially vol. 4, no. 4 (1988). Meanwhile, several of the nation's larger school districts moved toward elements of local site control. But as education specialist Ted Kolderie had pointed out, "site control" of schools—which in a serious way must involve a delegation of authority and power to local schools over such key issues as budget, hiring, curriculum, and control of use of time—has become a rhetorical buzzword; very few efforts have actually been made toward its implementation. See for instance Kolderie, "School-Site Management: Rhetoric and Reality" (Minneapolis: Humphrey Institute Public Services Redesign Project, 1988).

For an overview of the democratic argument and the clashing educational visions, see Leon Botstein, "Education Reform in the Reagan Era," *Social Policy,* 18:4 (1988), pp. 3–11; for Sizer's view, see Theodore R. Sizer, *Horace's Compromise: The Dilemma of the American High School* (Boston: Houghton Mifflin, 1984); also Alice Digilio, "Theodore Sizer: Man with a Mission," *Washington Post,* April 15, 1987. In Rochester, N.Y., for instance, the 1987 "Career in Teaching" agreement between the school district and the Rochester Teachers Association represented both a significant devolution of authority to teachers and an upgrading of teacher responsibilities and remuneration. Lead teachers were seen as mentors to others, in addition to their teaching responsibilities. They and other professionals would be assigned to areas with the most need—especially poorer districts—rather than the most affluent schools. Each secondary teacher assumed responsibility for regular interaction with up to twenty students, including conferences, advice, and contact with homes. In Miami's Dade County, an experiment in "school site control" delegated authority in the critical areas of budget, curriculum, and staffing decisions to local site committees involving administrative staff, teachers, and parents—a plan that formally resembles the process envisioned for Baltimore. In Chicago, under legislation passed by the state, inner-city schools beginning in 1990 will be governed by school councils of eleven members, including six parents, two teachers, two community residents, and a principal; councils will hire principals for a three-year term. See Will Astor, "Final Addition," *Rochester City,* September 3, 1987; Rochester agreement details taken from "Synopsis," Contract Settlement, July 1, 1987–June 30, 1990; the New York State Chapter of the National Education Association hotly attacked the seniority provisions. Kolderie, "School-Site Management."

12. Fruchter, "History of Community Education"; for a depiction of the more authoritarian and more democratic sides of the debate over a number of years, see James Wm. Noll ed., *Taking Sides: Clashing Views on Controversial Educational Issues* (Guilford, Conn.: Dushkin Publishing, 1983).

13. Interview with Ed Chambers, June 1, 1988.

14. Ira De Reid, *The Negro Community of Baltimore: A Social Survey* (Baltimore:

Urban League, 1934), pp. 207–8; interview with Gerald Taylor, Baltimore, November 11, 1987.

15. Reid, *Negro Community of Baltimore;* Suzanne E. Greene, *Baltimore: An Illustrated History* (Woodland Heights, Calif.: Windsor Publications, 1980); interview with Vernon Dobson, Baltimore, November 13, 1987.

16. Reid, *Negro Community,* especially pp. 191–205; Leroy Graham, *Elisha Tyson, Baltimore and the Negro* (Baltimore: Morgan State College Press, 1975).

17. Dobson, November 13 interview; Miles, November 14 interview.

18. Miles interview.

19. The story of the inner harbor and center city is detailed in Greene, *Baltimore;* interview with Michael Fletcher, Baltimore, November 13, 1987; interview with Michael Ollove, Baltimore, November 13, 1987; Miles interview.

20. Figures on schools and unemployment from DeWayne Wickham, *Destiny 2000: The State of Black Baltimore* (Baltimore: Baltimore Urban League, 1987); and also Frank Defillippo, "'Baltimore 2000' Revives the Notion of Two Baltimores," *City Paper,* February 13, 1987; interviews with Irene Dandridge and Alice Pinderhughes, Baltimore, November 16, 1987.

21. Interview with Carl Stokes, Baltimore, November 5, 1987; with Robert Keller, Baltimore, November 16, 1987.

22. Accounts of the convention based on firsthand observation and taped recordings of speeches; on BUILD's power in previous years, see for instance "BUILD Grows Stronger as Voice for Voiceless," *Baltimore Evening Sun,* December 3, 1984; "BUILD Flexes Its Political Muscle, " *Baltimore News American,* November 4, 1985; BUILD to Enter Mayor's Race," *Evening Sun,* November 17, 1986; On the expansion of the Baltimore Commonwealth," lead editorial, *The Sun,* February 29, 1988, and "Businesses to Help More Kids Get Jobs," *Evening Sun,* February 25, 1988.

23. This kind of evaluation includes ample praise for what worked well and for individuals who accomplished their agreed-upon tasks. But it is also tough and rigorous, incorporating both criticism and detailed discussion about what should be done in similar situations in the future. The consensus of the evaluation was that other key members of the Action Team besides Reckling, who was chairing the event, should have caucused with Taylor in the back of the auditorium as soon as it was apparent that the convention was running late and made an on-the-spot decision about what should be dropped from the program. The whole exercise was a strong indication of the immense importance IAF groups place on beginning and ending meetings on time, which they feel creates a culture of respect for people's commitments and an indispensable practice of accountability.

24. Interview with Father Joe Muth, Baltimore, November 13, 1987, Graf acknowledged that when he arrived, the organization was deeply in debt and had a core of only six to eight leaders.

25. Interviews with Arnie Graf, Baltimore, November 6 and 16, 1987.
26. *Baltimore Morning Sun,* July 10, 1981.
27. Interview with Gary Rodwell, Baltimore, November 13, 1987; the campaign was also described in the *Afro American;* see especially "BUILD Reaches Agreement with Baltimore Federal," June 30, 1981.
28. *Sun,* July 10, 1981.
29. Rodwell interview; Miles interview.
30. Miles interview.
31. Interview with Marian Dixon, Baltimore, March 31, 1988.
32. John Langston Gwaltney, *Drylongso* (New York: Vintage Books, 1981), p. 6; Dixon interview.
33. Interview with Mike Gecan, Baltimore, November 11, 1987.
34. Gecan interview.
35. "BUILD Convention Attracts Politicians, Gains Credibility," *The Sun,* October 22, 1984.
36. Graf interview, Baltimore, November 16, 1987.
37. Ibid.; also Pinderhughes interview, November 16; information on school supplies from "Schools Need Paper," *The Sun,* March, 7, 1984.
38. Interview with Alan Hoblitzel, Baltimore, April 18, 1988.
39. Miles interview; Hoblitzel interview; also interviews with Graf, Bob Keller, Baltimore, November 16.
40. Interviews with Gerald Taylor, Baltimore, November 11 and 12, 1987; Keller interview.

The initial *Commonwealth Agreement* was signed April 24, 1985. Its preamble read:

> The Commonwealth Agreement evolved out of a series of meetings held between leaders of the Baltimore City Public Schools, the Greater Baltimore Committee and BUILD over the course of the past six months. It represents a partnership between these parties to take dramatic steps to improve public educational opportunities.
>
> The largest segment of today's work force is composed of high school graduates who will not attend college. Numerous national studies indicate that many of these graduates lack the basic skills necessary for the employment opportunities open to them. Other students do not graduate from high school, further restricting their opportunities for the future. Well-educated citizens are essential to the economic well-being of our metropolitan area; our vitality is linked to our youth gaining appropriate job skills.
>
> The Commonwealth Agreement commits the Baltimore City Public Schools, the Greater Baltimore Committee (GBC) and BUILD (Baltimoreans United in Leadership Development) to improve educational opportunities, to prepare students for careers, post secondary education and to improve access for jobs. The Commonwealth Agreement is about a common vision, a common focus, a common wealth—One Greater Baltimore.

Document in author's possession.

41. On the Baltimore Commonwealth, see Carol Steinback, "Investing Early: Education Report on Baltimore," *National Journal.* September 3, 1988, pp. 2192–95; interview with Charlotte Brown, Baltimore, November 16, 1987.

42. Interview with Taylor, Baltimore, October 1, 1988; document on "A Public Understanding of Schools," developed by the collaborative committee for fundamental school reform, in author's possession. On difficulties, see Kolderie, "School-Site Management."

43. Interviews with Richard Hase, Baltimore, November 16, 1987 and June 1, 1988; with Carol Reckling, Baltimore, November 15, 1987; with Marian Dixon; and with Ted Kolderie, Minneapolis, August 22, 1988.

44. Interview with Gerald Taylor, April 2, 1988.

45. Interview with Taylor, Baltimore, November 12, 1987.

46. Interview with Hoblitzel, Minneapolis-Baltimore, April 18, 1988; interview with Kurt Schmoke, Minneapolis-Baltimore, May 5, 1988.

Chapter 8
The Larger Lessons of Community Initiative

1. In 1988—building on the BUILD electoral strategy of 1987, where the organization's announcement of its "own" candidate, an agenda of issues, strongly shaped the parameters of subsequent political debate— IAF groups for the first time joined together nationally to develop an overarching campaign, "Sign Up and Take Charge." In the campaign, which local groups adapt to their areas and particular issues, volunteers collect hundreds of thousands of signatures in each area of the country where IAF has concentrated strength, in an effort to begin setting the political agenda for future elections. Ed Chambers saw the effort as the beginning of a new IAF interest in finding ways to reach people who are "not members of mediating institutions" like religious congregations and unions. Interview with Chambers, Minneapolis-New York, June 1, 1988. IAF has been asked to develop organizing projects in several other countries, Mexico, Great Britain, and South Africa among them.

In the IAF training session in Baltimore in 1987, Ernie Cortes speculated about how much their "universals" of organizing could be applied elsewhere, especially beyond cultures strongly shaped by Jewish and Christian traditions. "My guess is you could do it with any cultural tradition built around engagement in the world (I'm not sure of Buddhism, where withdrawal seems to be the ideal), any culture which values relationships, community, inclusiveness," he argued. "It would be very difficult in an environment of 'church triumphalism'—of whatever faith— where the point is to get power and wipe out opposing points of view. Our approach is strongly shaped by the tension between religious and democratic values, themes like diversity, openness, pluralism." Cortes comments, Baltimore, November 10, 1987.

2. In certain states like Texas and perhaps Maryland, moreover, the IAF groups may well begin reshaping the political agenda. As Peter Apple-bome recently put it in the *New York Times,* "Ernie Cortes ... over the past fifteen years has helped build a remarkable network that, in ways large and small, is changing politics in Texas" ("Changing Texas Politics at Its Roots," *New York Times,* May 31, 1988). On the other hand, some of the more ambitious IAF claims—like Chambers's remark that he thought IAF groups could soon pick a winning candidate for the presidency—seem overblown. See Michael Ollove, "Community Organizers Carry Saul Alinsky's Message of Power to the Poor," *Baltimore Sun,* February 7, 1988, for Chambers comment, as well as an overview of the IAF projects across the country.

3. The language of public life used by groups like BUILD reminds us of Hannah Arendt (the IAF's favorite political theorist), who once observed that

   the history of revolutions ... which politically spells out the innermost story of the modern age could be told in parable form as the tale of an age-old treasure [once called 'public happiness' in America, 'public freedom' in France] which, under the most varied circumstances, appears abruptly, unexpectedly, and diappears again, under different mysterious conditions, as though it were a fata morgana.

   Today, intimations of public life emerge even in arduous and authoritarian circumstances. Soviets, for instance, are gripped by questions like the meaning of "citizenship," "public," and "common good"—and how such things might be achieved in technologically advanced, diverse modern societies—which grow less from practice of democracy than its imagining. Hannah Arendt, *Between Past and Future: Eight Exercises in Political Thought* (New York: Viking Press, 1954), p. 5.

4. John Dewey, *The Public and Its Problems* (Athens, Ohio: Swallow Press, 1954), p. 185.

5. For a rendering of public and private in Greek thought, see especially Foley's essay "The Conception of Women in Athenian Drama," in Helene P. Foley, ed., *Reflections on Women in Antiquity* (New York: Cordon and Breach Science, 1981); for a tracing over time, Jean Bethke Elshtain, *Public Man, Private Woman: Women in Social and Political Thought* (Princeton: Princeton University Press, 1981). Linda Kerber has explored the way in which eighteenth- and nineteenth-century Americans drew upon, recast, and developed a distinctively female understanding of republican themes in her splendid *Women of the Republic: Intellect and Ideology in Revolutionary America* (Chapel Hill: University of North Carolina Press, 1980).

6. Dewey, *The Public,* pp. 212–13; *Culture and Freedom* (New York: G. P. Putnam's Sons, 1939), pp. 160–61. Though he struggled to adapt older conceptions of democratic politics and public life to a modern environment (and in the process generated many creative insights, such as the

stress on learning through experience that constantly informs his work), Dewey's construction of "public" remained the captive of his critique of Aristotle. Instead of seeking to recreate the concept of public out of a never-resolvable tension between ideals and the realities of difference, self-interest, and interplays of power, Dewey's strategy would widen still further the distance between ideal and real; indeed he criticized Aristotle for distinguishing between ethics and politics. In Dewey's view, there should be no such distinction. See the treatment in James T. Kloppenberg, *Uncertain Victory: Social Democracy and Progressivism in European and American Thought, 1870–1920* (New York: Oxford University Press, 1986), chapter 8. Dewey's arguments are paralleled in the work of critics like G. D. H. Cole and, today, C. B. MacPherson. See for instance, Cole, *Self-Government in Industry* (London: G. Bell and Sons, 1919).

"Public" as a word first appeared in English with strong republican overtones, identified with the common good, or "publyke wele," as Thomas Malory put it in 1470. By the sixteenth century, it also had overtones of openness, visibility, and accessibility, an arena of diversity (especially with urban connotations), in contrast to "private," which increasingly came to mean the smaller world of family and friends that was sheltered from public view. American social history added unique overtones to the concept, associating public not only with formal governmental institutions but also with voluntary activity through which citizens expressed continuing involvement in community affairs.

The history of "public" in the first two senses is traced well in Richard Sennett, *The Fall of Public Man* (New York: Alfred A. Knopf, 1977); Malory quoted pp. 16–17. In French, too, *le public* similarly suggested the sense of common good, or body politics, and acquired additional meanings suggesting a "region of sociability" by the end of the seventeenth century. As Sennett put it, "By the time the word . . . had taken on its modern meanings . . . it meant not only a region and social life located apart from the realm of friends and close friends, but also that this public realm of acquaintances and strangers included a relatively wide diversity of people"—associations acquired especially in urban centers like London and Paris. *Fall*, p. 17.

Associations with voluntary life were especially the products of nineteenth-century social and reform movements, most particularly the efforts of women. See, for instance, Sara M. Evans, *Born for Liberty: A History of American Women* (New York: Free Press, 1989).

The IAF seeks to rehabilitate both "public" and "politics" in ways that expand the older meanings of the words and add new dimensions, like the intensive interplay between public and everyday life-worlds, the varied *sorts* of public environments, and an implicit understanding of public life as always involving ongoing tension between "commons," understood as here-and-now obligations of citizenship, and "commonwealth" (the "New Jerusalem" or other formulations), understood as an ideal. See chapter 9.

7. "Republican" discussions of public life have classically rested upon a

sharp separation of the world of the public from the private and self-interested. As Isaac Kramnick described the American republican sense of citizenship drawn from this tradition:

> Man was a political being who realized his telos [purpose] only when living in a *vivere civile* with other propertied, arms-bearing citizens, in a republic where they ruled and were ruled in turn. . . . The pursuit of public good is privileged over private interests, and freedom means participation in civic life rather than the protection of individual rights from interference.

Politics, the activity of the citizen, also had such overtones, conveying in classical terms a "horizontal" concept of collaboration with fellow citizens that, as Giovanni Sartori put it, "goes into the English common weal and commonwealth, and is rendered today by the notion of common good, public good and general interest." But especially with the rise of the modern state, the dominant meaning of "politics," like that of "republic," increasingly acquired implications of hierarchy, distance, and corruption. Isaac Kramnick, "The 'Great National Discussion': the Discourse of Politics in 1787," *William and Mary Quarterly*, 3:45 (1988), pp. 4–5; Giovanni Sartori, "What Is Politics?" *Political Theory:* 1:1 (1973), p. 9.

For a similar view now, see William M. Sullivan, *Reconstructing Public Philosophy* (Berkeley: University of California Press, 1986), pp. 159, 157, 163, 215. Sullivan's arguments are similar to a wide range of other neo-republican writers today. See for instance, Joseph Tussman, *Obligation and the Body Politic* (New York: Oxford University Press, 1960); Ralph Ketcham, *Individualism and Public Life: A Modern Dilemma* (New York: Basic Books, 1977); James Gouinlock, *Excellence in Public Discourse: John Stuart Mill, John Dewey and Social Intelligence* (New York: Teachers College Press, 1986); and Mary Stanley, "Six Types of Citizenship," *Civic Arts Review*, Fall 1988, pp. 12–15.

The main contemporary communitarian arguments are given by Michael Sandel, *Liberalism and the Limits of Justice* (Cambridge: Cambridge University Press, 1982); and Alasdair MacIntyre, *After Virtue* (Notre Dame: University of Notre Dame Press, 1981); Parker J. Palmer, *The Company of Strangers: Christians and the Renewal of America's Public Life* (New York: Crossroads Publishing, 1985). For a very articulate reading of the "public" dimensions of America's civil religion, see Fred R. Dallmayr, *Polis and Praxis: Exercises in Contemporary Political Theory* (Cambridge, Mass.: M.I.T. Press, 1984), and Sullivan, *Reconstructing Public Philosophy; Political Theory's* symposium on the republican revival, "Civic Republicanism and Its Critics," 14:3 (1986), summarizes the arguments. Michael Sandel, "The Democrats and Community," *New Republic*, 198 (February 22, 1988), pp. 20–23, is an effective, well-crafted translation of this body of theoretical literature into political terms. For a sympathetic but critical treatment, see Boyte, "On the Commonwealth," *Tikkun*, May 1988.

8. In a number of cases, republican arguments today sound too much like

a different *language* for describing essentially liberal and social democratic programs. In particular, the liberal left, whose recent calls for a
spirit of "national community" are far removed from the local level,
still shares with republicans an idealized view of what politics *should*
entail. Some of the most thoughtful and effective conservative writing
in recent years has pointed to the "nationalization" of communal
themes as the source of the liberal crisis. "Mondale's notion of community," wrote George Will, "was [that] the people would be prodded by
the central government into a 'national' community." Will, "The Real
Campaign of 1984," *Newsweek,* September 2, 1985; for a more elaborate
version of this argument, see William A. Schambra, *The Quest for Community and the Quest for a New Public Philosophy* (Washington: American Enterprise Institute, 1983).

9. Stephens and Anaya quoted from Geoffrey Rips, "A New Spirit Flows
   Along the Rio Grande," *In These Times,* May 18–24, 1988.

10. Interview with Ernie Cortes, Los Angeles, July 23, 1977.

11. For a telling description of the tightening elite control over American
    political institutions that took place in the 1980s, see Thomas Byrne
    Edsall, *The New Politics of Inequality* (New York: W. W. Norton, 1984); on
    long-range trends, see "U.S. Economic Role May Face Long Decline,"
    Wall Street Journal, August 17, 1987; on a fantasy of a world in which
    America has become an impoverished "Third World" nation, Mark Pan-
    tinkin, "2088: How Our Grandchildren May Reap the Benefits of Our
    Foolishness," reprinted in *Minneapolis Star and Tribune,* February 24,
    1988; on the growing public unease with the greed and selfishness of
    the 1980s, "The '80s: Goodbye to All That," *Newsweek,* January 4, 1988;
    on worries about the future, Steven Roberts, "Poll Finds Less Optimism
    in U.S. on Future, a First Under Reagan," *New York Times,* February 21,
    1988.

12. Cortes interview, July 23, 1977; in the IAF 10 Day Training, Cortes ar-
    gued that "conservatives often understand the deep human need for
    roots far better than liberals or leftists," pointing to Indian peoples,
    blacks, and Hispanics as confounding traditional political categories in
    this regard.

13. *The Tent of the Presence: Black Church Power in the 1980s* (New York: IAF,
    1981), p. 8.

14. Bernard Crick, *In Defense of Politics* (Chicago: University of Chicago
    Press, 1972); Hannah Fenichel Pitkin, *Fortune Is a Woman: Gender and
    Politics in the Thought of Niccolo Machiavelli* (Berkeley: University of Cali-
    fornia Press, 1984). For perspectives on public life which also continue
    to urge a sense of the specificity of politics and its diversity, see Benja-
    min Barber, *The Conquest of Politics* (Princeton: Princeton University
    Press, 1988); Michael Walzer, *Spheres of Justice: A Defense of Pluralism and
    Equality* (New York: Basic Books, 1983); and Mary Dietz, *Between the
    Human and the Divine: The Political Thought of Simone Weil* (Totowa, N.J.:
    Rowman and Littlefield, 1988).

    Crick, for instance, distinguished politics from ideology, which he argued seeks to refashion and reconstruct society according to a particular aim or vision. Politics "is concerned with limited purposes" and occupies a particular region: it "is not religion, ethics, law, science, history or economics; it neither solves everything nor is it present everywhere; and it is not any one political doctrine, such as conservatism, liberalism, socialism, communism or nationalism. Politics is politics." In Crick's reading, political action is the specific way of resolving conflicts and making decisions in relatively complicated, technologically sophisticated societies where traditional beliefs and codes of behavior are no longer universally shared. It depends on negotiation, bargaining, disagreement, collaboration, and discussion, but ultimately on a certain respect for the process of practical public life itself: "Politics may be a messy, mundane, inconclusive, tangled business, far removed from the passion for certainty and the fascination for world-shaking quests which afflict the totalitarian intellectual." Politics does give citizens experiences of autonomy, commonality, and power not found elsewhere: "some choice in what role to play, some variety of corporate experience and some ability to call [their] soul [their] own." It amounts to "a way of ruling divided societies without undue violence" that deserves an honoring on its own terms. But "ruling" is not as apt a word for the IAF's view of politics as is "sovereignty." Crick, *Defense of Politics,* pp. 35, 42, 15–16, 56, 34.

Pitkin's work develops a similar view. "The Citizen image [in Machiavelli]," Pitkin argued, "is . . . a way to 'give thought to private and public advantages' together. It concerns the transformation of narrowly defined self-interest into a larger awareness of one's ties to others, one's real stake in institutions and ideals." The change involved is not so much movement from self-interest to self-sacrifice, nor short- to long-range self-interest, but rather a deepening understanding of identity, "a transformation . . . in the understanding of what the self *is,* of the limits of the self." Pitkin, *Fortune Is a Woman,* pp. 240, 93, 95, 299–300.

15. As Nelson Polsby put it, it can be examined by looking at "who participates, who gains and loses and who prevails in decision-making." Robert Dahl, "The Concept of Power," in Robert Bell, David M. Edwards, and R. Harrison Wagner, eds., *Political Power: A Reader in Theory and Research* (New York: Free Press, 1969), p. 80; Dahl, *Who Governs? Democracy and Power in an American City* (New Haven: Yale University Press, 1961), pp. 91, 93; Nelson W. Polsby, *Community Power and Political Theory* (New Haven: Yale, 1963), p. 5.

16. In his great dissenting work *The Power Elite,* published in 1956, C. Wright Mills sketched the way power operates in modern society to render most people spectators:

> The powers of ordinary men are circumscribed by the everyday world in which they live, yet even in these rounds of job, family, and neighborhood they often seem driven by forces they can neither understand nor govern. "Great changes" are beyond their control, but affect their conduct and outlook none the less. The

very framework of modern society confines them to projects not their own, but from every side, such changes press upon the men and women of the mass society, who accordingly feel that they are without purpose in an epoch in which they are without power.

But not all men are in this sense ordinary. As the means of information and of power are centralized, some men come to occupy positions in American society from which they can look down upon, so to speak, and by their decisions mightily affect, the everyday worlds of ordinary men and women.

C. Wright Mills, *The Power Elite* (New York: Oxford University Press, 1956), p. 31; for similar arguments, see Peter Bachrach and Morton Baratz, "The Two Faces of Power," *American Political Science Review,* 56 (1962), pp. 947–52; E. E. Schattschneider, *The Semi-Sovereign People: A Realist's View of Democracy in America* (New York: Holt, Rinehart & Winston, 1960).

In more recent years, critics have not only pointed to the operation of "rules of the game"—values, institutional procedures, rituals, and other means that operate to shape the sort of discussion and issues considered a part of normal "politics"—they have also drawn attention to the fashion in which meanings, symbols, and language itself are constituted by power relations. Even the terms and themes of popular consciousness may mystify or preclude explicit recognition of certain basic interests, argue the newer theorists of culture and language. To explore such patterns of the social construction of meaning and culture requires a more complex and subtle process.

According to John Gaventa, power analysis

> involves specifying the means through which power influences, shapes, or determines conceptions of the necessities, possibilities and strategies of challenge in situations of latent conflict. This may include the study of social myths, language and symbols, and how they are shaped or manipulated in power processes. It may involve the study of communication or information—both of what is communicated and how it is done. It may involve a focus upon the means by which social legitimations are developed.

Attention to the patterns of power relations that operate systematically through a variety of cultural mechanisms can highlight the ways "the oppressed" participate in their oppression through long-inculcated modes of avoidance and self-censorship, developing what the educator Paulo Freire calls a "culture of silence" in which politics becomes a spectacle, not a participatory activity. John Gaventa, *Power and Powerlessness: Quiescence and Rebellion in an Appalachian Valley* (Urbana: University of Illinois Press, 1980), p. 15; Paulo Freire, *Cultural Action for Freedom* (New York: Penguin Books, 1972), p. 58; see also Murray Edelman, *Politics as Symbolic Action: Mass Arousal and Quiescence* (Chicago: Markham Publishing, 1971. Edelman, in a fashion paralleling Gareth Stedman Jones, points to the way political action and language are constitutive of power relations: "Political actions chiefly arouse or satisfy people not by granting or withholding their stable, substantive demands but rather by changing their demands and expectations" (p. 8).

17. The title of Gaventa's book—*Power and Powerlessness*—suggests the dominant intellectual approach. In a recent work, the feminist author Marilyn French expressed the pessimism underlying a broad range of modern intellectual effort. "Power worship is contagious," French writes.

> If a worshiper of power decides to extend his power over your society, your choices are between surrendering and mounting an equal and opposite power. In either case, the power worshiper wins—he has converted your society into a people who understand that power is the highest good. Over the millennia [the power lovers' view] spreads to all corners of the planet, and only a couple of tiny societies still exist that appear not to have been influenced by it.

> Marilyn French, *Beyond Power: On Women, Men and Morals* (New York: Ballantine Books, 1985), p. 19; the despair over loss of agency and a capacity to act that emerges from feminist poststructuralism is well described in Linda Alcoff, "Cultural Feminism Versus Post-Structuralism: The Identity Crisis in Feminist Theory," *Signs: Journal of Women in Culture and Society,* 13:3 (1988), pp. 405–36. Postmodernist and poststructuralist thought overwhelmingly reflects what the IAF terms a "unilateral" understanding of power. See for instance the collection of essays edited by Andrew Ross, *Universal Abandon? The Politics of Postmodernism* (Minneapolis: University of Minnesota Press, 1988).

18. Intellectuals are not normally alert to what ordinary citizens are already doing in the way of "political" participation. Thus Gaventa, an astute observer, was surprised when he went to study an actual community in order to test recent critical thought about the operation of power: "As one draws closer . . . the silence is not as pervasive as it appears from other studies, or even from initial inquiry within this one." Gaventa, *Power and Powerlessness,* p. 252.

On alternative, relational theories of power, see for instance Elizabeth Janeway, *Powers of the Weak* (New York: Alfred A. Knopf, 1980); James Scott, *Weapons of the Weak: Everyday Forms of Peasant Resistance* (New Haven: Yale University Press, 1986); Linda Gordon, "Family Violence, Feminism and Social Control," *Feminist Studies,* 12:3 (1986), pp. 452–78, and *Heroes of Their Own Lives: The Politics and History of Family Violence* (New York: Viking Press, 1988).

19. Bernard Loomer, "Two Conceptions of Power," *Criterion,* 15:1 (1976), pp. 12–29.

20. IAF 10 Day Training session in Baltimore, November 12, 1987; shortly before the session, Cortes had been "trying out" such arguments in Texas workshops. IAF organizers have long referred to "informed judgment," and have drawn on Hannah Arendt's conceptions of judgment as a kind of representational thinking, expressing the "civic common

sense" of a community, but never exploring the concept in much detail. For a discussion of Arendt's conception of judgment, see Richard Bernstein, *Beyond Objectivism and Relativism* (Philadelphia: University of Pennsylvania Press, 1985), pp. 207–23.

21. In Arendt's words,

> As distinguished from "objectivity," whose only basis is money as a common denominator for the fulfillment of all needs, the reality of the public realm lies on the simultaneous presence of innumerable perspectives and aspects in which the common world presents itself and for which no common measurement or denominator can ever be devised. For though the common world is the common meeting ground of all, those who are present have different locations in it . . . the word "private" in connection with property, even in terms of ancient political thought, immediately loses its privative character and much of its opposition to the public realm in general; property . . . possesses certain qualifications which . . . were always thought to be of utmost importance to the political body *(Human Condition,* pp. 57, 61).

22. For an interesting exploration of the contingency of the modern citizenry which, however, has lost the concept of public life almost entirely, see Benjamin Ginsberg, *The Captive Public: How Mass Opinion Promotes State Power* (New York: Basic Books, 1986).

23. Robert Nisbet, "The Total Community," in Marvin E. Olson, ed., *Power in Societies* (New York: Macmillan, 1970), p. 423.

24. Peter Berger and Richard John Neuhaus, *To Empower People: The Role of Mediating Structures in Public Policy* (Washington, D.C.: American Enterprise Institute, 1977); see also Peter Berger, *Facing Up to Modernity: Excursions in Society, Politics and Religion* (New York: Basic Books, 1977). On IAF use of the language of mediating institutions, see *Organizing for Family and Congregation,* and "Organizing," a presentation by Edward T. Chambers to the 1988 Church and City Conference, Philadelphia, May 9, 1988.

25. The meanings of free spaces and their centrality in American democratic movements (especially the black freedom struggle, women's movements, workers' struggles, and populist farmers' movements) are explored in Sara M. Evans and Harry C. Boyte, *Free Spaces: The Sources of Democratic Change in America* (New York: Harper & Row, 1986).

26. Chambers in IAF training session in Baltimore, November 5, 1987. In a workshop of the "Sister's Caucus" of UNO, the Los Angeles group, Ernie Cortes contrasted a growing, autonomous person with compulsivity, addictions, and obsessiveness, and argued that a healthy sense of one's self-interest and the self-interest of the other is an essential way to move toward autonomy. Cortes notes on workshop, December 6, 1977, in author's possession.

27. Larry McNeil, 10 Day Training, Baltimore, November 11, 1987.

Chapter 9
Commonwealth in the Information Age

1. Lloyd quoted from Norman Pollack, ed., *The Populist Mind* (Indianapolis: Bobbs Merrill, 1967), pp. 69–70.

2. For a description of the dynamics behind populism's demise, see Lawrence Goodwyn, *Democratic Promise* (New York: Oxford University Press, 1976); and Steven Hahn, *Roots of Southern Populism: Yeoman Farmers and the Transformation of the Georgia Upcountry, 1850–1890* (New York: Oxford, 1983). Bruce Palmer, *Man Over Money: The Southern Populist Critique of American Capitalism* (Chapel Hill: University of North Carolina Press, 1980), describes in detail the populist ideas of politics and a commonwealth of producers.

3. See Joseph Campbell, *The Power of Myth* (New York: Doubleday, 1988), pp. 22, 25.

4. Hans-Georg Gadamer described the essence of a utopian—as contrasted with an immediately practical—aim in Richard Bernstein, *Beyond Objectivism and Relativism* (Philadelphia: University of Pennsylvania Press, 1983), p. 212.

5. Taylor, "Lessons from Organizing in the 1980s," *Democracy Notes* discussion bulletin #1, January 1989; for an interesting exchange on the ways political language is both constitutive and reflective of power, politics, and social reality, see Joan W. Scott, "On Language, Gender, and Working-Class History," and her critics in *International Labor and Working-Class History,* 31 (Spring 1987), pp. 1–45.

   The reform establishment of politics in America goes under the name of "liberalism." But since liberalism is a term with such diffuse and different meanings, Michael Harrington, author of *The Other America,* described the liberal mainstream perhaps more accurately as "America's invisible social democratic movement." The problem is that social democracy, in American guise and European contexts alike, has become increasingly associated with efficient administration of the economy-as-is, and the effective delivery of services. And while the broad public shows no signs of following a right-wing crusade for its dismantling, the welfare state, even in more participatory variants, has lost its power to stir popular passion or generate imaginative reconstructions of the future. One can see the dramatic effects of the loss in socialist "faith"—especially in the aftermath of the decay of hopes for the Mitterand government in France through the 1980s—in Harrington's own work. Earlier books brimmed over with confidence; his newest ideas for reform have retreated significantly from what he once imagined possible. Contrast *Socialism* (New York: Bantam Books, 1972) or *The Twilight of Capitalism* (New York: Simon & Schuster, 1976) with his latest proposals for action, such as "The First Few Steps—and a Few Beyond," in Robert Kuttner and Irving Howe, eds., *The Democratic Promise* (New York: Foundation for the Study of Independent Ideas, 1988), pp. 16–28.

   Left theorists of reform today reflect a widespread discouragement.

Thus political scientist William Connolly conjures up the sad image of "political theorists ... wandering through the debris of old doctrines searching for stray material" with which they might be able to understand the modern predicament. Harvard economist Julie Schor, a pioneer in proposals to adapt sixties-style themes of participation to the modern economy, acknowledges that "economic democracy," a concept that a decade or so ago seemed to offer fresh hopes for the left, has failed to stir popular interest. The populist tradition in America here, as elsewhere, has resources to offer. William Connolly, *Politics and Ambiguity* (Madison: University of Wisconsin Press, 1987); Julie Schor, "The Political Economy of Economic Democracy," paper delivered to the International Sociological Conference Group 10 Conference, Boston College, August 7, 1987.

There is no small irony that Richard Rorty identifies a broad "consensus" he sees in the mainstream of political theory—extending to "Rawls, Habermas, Berlin, Robert Bellah, Daniel Bell, Irving Howe, Sidney Hook, John Dunn, Charles Taylor"—around a social democratic politics in the very issue of the magazine *Political Theory* that extensively reviews the public's loss of passion for welfare state reform, in essays by Claude Offe and Sheldon Wolin. See Rorty, "Thugs and Theorists," *Political Theory*, 15:4 (1987), p. 567; also John Dunn, *Rethinking Modern Political Theory: Essays 1979–83* (Cambridge: Cambridge University Press, 1985), on the dead-end quality of much current theory.

6. The quotes from Pettus are taken from interviews in Seattle, March 14, 17, 18, 1983. Other accounts of the houseboat story are found in "Subversive?" a special documentary by John de Graaf for station KCTS, aired in Seattle, September 5, 1983; and Howard Droker, *Seattle's Unsinkable Houseboats* (Seattle: Watermark Press, 1977). For a detailed description of the Lake Union effort and other "commonwealth" stories of the 1970s and '80s, see Harry C. Boyte, *Community Is Possible: Repairing America's Roots* (New York: Harper & Row, 1984).

7. Steinbrueck's battle is described in detail in Alice Shorett and Murray Morgan, *The Pike Place Market: People, Politics and Produce* (Seattle: Pacific Search Press, 1982); Ellis quoted from Leonard Silk, "Seattle Looks for Its Future," *New York Times*, April 22, 1983.

8. Garrett Hardin, *Science*,162 (1968), p. 1244. On the origins of commons, see for instance, Warren Ortman Ault, *Open Field Farming in Medieval England* (London: Allen and Unwin, 1972); Robert Dodgshon, "The Interpretation of Subdivided Fields: A Study in Private or Communal Interests," in Trevor Rowley, ed., *The Origins of Open-Field Agriculture* (London: Croom Helm, 1981). See Paul Starr, *The Limits of Privatization* (Washington, D.C.: Economic Policy Institute, 1987) for an excellent description of some of the hidden costs of privitization today.

The historian of American populism Lawrence Goodwyn enjoys pointing out that most political theorists, whatever their intellectual range, however brilliant their insights into contemporary ills or creative their proposals for change, have stalled at the first point of political action: they never get beyond the "kitchen table" of self-absorbed conversation. Goodwyn formulated a principle he believed the key to the success of populist organizers in the 1880s with broader applicability: "Movements begin when unresigned and self-respecting activists find a way to connect with people *as they are in society,* that is to say, in a state that sophisticated modern observers are inclined to regard as one of "insufficient consciousness." Lawrence Goodwyn, "Organizing Democracy," *democracy,* 1:1 (1981), p. 51.

It is ironic but useful to note that the founders of classical economics themselves were fully aware of the existence of essential public goods. "The third and last duty of the sovereign or commonwealth," wrote Adam Smith,

> is that of erecting and maintaining those public institutions and those public works which, though they may be in the highest degree advantageous to a great society, are, however, of such a nature that the profit could never repay the expense to any individual or small number of individuals, and which it therefore cannot be expected that any individual or small number of individuals should erect or maintain.

Adam Smith, *An Inquiry into the Nature and Causes of the Wealth of Nations* (Chicago: University of Chicago Press, 1976), p. 244.

9. Political theorist William Connolly has effectively argued that individualist approaches to such basic "consumption needs" on left and right create an insoluble crisis in physical and social infrastructure:

> The forms of health care, transportation, housing and food available in this country approach the status of exclusive goods: if restricted to the affluent they create hardships for the remaining populace that provides infrastructural support for these forms ... if extended to the entire populace they damage the social and natural environment, increase social expenses borne by the state, and fuel inflationary wage demands.

Although he suggests little mechanism through which common action might be effected, Connolly's argument for "more inclusive forms" that "if well designed, would drain electoral support from repressive strategies ... and encourage constituencies now divided to draw closer together in a progressive political movement" finds a counterpart in IAF practice. Connolly, *Politics and Ambiguity,* p. 39.

For a discussion of the privileged access to information enjoyed by large private corporate institutions and the disadvantage it works on communities and local governments, see for instance Robert Warren and Mark S. Rosentraub, "Information and the Control of Local Decisions," *Journal of Urban Affairs,* fall 1986, pp. 41–50.

10. The public world, defined as the world we have in common, has suffered in the modern era from the sharp erosion of any agreed-upon, transcendent *authority.* As Hannah Arendt said in a 1958 essay,

Historically we know of a variety of sources to which authoritative rulers could appeal in order to justify their power; it could be the law of nature, or the commands of God, or the Platonic ideas or ancient customs, or a great event in the past . . . in all these cases legitimacy derives from something outside the range of human deeds.

Hannah Arendt, "What Was Authority?" in Carl Friedrich, ed., *Nomos* (Cambridge, Mass.: Harvard University Press, 1958), p. 82. The change grew far more acute in the twentieth century. The relatively homogeneous, face-to-face world of small towns and rural communities in which those who sought authority could find common cultural and historical sources gave way to massive urban areas where people no longer even knew their neighbors, much less other cultural and racial groups across town. Communications systems spanned whole continents. Institutions of business, government, and professions became centralized far beyond the local area. In such a world, establishing *consensus* about the common ends of public life became a task to be achieved, rather than a "given" imported, even imposed, on public life from some realm outside of politics itself. Chaos combines with freedom in an uneasy mix that often seems to make the two synonymous—which, from the perspective of "authority," in a way they are. I am indebted to Elizabeth Minnich for this particular insight, among her many contributions to *CommonWealth.*

11. Robert N. Bellah et al., *Habits of the Heart: Individualism and Commitment in American Life* (Berkeley: University of California Press, 1986), p. 72.

12. In this sense, BUILD's commons are like the goals that Bernard Crick described as the essential rationale of politics: "Diverse groups hold together, first, because they have a common interest in sheer survival and, secondly, because they practice politics—not because they agree about 'fundamentals.'"

    Crick argued that it is through the process of politics itself, "not something mysteriously prior to or above politics," that a "moral consensus" develops. Bernard Crick, *In Defense of Politics* (Chicago: University of Chicago Press, 1972), p. 24.

13. For an account of COPS's drainage campaigns, see Boyte, *Community Is Possible,* chap. 5.

14. IAF 10 Day training session, Baltimore, November 5, 1987.

15. Interview with Gary Rodwell, Baltimore, November 13, 1987; Cortes also makes many of these points in Ripps's article, "A New Spirit."

16. Except in Baltimore and in a campaign against a local effort to impose government spending limitations in San Antonio, IAF groups have generally not explicitly used the older vocabulary of "commonwealth," substituting instead biblical imagery like Nehemiah, Jerusalem, and Genesis to describe their visionary objectives. But cabinet members Ed Chambers, Ernie Cortes, Arnie Graf, and Mike Gecan all agreed that

the concept of "commons" is particularly useful for describing the larger infrastructural issues around which IAF groups create public occasions and a sense of visionary purpose.

BUILD's commonwealth language draws from religious as well as secular political traditions, but it is important to note that religious themes in politics for BUILD, like others of the IAF groups, have vividly illustrated the egalitarian, popular democratic strands that can be found in the Bible. IAF leaders do not imagine all will share in their images or understandings—their concepts of "public life" are very far from a theocracy. Indeed, IAF groups actively seek out as members organizations founded on secular bases, like trade unions and tenant associations; they have also vigorously sought to enlist synagogues in membership as well as churches. In this regard, BUILD's use of religious themes illustrates the arguments of Alexis de Tocqueville: although American religious passions could and sometimes did lead to intolerance, when expressed in the context of many traditions and democratic values, they could, alternatively, become great resources for a democratic public life. See John A. Coleman, "The Christian as Citizen," *Commonweal*, September 9, 1983, p. 457–62, for an excellent description of Tocqueville's arguments about religion and politics.

17. Interview with Vernon Dobson, November 13, 1987; with Doug Miles, November 14, 1987.

18. In *The Human Condition*, Hannah Arendt defined "public" as constituted of two elements. First, public life entails visibility among those who—putting aside the ways in which they are radically different and unequal in private life—agree to be "equals" in a process of action and talk: "everything that appears in public can be seen and heard by everybody and has the widest possible publicity." Second, public means the common world, "in so far as it is common to all of us and distinguished from our privately owned place within it." The common world, in Arendt's terms, involves both the built environment that is commonly shared and the "affairs which go on among those who inhabit the man-made world together." What Arendt neglected was the interplay between what she called the "social realm"—where in her view questions of poverty, injustice, hunger, and the like are decided—and a public life where conflict and debate, challenge as well as collaboration, can over time *make* issues that were previously seen as "prepolitical" or "special interest" matters of common concern. Such a process constantly reworks and revitalizes the common world itself. This is the essence of the kind of populist vision of public that grows from active, effective political practice by groups of the citizens. Arendt's views on public life as an arena of equals ("the equality of the Greek polis, its isonomy, was an attribute of the polis and not of men, who received their equality by virtue of citizenship, not by virtue of birth") are set forth in *On Revolution* (New York: Viking Press, 1963), p. 23; also *The Human Condition* (Chicago: University of Chicago Press, 1958), pp. 50, 52; her understanding of the difference between the "social" and the "political" is discussed in Bernstein, *Beyond Objectivism*, pp. 213–15.

19. Interviews with Gerald Taylor, Baltimore, April 2 and June 1, 1988; Bob Moore, Minneapolis-Baltimore, April 12, 1988.

20. Jackson's appeal beyond the black community was not as wide in the 1984 race, but it had clear populist overtones that went almost entirely unremarked. In the New Hampshire debate that year on the eve of the primary, despite a campaign then besieged by questions about Jackson's "Hymietown" remark and associations with Louis Farrakan, I watched while he got a standing ovation when he remarked that he was running "to empower the people." For an account of the campaign (which neglects that revealing moment) see Bob Faw and Nancy Skelton, *Thunder in America: The Improbable Presidential Campaign of Jesse Jackson in 1984* (New York: Paperjacks, 1986). Robert Kuttner, *Life of the Party* (New York: Penguin Books, 1988) details the powerful appeal of Jackson's populism in 1988.

21. E. J. Dionne, chief political reporter for the *New York Times,* gave a thoughtful, detailed treatment to his coverage of the Jackson campaign. "Populism may be an overused word in the 1988 campaign," wrote Dionne.

    But it goes to the heart of what Mr. Jackson has accomplished. As a movement in American history, populism has always been a Janus creature, looking both forward and backward. On the one hand, its adherents—the downtrodden in search of a better deal—were years ahead of the powers-that-be in advocating social reforms on wages, hours, and working conditions, farm supports and the popular election of United States senators. But populism has often succumbed to the mistrusts and hatreds of race, religion and nationality—hatreds sometimes aggravated by the authorities whom the populists threatened. . . . Jackson's speeches are full of indirect references to this history.

    Dionne points out that 22 percent of whites in Wisconsin who called themselves conservative backed Jackson—to show that populism does not fit conventional left-right divisions. "Black and White: How Jesse Jackson Made History While Losing Wisconsin," *New York Times* Week in Review, April 10, 1988.

22. See Leslie Phillips, "Convention Belongs to Jackson," *USA Today,* July 20, 1988.

23. "Analysis of Michigan," *Minneapolis Tribune,* March 25, 1988.

24. "Jackson's Speech: Let's Find Common Ground," *New York Times,* July 21, 1988.

25. For the popular mood, see "The '80s: Goodbye to All That," *Newsweek,* January 4, 1988; on Jackson's funding and his "flesh and blood" campaign, see "Analysis" in *Minneapolis Tribune;* Douglas David, "Zapping the Myth of TV's Power," *New York Times,* May 20, 1988, and Jeff Greenfield, "Beware Pundits' Words on the Campaign," *New York Times,* April 5, 1988, discuss the low-budget campaign and Jackson's "human" appeal.

26. *New York Times,* July 21, 1988.
27. For a good summary of Jackson campaign themes, see Dionne, "Black and White"; see also his "Twin Messages of Protest," *New York Times,* February 10, 1988; Joseph Sullivan, "Jersey Democrats See Two Sides of Presidential Race," *New York Times,* May 16, 1988; and "Jackson Outlines Budget, Jabs at Dukakis," *Minneapolis Tribune,* May 24, 1988. The carelessness about basic infrastructural elements in American society is extensively documented in the National Council on Public Works Improvement report, *Fragile Foundations: A Report on America's Public Works* (Washington, D.C.: Government Printing Office, 1988).
28. For a treatment of North American commonwealth politics in the 1920s, '30s, and '40s, see for instance Seymour Martin Lipset, *Agrarian Socialism* (Berkeley: University of California Press, 1950); Robert L. Morlan, *Political Prairie: The Nonpartisan League, 1915–1922* (Minneapolis: University of Minnesota Press, 1955); and Walter Young, *The Anatomy of a Party: The National Cooperative Commonwealth Federation* (Toronto: University of Toronto Press, 1969).

    Populist politics today, expressing the theme of "commonwealth" as the concerns of the whole people, do suggest different ways of casting issues of poverty, discrimination, and injustice—basically by stressing programs of universal entitlement and rights, rather than particular remedies. For this sort of argument, see for instance, Kuttner, *Life of the Party;* and William Julius Wilson, *the Truly Disadvantaged: The Inner City, the Underclass and Public Policy* (Chicago: University of Chicago Press, 1987).

    For a discussion of strategies and approaches toward a recommunalization of urban spaces along these lines, see for instance Dolores Hayden, *Redesigning the American Dream: The Future of Housing, Work and Family Life* (New York: W. W. Norton, 1984), especially chap. 8, "Domesticating Urban Space."

    This perspective on the interdependence of the individual and the communal life as a whole is closely paralleled by the "land ethic" advanced by Aldo Leopold: "A thing is right when it tends to preserve the integrity, stability and beauty of the biotic community. It is wrong when it tends otherwise." Aldo Leopold, *Sand County Almanac* (New York: Oxford University Press, 1949), pp. 224–25; see also J. Baird Callicott, *In Defense of the Land Ethic: Essays in Environmental Philosophy* (Albany: SUNY Press, 1989). Callicott argues, in ways that have clear resonance here, that "a society is particularly vulnerable to disintegration when its members become preoccupied totally with their own particular interests, and ignore those distinct and interdependent interests of the community as a whole" (p. 24).

Index